Reason in Law

Reason in Law

SECOND EDITION

Lief H. Carter J.D., Ph.D.
UNIVERSITY OF GEORGIA

Little, Brown and Company
Boston   Toronto

Library of Congress Cataloging in Publication Data

Carter, Lief H.
    Reason in law.

    Bibliography: p.
    1. Judicial process—United States.   2. Law—
United States—Interpretation and construction.
3. Law—Philosophy.   I. Title.
KF380.C325   1984   340′.11   84-5646
ISBN 0-316-13049-4

Library of Congress Catalog Card Number 84-5646

ISBN 0-316-13049-4

9 8 7 6 5 4 3 2 1

ALP

Published simultaneously in Canada
by Little, Brown & Company (Canada) Limited

Printed in the United States of America

Credits are listed on page 345.

For my wife, Nancy,

and

*For Sandy Muir and
all teachers who care*

Preface to the
Second Edition

The task of creating a new edition of *Reason in Law* proved, quite unexpectedly, a particularly satisfying one. Part of the satisfaction arises, as it so often does at many points in our lives, from confessing and atoning for sin. Through teaching the first edition, I became painfully aware of expressive infelicities and opaque passages that confused students and revealed my own confusion. In this edition I hope I have removed more causes of confusion than I have added. I have, for example, clarified the critical distinction between vertical and horizontal stare decisis. More important, I hope that the new Chapter III, which highlights the significance of social background facts in judicial decision making, will help readers appreciate more readily the book's many illustrations of judicial use and misuse of what I call "fact freedom."

The main source of satisfaction, however, arises from my good luck (and it was at least as much luck as it was exhaustive scholarship) discovering very recent and usually unresolved newsworthy legal puzzles plus illustrative case opinions. I hope these will capture the layperson's imagination when they appear at the ends of chapters. I hope also that you will gain as much intellectual fun and profit as I have when you speculate with colleagues and students about the contentions, outcomes, and justifications in these cases.

Although the second edition primarily expands rather than alters the first, emphasis on some points does shift significantly. The major changes are:

1. More explicit enthusiasm for "non-interpretivist" approaches to legal reasoning. This enthusiasm appears particularly in the last two chapters. If space permitted, I would explore more fully how my model for constitutional reasoning differs from John Hart Ely's essentially interpretivist model. I fear my presentation here is still uncomfortably "Carolenean," but I must attempt that clarification another day.

2. An explicit endorsement of the thesis that most judicial opinion "failures" are characterized by reasoning from a factual premise which an informed layperson in our culture would not hesitate to find false. In other words, I believe the appellate process works well when judges seek to make their hunches about the social relationships exemplified in the case before them as factually plausible as possible. In the practical enterprise of law, the fact/value distinction and philosophical "objectivity" have much to offer. Alfred North Whitehead describes the process as "the concrete contemplation of the complete facts." To illustrate with respect to the court decisions I have reproduced in this edition, the factual contemplations underlying the opinions for the courts in *Francioso*, *Craig*, and *Soldano* seem completely plausible; those implicit in *Repouille*, *Prochnow*, *Whiteley* and *Michael M.* do not.

3. Sharper focus, primarily near the book's close, on the ethical bases of legal practice. I hope I communicate to law and prelaw students that lawyers are first and foremost peacemakers and that acceptable justifications for the adversary system can be found only within a larger peacemaking framework.

ACKNOWLEDGMENTS

A few weeks before I completed this edition my wife introduced me to Lewis Hyde's beautiful (and beautifully titled) book, *The Gift: Imagination and the Erotic Life of Property* (Vintage Books, 1983). In this poetic anthropology of gift practices, Hyde speculates that refereed journal articles "count more" than books in the ranking of academic achievements because articles are true gifts. Their authors receive no royalties for their efforts. I am inclined for many reasons to think Hyde overgeneralizes on the point. His dichotomy certainly underestimates the selfish rewards of article-writing and overestimates those of book-writing. In any event, his book reminded me most forcefully that in both books and articles scholars beyond counting have unknowingly given me extraordinary gifts. Thomas Shaffer provided the telling quote from Karl Barth (Chapter VII) in his *On Being a Christian and a Lawyer* (Brigham Young University Press, 1981). I am sure I met the *Repouille* case a decade ago in Walter Murphy and C. Herman Pritchett's *Courts, Judges and Politics* (Random House, 1974). I am almost sure I encountered *Fox v. Snow* before that in Cataldo et al.'s *Introduction to Law and the Legal Process* (John Wiley, 1965). And, as in the first edition, I am especially grateful to the late Henry Hart and Professor Albert Sacks, this time for giving me *Whiteley v. Chappell.*

Al Matheny, Rodney Grunes, Larry Baum, and Scott Turnbull gave most valuable suggestions for this edition. Wes Wynens and Brian Wahl did library leg work most ably. Little, Brown's staff, especially Don Palm and Julie Winston, and their independent contractors—Gail Hapke, Terri Gitler, and Diana Scott—gave extra measures of constructive help at every step.

Lewis Hyde finds that a recipient's most constructive response to a gift is not to repay it but rather to pass it on. I hope this edition, built as it is upon innumerable gifts, in small measure does so.

Athens, Georgia

Preface to the First Edition

When we study legal reasoning we confront important—and often perplexing—questions that reach far beyond the legal system as we conventionally define it. We must understand some psychology and philosophy in order to perceive what reason is in the first place, or to tell a reasoned and an unreasoned choice apart, or to decide whether a well reasoned choice is necessarily "right." And we must know something about political and social life in order to determine whether those who reason in law—lawyers and judges—do so wisely.

This book, like its subject, ranges broadly and refuses to reduce to neat categories of questions and answers. I justify such a book in three ways. First, I believe that, in an increasingly legalized society, laypeople can and must understand the legal process more fully. I believe that, since our understanding of law is essentially a reflection of our understanding of life, any literate and motivated reader can, without special legal training, deepen his or her understanding of law. The choices that lawyers and judges make, and the way in which they make them, resemble the choices we make in our daily lives more than we think.

Second, I have written this book because I sense that educators have failed to communicate to laypeople the nature of legal thinking. The problem has been equally one of medium and of message. Law professors too often write only to and for each other. Social scientists who rely on systems theory and quantitative analysis of outcomes and judicial votes often seem to me to end at the beginning. The medium may be clear, but the message is the beginning: Cases before appellate judges usually have more than one "right" answer.

Third, and most important to me, lawyers, judges, and law professors themselves do not fully understand the nature of legal reasoning. Studying law in the United States too often stresses the search for narrowly drawn legalistic answers. It focuses only briefly and dimly on the nature of reason and on the social and political roles of lawyers, judges, and rules.

In a nutshell, then, *Reason in Law* presumes only literacy and motivation. It supplies the definitions and descriptions of law in action that the layperson needs to understand the world of appellate court decision-making. The reader should not, however, approach these pages as a text. I offer no comprehensive descriptions of the legal process and no canvass of all jurisprudential points of view. Instead, this book asks questions. Asking the right question is equally important for judges and lawyers and for people who try to think about what judges and lawyers do. In many instances I am confident that both my question and my answer are correct. In many more instances, however, the answer—maybe even the question itself!—only serves to stimulate thoughts that carry you, both in space and time, beyond the pages of this book. Lawyers, judges, and students who grapple and sweat in close engagement with these materials—readers, in other words, who think as they read—will meet my expectations regardless of the proportion of my views they reject.

Finally, a word about teaching. I hope the didactic approach here well suits the needs of teachers. It certainly has served my own. I trust that undergraduate and graduate students in a variety of courses—legal process, constitutional law, judicial behavior, indeed, any law-related course—will see the issues in these courses more clearly by virtue of their combat on the field of legal reasoning. I do feel, however, that in courses where most students have no prior legal exposure the teacher must teach this book, not assign it as background reading; hence, I have included the questions at the end of each chapter, which allow both review and exploration in class discussions and independent study. Both students and teachers will profit from taking *Reason in Law* a step at a time and discussing issues and questions chapter by chapter. Above all else, teachers must realize that I have attempted to create both a teaching book and a short treatise. They will find a progression from the straightforward descriptions of the first two chapters through the personal essays on statutory interpretation, common law, and constitutional law to the final chapter's jurisprudential synthesis that leans heavily on political science, psychology, and philosophy.

In short, I am not trying primarily to describe how judges think. I am prescribing how they ought to think.

ACKNOWLEDGMENTS

Modernism, which shakes our confidence in causation, poses problems in legal reasoning. It also poses a problem in acknowledging debts. Clark Byse, who taught me contract law at Harvard fifteen years ago, and Leonard Nash, from whom I learned something of the history of science at Harvard College nearly twenty years ago, taught me a way of thinking and communicating that influenced this book. So, for that matter, did Martha Hardy, John Terrey, William Lamont, and John Sorensen of

Bellevue (Washington) High School. I hope that reflecting on such debts, remote in time yet immediate in memory, reminds us of the depth of our interconnectedness and our mutual dependence.

Fortunately, there can be no doubt about the size of my debt to this book's more proximate causes. Above all thanks go to the late Henry M. Hart and the very current Dean Albert M. Sacks, both of Harvard Law School. Readers familiar with their unpublished materials on the legal process will find that, especially in chapters three and four, I have adopted—though occasionally with an altered interpretation—several of their illustrative cases. I would be excessively presumptuous if I attempted to improve upon their selections.

Perhaps only other authors fully appreciate how dramatically readers of preliminary manuscripts can improve final products. Many have maintained my faith in the project at the same time they gently rescued me from appearing alternately dull, naive, ignorant, and wrong. The list includes Professors Joel Grossman, David Danelski, Stephen Wasby, Herbert Jacob, Edward Epstein, Loren Beth, Catherine Krendl, and Paul Kurtz. Judge Robert Winsor, Superior Court of King County, Washington and James Krendl, of the Colorado Bar, unhampered by academic habits and abstractions, strove mightily, and with partial success, to keep me honest and realistic, as did the graduate students in my seminar at the University of Washington in the spring quarter, 1978. All have caused much of what is good here, I alone am the necessary (but I hope not always a sufficient) cause of all the defects.

Finally, Cheryl Bilgin, Sue Willis, and Jack Call did much of the mundane work of typing and proofing. They were as indispensable as they were undercompensated. My thanks also to Greg Franklin, Barbara Garrey, and Wayne Ellis of Little, Brown and Company.

Athens, Georgia

Contents

Reason in Law

*I was much troubled in spirit, in my first years upon
the bench, to find how trackless was the ocean on
which I had embarked. I sought for certainty. I was
oppressed and disheartened when I found that the
quest for it was futile. I was trying to reach land, the
solid land of fixed and settled rules, the paradise of a
justice that would declare itself by tokens plainer and
more commanding than its pale and glimmering
reflections in my own vacillating mind and conscience.... As the years have gone by, and as I have
reflected more and more upon the nature of the judicial process, I have become reconciled to the uncertainty, because I have grown to see it as inevitable. I
have grown to see that the process in its highest
reaches is not discovery, but creation; and that the
doubts and misgivings, the hopes and fears, are part
of the travail of mind, the pangs of death and the
pangs of birth, in which principles that have served
their day expire, and new principles are born.*

 *What is it that I do when I decide a case? To
what sources of information do I appeal for guidance? In what proportions do I permit them to contribute to the result? In what proportions ought they
to contribute? If a precedent is applicable, when do I
refuse to follow it? If no precedent is applicable, how
do I reach the rule that will make a precedent for the
future? If I am seeking logical consistency, the symmetry of the legal structure, how far shall I seek it? At
what point shall the quest be halted by some discre-*

*pant custom, by some consideration of the social wel-
fare, by my own or the common standards of justice
and morals? Into that strange compound which is
brewed daily in the caldron of the courts, all these
ingredients enter in varying proportions. I am not
concerned to inquire whether judges ought to be
allowed to brew such a compound at all. I take judge-
made law as one of the existing realities of life. There,
before us, is the brew. Not a judge on the bench but
had a hand in the making.*

  –Judge Benjamin N. Cardozo,
  The Nature of the Judicial Process (1921)

Chapter I

INTRODUCTION: THINGS ARE SELDOM WHAT THEY SEEM

Curriculum jurisprudentiae tres annos poscit, et scientia vera aetatem.
— Professor Richard LaFleur

I have grown to see that the [legal] process in its highest reaches is not discovery, but creation....
— Benjamin N. Cardozo

Many Americans, including more than a few lawyers and judges, do not properly understand how and why the legal process in the United States operates as it does. They believe, with the young Cardozo, that the legal process "discovers" life's truths and certainties. This book, in contrast, explores the creative character of law. Investigating the creative nature of our legal system can, I believe, improve the quality of justice that the legal system produces. Greater understanding may enable us to demand those improvements which lawyers and judges can realistically make without spinning our wheels searching, as even Judge Cardozo confesses to doing, for the impossible.

1

Our misunderstandings of the legal process persist primarily because we do not understand "legal reasoning." Legal reasoning embodies the ways in which lawyers and judges combine their beliefs about facts, events, and conditions in the word (beliefs about the actuality of things) with their moral beliefs and values (beliefs about right and wrong) to make legal choices. All of us—lawyers, judges, and college professors included—sometimes reason poorly. We make decisions by assuming that some facts are true when we should know they are false. We choose on the basis of one set of moral beliefs without realizing that a different choice resting on an entirely different moral approach would satisfy us more if only we had thought of it in time. Studying when and how lawyers and judges reason well and reason poorly provides us with the key to unlock a more realistic and constructive view of the legal process.

Particularly if you are grappling with the mysteries of law for the first time in your life, you may now feel that you are standing, a bit wobbly in the knees, at the edge of a pit of legalistic double-talk and arcane philosophy. If this is so, you deserve some reassurance: Our awe of law, lawyers, and judges creates unnecessary confusion. We tend to think of law as a science, just as complicated and removed from our daily lives and experiences as quantum mechanics. We also tend to think of both law and science as masses of complex rules and principles that, if we could only memorize them, would allow us to deliver "right answers" like a perfectly programmed computer. If the practice of law amounted to no more than "finding the right rule," law school training would hardly require three years as stated in this chapter's Latin epigraph. A few months of law library training or computer school would suffice.

But neither law nor science really operates that way. Legal reasoning resembles your own experience more than you realize. We make decisions every day by applying to the facts and values around us the tools of common sense, elementary logic, empathy, and personal honor. These factors influence common decisions, such as the family's debate over which of several desired television programs to watch at 8:00 Thursday night or the matron's choice of which of her many friends to invite to tea. These same basic forces in decision making—common sense, logic, empathy, and honor—drive the lawyer's advice to a client or the judge's resolution of a lawsuit. Our culture encourages us to take these values and others like them seriously. Sometimes these values conflict and we must then sort them out and choose among them. The combination of facts and values to make legal choices works in the same way.

This book makes no effort to disguise or hide the complexities of legal reasoning. Sometimes legal reasoning is unavoidably complicated. The facts that the judge must take into account seem to run on for endless pages. The values, the right and wrong issues the case raises, seem to crash headlong against each other. You will therefore need to take the subject of legal reasoning one step at a time. Throughout this book, however, you must keep in mind my main objective. I am *not* trying to reveal to the layperson the unique world of lawyers and judges. I am trying to tell lawyer, judge, and layperson alike that they live and work in the *same* world. This is what too many of us do not understand.

You should approach the study of legal reasoning as you would a jigsaw puzzle. Each chapter will turn some pieces right side up and allow you to fit more of them together. Some pieces uncovered in early chapters may not, however, finally find their fit until the last. Like the challenge of assembling a puzzle, the challenge of this book leaves much of the work to you.

We begin in the next section to work toward a definition of law. In successive sections of this chapter, we shall examine several ways of classifying law and describe the place of this book in a broader overview of law. Having thus laid at least a primitive foundation, we shall return to the main themes of this book.

A DEFINITION OF LAW

Thus far I have deliberately used the word "law" and the phrase "legal process" interchangeably. Law is indeed a process, not a collection of rules. This section works inductively toward a clarified definition of what that process is and what it does. This inductive approach will lead the beginner to unexpected conclusions because it will produce a working definition of law that resembles only slightly what law seems to be, at least on television.

What distinguishes the legal process from other ways of coping with life? Lawyers and judges attempt to prevent and solve other people's problems, but so do physicians, priests, professors, and plumbers. "Problem solving" therefore defines too much. Lawyers and judges work with certain kinds of problems, problems that can lead to conflicts, even physical fights, among people. It is the *kind* of problem with which judges and lawyers work that helps define law.

Contrary to the impression that television drama gives, with its emphasis on courtroom battles, most lawyers generally practice "preventive law." They help people discover ways to reduce their taxes or write valid wills and contracts. They study complex insurance policies and bank loan agreements. Such efforts reduce the probability of conflict. Most lawyers usually play a planning role. They help people create their own "private laws," laws governing their personal affairs and no more.

But, of course, some conflicts start anyway. Why? Sometimes they start because a lawyer did the planning and preventing poorly or because the client did not follow a lawyer's good advice. Sometimes lawyers cannot find in rules of law a safe plan with which to prevent a conflict. Many conflicts, however, such as the auto collision, the dispute with a neighbor over a property line, or the angry firing of an employee, begin without lawyers. Then people may call them in after the fact, not for an ounce of prevention but for the pounding of a cure.

If a battle erupts spontaneously, lawyers may find a solution in the rules of law, though once people get angry at each other they may refuse the solution lawyers offer. If a struggle arises, however, and the lawyers don't find a solution or negotiate a compromise, then either one side gives up or the opponents go to court; they call in the judges to give their solution.

You may now think you have a solid definition of law: Law is the process of preventing or resolving conflicts between people. Lawyers and judges do this; professors, plumbers, and physicians, at least routinely, do not.

But wait. Parents prevent or resolve conflicts among their children daily. And parents, perhaps exasperated from coping with family fights, may turn to a marriage counselor to deal with their own conflicts. Many ministers too no doubt define their goals as reducing conflict. Lawyers, then, aren't the only people who try to resolve conflicts. We have yet to define law precisely.

Law, like the priesthood and professional counseling, involves an immense variety of problems. Law requires the ability to see specifics and to avoid premature generalizing and jumping to conclusions. So do good counseling, good "ministration," and good parenting. But what distinguishes the conflict solving of lawyers and judges from the conflict solving of parents, counselors, or ministers? Consider these three not-so-hypothetical cases. What makes them distinctively *legal* problems?

- A Massachusetts supermarket chain's order of a carload of cantaloupe from Arizona arrives two weeks late and partially rotten. The supermarket chain refuses to take delivery of the melons and refuses to pay for them. Did the seller in the contract of sale guarantee their safe arrival? Did the delay cause the decay, or had some spore infected the melons before shipment? Did the railroad act negligently in causing the delay, thus making it liable for the loss? Should the supermarket chain try to recover the profit it didn't make because it had no melons to sell? From whom? Do any regulations made by the Department of Agriculture of the Interstate Commerce Commission speak to the problem?[1]
- A young man, entranced by the thought of flying, steals someone's Cessna from an airstrip in Rhode Island and manages to survive a landing in a Connecticut corn patch. He is prosecuted under the National Motor

[1]Real life provides us with a much more complicated version of this case of the rotten cantaloupe. See *L. Gillarde Co. v. Joseph Martinelli and Co., Inc.*, 168 F.2d 276 (1st Cir. 1948) and 169 F.2d 60 (1948, rehearing). The case has introduced a generation of students at Harvard Law School, myself among them, to the complexities of the legal process in Henry M. Hart, Jr., and Albert M. Sacks, *The Legal Process* (Cambridge: Harvard Law School, 1958), pp. 10–75. This mammoth unpublished work is one of the finest sources of ideas and problems in the field of legal reasoning ever written. It is available in many university law libraries.

Vehicle Theft Act, which prohibits transportation "in interstate or foreign commerce [of] a motor vehicle, knowing the same to have been stolen...." The statute defines motor vehicle to "include an automobile, automobile truck, automobile wagon, motorcycle, or any other self-propelled vehicle not designed for running on rails." Does the pilot's brief flight amount to transportation of the plane "in interstate...commerce?" Is an airplane a "vehicle" within the meaning of the act?[2]

- A United States president seeks to protect the confidentiality of his private conversations in office from prosecutors who suspect the conversations will reveal evidence of a criminal conspiracy. In what circumstances does the Constitution allow a president to withhold such information?[3]

These are legal problems, not counseling or psychological or parental problems, because we define their nature and limits—but not necessarily their solution—in terms of rules that the state, the government, has made. The laws of contract and of negligence help define the problem or the quarrel between the melon seller and the melon buyer. So, as it turns out, do shipping regulations for farm produce made by the Department of Agriculture. Criminal statutes passed by legislatures define, among many concepts, how the government may deal with thieves. The Constitution sets limits on presidential power. The government has made these rules; they are laws. The process of resolving human conflicts through law begins when one person or several persons decide to take advantage of the fact that the government has made rules to prevent or resolve such conflicts.

---

[2]Cf. *McBoyle v. United States*, 283 U.S. 25 (1931). The letter abbreviations following the names of cases identify the series of books that contains the judicial opinion deciding the case. The first number indicates the volume in the series that contains the opinion, and the second number is the starting page of the opinion. These letters and numbers may bewilder laypersons. If you want to follow up any of my cases, don't hesitate to ask a librarian to help you get started. Most of us like to feel useful, and librarians are no exception. Besides, that's what they're paid to do. At the end of each chapter in this book, you will find actual judicial opinions that illustrate the points just covered. *McBoyle* appears at the end of Chapter 1, pages 22–23.

[3]*United States v. Nixon*, 418 U.S. 683 (1974).

When people convert a problem into a legal conflict by taking it to court, the court's resolution of the problem has the force of the government behind it. Even in a noncriminal case, if the loser or losers don't pay up, the judge may order them to jail.

For centuries judges have, with little help until recently from legislatures, created "the law" of contracts and of negligence through a process we call "common law."[4] Judges are very much a part of the government: they speak with the authority of the state just as legislators and executives do. Of course, legislatures pass statutes, administrative agencies write regulations, and executives issue executive orders and make law, too. And constitutional conventions and amendments to constitutions create the law that governs the government: constitutions. Lawyers and judges often have a difficult time deciding exactly what various arms of the government may have said about their case, but their legal training enables them to discover whether the state has tried to say something.

The legal process, then, is the process lawyers and judges use when they try to prevent or resolve problems—human conflicts—using rules made by the state as their starting point. To study reason in this process is to study how lawyers and judges choose, as they so often must, between alternative legal solutions. For example, legal reasoning studies how they decide whether an airplane is or is not a "vehicle" in the context of the National Motor Vehicle Theft Act. Throughout this book we shall study the legal process by asking the central question lawyers and judges ask themselves as they do their work: What does the law mean as applied to the problem before me? What different and sometimes contradictory solutions to the problem does the law permit? How shall I choose among them?

Now stop and compare this definition of law and legal reasoning with your own intuitive conception of law, with the definition of the legal process you may have developed from television, movies, and other daily experiences. Do the two overlap? Probably not very much. The average layperson usually thinks of law as trials, and criminal trials at that. But trials, by our definition, are one of the less legal, or "law-filled," parts of

---

[4]Karl Llewellyn's *The Common Law Tradition* (Boston: Little, Brown, 1960) remains one of the finest treatments of the subject.

the legal process. Why? Much of the conflict-settling work of lawyers and judges involves deciding not what law means but what happened. In a sense this part of conflict solving is really not law at all but a peculiar kind of historical research: Did the deceased pull a knife on the defendant before the defendant shot him or didn't he? Did that witness really see the defendant run the red light just before he hit the police car? We are confident enough that these historical problems do not require legal reasoning that we often turn the job of solving them over to groups of amateur historians, juries. (Consult Chapter III for more information about juries and fact finding in law.)

Laws do tell these historians what facts to seek. Pulling the knife *could* excuse the shooting through the law of self-defense, though if the deceased were a child of three it would almost surely not. Running the red light *could* establish legal negligence, though it presumably would not if the defendant were driving his car in a funeral procession at the time.

We cannot totally separate law and facts, but the heart of the reasoning part of law, and the subject of this book, lies not in analyzing what happened but in analyzing what facts the rules allow us to seek and what to do with these facts once we "know" them. Turning to the eager flyer, the historical problem we must solve is whether or not that particular defendant at some specified point in the past actually flew someone else's airplane to another state without permission. The legal reasoning problem, on the other hand, requires deciding whether or not we "ought" to call the plane a "vehicle" in this statute's context. Notice that, although this is a statutory rule, the judge, not the legislature, must decide whether an airplane is or isn't a vehicle. The judge has no authority to stop the case and command the legislature to clarify its statute. He must make his own decision. If the judge's decision makes legislators unhappy, they can amend the statute, but that is their concern, not the judge's.

The word "ought" appears intentionally in the last paragraph. Throughout this book you will see that legal decisions inescapably mix factual beliefs with ethical and moral values. This ethical quality makes reason in law very different from reason in arithmetic, whereby a problem involving square roots can be solved simply by following the rules for finding square roots.

You may not yet appreciate the ethical quality in legal reasoning, and you probably do not see law as a process of ethical reasoning rather than rule following. I hope that when you have finished this book you will. The next section helps you with the more immediate task of classifying law so that its many facets do not become a mind-boggling blur.

THREE WAYS TO CLASSIFY LAW

Sources of Law: Where Laws Originate

The range of legal problems and conflicts is practically infinite, but lawyers and judges will, one way or another, resolve the issues by referring to and reasoning about rules of law. Despite the endless variety of legal problems, lawyers and judges usually resort to the four categories of law mentioned in the preceding section: *statutes, common law, constitutional law*, and *administrative regulations*.

The easiest category to understand is what we often call "laws"—the *statutes* passed by legislatures. Laymen tend to think of statutes as the rules that define types of behavior that society wishes to condemn: crimes. However, legislatures enact statutes governing (and sometimes creating!) many problems without enacting criminal statutes—no-fault insurance, income tax rates, social security benefit levels, for example. For our purposes this statutory category also includes the local ordinances passed by the elected bodies of cities and counties.

But there is a problem here. Despite their freedom, legislatures do not enact statutes to cover everything. And when lawyers and judges face a problem without a statute, they normally turn to that older set of rules called *common law*.

Judges, not legislators, make common law rules, but not by calling together a judicial convention to argue, log-roll, draft, and finally vote on (or bury) proposed laws. Common law rules have emerged through a process introduced in England before the discovery of the New World. The process began essentially because the Crown in England chose to assert national authority by sending judges throughout the country to act, to decide cases, in the name of the Crown. The king did not in fact write rules to govern all judges' decisions. It was because the judges *acted* in the name of the central government, certainly a shaky government by our standards, that their decisions became law common to all the king's domain. Many of the rules for decision making originated in local custom or the minds of the judges themselves.

The process by which these decisions became "law" took a surprisingly long time. In the beginning, the reasons for judicial decisions were murky, and judges applied them inconsistently. But observers of the courts wrote descriptions of the cases, often just the facts and the result, and judges began to look to these descriptions for past examples to guide current judicial action. The formal practice whereby judges write opinions explaining their choices, which other judges in turn treat as legal authority called "precedents," is only a few hundred years old, but it is a powerful and stabilizing force in legal reasoning today. Precedents will receive much attention in this book because the facts and values embedded in the examples of precedents are fundamental tools of legal reasoning.

In Chapters IV and V we examine reason in statutory and common sources of law, and Chapter VI explores the third source of law: *constitutional law.* The Constitution of the United States and the 50 state constitutions set out the structure and powers of government. They also place legal limits on the way those who govern can use their power. While statutes (and common law where statutory law is silent) can govern anybody, constitutions govern the government.[5] The Constitution even governs presidents, although most constitutional cases involve an alleged conflict between the national or state constitutions and a decision made and enforced by lesser public administrators who claim to act under statutory authority.

Administrative regulations, of the Internal Revenue Service, or the San Francisco Zoning Board, or any of the thousands

---

[5]If I, as a private citizen, don't like a speech of yours and forcibly remove you from your soapbox, I will probably violate a principle of common or statutory law. And I would violate a normative principle favoring free exchange of ideas. This principle is what makes the heckling of public speakers by antagonists in the audience so despicable. I will not violate the First Amendment of the Constitution. If I did this to you while working as a government official, such as an FBI agent, however, that would be another matter.

of national, state, and local administrative agencies, make up the fourth source of law. Executives and non-elected administrators can make rules only when a constitution or a statute gives them the authority to do so. Problems in administrative law can fascinate and perplex as much as any. Because the length of this book and your time have limits, we shall examine reasoning about administrative regulations only slightly. You should not, however, let this deliberate neglect mislead you into thinking the subject is unimportant. Administrative regulations are shaping law and our lives more and more.[6] The scope of this book is confined to historically more developed sources of law: *statutes, common law,* and *constitutional law.*

Before concluding this discussion of the sources of law, I want to emphasize this central truth: Judges write opinions explaining their legal choices. They do so not only when they apply older, judge-made common law rules but also when they choose among alternative possible meanings of statutes, constitutional provisions, and administrative regulations. All these opinions create precedents, guides to help judges in similar future cases make similar kinds of decisions. *Judicial opinions, therefore, give meaning to all types of legal rules.* A judge who chooses to interpret a statute in a certain way creates a precedent that judges in future similar cases may incorporate into their own decisions. This is why we say that judges make law.

Note carefully, however, that the source of a given law does not solve any individual's legal problem that arises under the rule. Understanding the sources of law may explain the why of legal reasoning, but not the how. Is the following method of classifying law more helpful in this regard?

Functions of Law: The Problems That Laws Solve

The second way of classifying laws examines the various social objectives that different laws try to achieve. It examines the problems that laws try to solve.

Scholars classify these so-called "functions" of laws in varying ways. In one common method, examples of the kinds of

---

[6]See my *Administrative Law and Politics* (Boston: Little, Brown, 1983).

problems laws attempt to prevent or resolve are simply listed. Some laws (but only a small fraction of the total) deter crimes by threatening punishments. These same criminal laws also diminish the occurrence of vigilante justice; they allow people outraged by crimes to vent their anger safely on the criminal through the punishments decided by the courts. Other laws, like those regulating the operation of radio and television broadcasters, do not prevent good people from doing bad things or punish bad people in hopes of making them good. Instead, these laws coordinate people with different but equally "good" wants, in this case the competing interests of broadcasters and listeners. Note that the problem here arises from a limited resource, the airwaves, which society must use wisely for its collective advantage.

Some laws promote government itself and keep it financially solvent by raising tax revenues. Other laws protect citizens from government. They preserve our freedoms not only to participate in politics but also to transact and enforce private economic agreements. Many laws, like building and sanitation codes, seek to protect our individual health. Others, like laws that prohibit racial discrimination, identify broad objectives for society as a whole.

Superficially, these classifications do seem important and useful. It *is* important to know the legal process helps people trust that government will try to make important immediate expectations about life come true. When this minimum trust collapses, societies quickly slip toward anarchy. Law *does* help people cope with many kinds of problems, and it will take more than a few simple formulas to understand law and legal reasoning. But, on closer inspection, how helpful is this classification of legal functions? Since policy makers in government generally (but not inevitably) express their policy choices as rules of law, the list of problems that laws address can become no more than a laundry list of public policies.

More to the point, a judge who knows that law X protects individual health or that law Y seeks to raise revenues does not, by that knowledge, move any closer to deciding the case before him.[7] Indeed, in the typical case, the judge must evaluate a

----

[7]Throughout this book the masculine gender, when I use it generically, refers

variety of legal rules with many functions—some directly opposing one another—all of which potentially apply to the case.

Thus the first two ways of classifying laws are not entirely satisfactory. In this book therefore we focus less on the sources and functions of law than on the choices judges must make when they decide legal cases and on the manner in which they can make such choices wisely. How can we begin to classify the kinds of choices judges make?

Dynamics of Law: The Choices That Laws Create

In most cases, judges must reconcile the competing pulls of constitutional values, the actual wording of legal provisions, prior judicial opinions, and their own views of the facts and values—the social realities—of the cases before them. Judges must make difficult choices such as these:

- Does the case before me call for continued adherence to the historical meaning of legal words? Must I do what the framers of statutory or constitutional language hoped their language would accomplish? When do social, political, and technological changes permit or require a different or revised interpretation?
- Does this case call for judicial deference to the literal meaning of the words themselves? In what circumstances do I decide more wisely by ignoring the actual dictionary definitions of the words in a statute or constitution?
- Does this case obligate me to follow a judicial precedent the wisdom of which I doubt? When am I free to ignore a relevant precedent?

Throughout the following chapters we shall see that the judge's choice of change or stability, judicial discretion or legislative judgment, and literal or flexible interpretation of words and precedents depends on the nature of the relationship a legal choice addresses. We shall see that it becomes crucial for

---

to women and men equally. For an effective corresponding generic use of the feminine gender, see Charles L. Knapp, *Problems in Contract Law* (Boston: Little, Brown, 1976).

judges to know to what extent people (1) probably relied on past statements of law; (2) had a justifiable reason to rely on past law; (3) can benefit from judge-made changes in law; and (4) can or cannot use the courts in the future to implement a planned effort to solve problems. Judges must know all of these, or at least guess at them as intelligently as possible, to reason wisely in law.

A BRIEF OVERVIEW OF LAW

The legal process encompasses a huge terrain. The boundaries include the political processes by which legislators, executive officials, and bureaucrats make laws. It also includes all the ways in which people, with and without the help of lawyers, make their own "private law" to govern their immediate affairs, and it equally includes all the methods, both deliberate and unconscious, that people use to avoid their legal responsibilities. The legal process incorporates the many complex requirements of legal procedure and jurisdiction that define when and how courts hear lawsuits in the first place.

In this book we will examine this huge terrain of the legal process from only one of many possible vantage points: Somehow a disagreement has occurred. Neither love nor negotiation nor a clear rule of law standing alone has produced a resolution. The parties have gone to court. The lawyers have urged competing and inconsistent interpretations of the law before the judge. The judge, whose decision will probably not be much better than the quality of the legal arguments he has heard, must make choices. *Legal reasoning* is the label I attach to this last point in the huge field of legal process, the point at which judges make legal choices.

Have I given this book a misleading title? Because the legal process is so much vaster than the point at which judges make choices among many possible interpretations of legal rules, should I not have chosen a title like *Reason in Courts*? No. The point of judicial choice is the centerpoint in the field. Whenever a lawyer works with a client to help him create his own private law or to help him prevent or resolve a conflict; whenever a legislative draftsman worries about the wording of a proposed statute; whenever an executive official designs a new regulation, all must decide as well as they can how courts will react to their creations. If they choose incorrectly, if the courts interpret and apply the rule in unanticipated ways, they may fail to achieve the purpose of their plan. Lawyers must reason about their clients' wishes, and legislators and officials must reason about policy needs, but they must also reason like judges or run the risk of failing. Because courts tend to have the last word, at least in the short and usually in the medium run, the law is what the judges say it is. Anyone who seeks to make and interpret official policy through law must, at some point, tailor his behavior to the realities of legal reasoning in a potential lawsuit in order to achieve his goals.

FIVE STARTLING STATEMENTS ABOUT LAW

Having thus laid the beginnings of an analytical foundation for studying law, we can now begin to grapple more directly with the subject of this book. Here are five important statements about the legal process. Each one may contradict what you now believe about law and thus startle you a bit. The legal process in the United States is not what it so often seems to be. If you are a beginner in the study of law, you should feel, when you finish this chapter, no more than a mixture of curiosity and confusion. After all, the great Benjamin Cardozo confessed to being confused even after he became a judge!

1. Rules of Law Do Not Resolve Legal Conflicts in Court

Posted speed limits tell us how fast we may legally drive. Speed limit laws authorize policemen to ticket us if we go faster. Statutes tell us that if we wish to create a valid will we must sign it. Often they tell us we must sign the will "at the end." If we don't so sign a will, a judge will disregard it entirely. The Supreme Court ruled that the Constitution forbids school systems deliberately to segregate students in classrooms by race.

Other judges follow the Court's ruling and compel schools that do so to integrate.

Each of these statements correctly describes a legal rule. How, then, can I assert that rules of law, rules about speed limits, wills, and racial segregation, do *not* resolve legal conflicts? The answer depends on the definition of a legal conflict and on what judges must do when they resolve legal conflict.

By a legal conflict I mean *litigation,* going to court and asking a judge or a jury or both to settle a dispute.

Occasionally, people go to court knowing they will lose. They go simply to delay the inevitable as long as possible, to delay going to jail or to delay repaying a debt. Courts, in other words, occasionally act as bill collectors. But most people who go to court—who engage in a legal conflict—do so in two other situations. In the first, they will disagree about the facts. "I *was* doing only 35 in the 35 zone," the motorist argues. "Fifty," answers the officer. "That signature is a forgery," argues the disinherited son. "The deceased's very own," responds the will's beneficiary. In the second situation, they will disagree about the meaning of the law. Each side will interpret the law differently. The speeder argues that the speed limit doesn't apply because he was rushing his very pregnant wife to the hospital at the time. The disinherited son argues that the will wasn't signed "at the end" because the mother added a clause, written below the signature line, just before she signed the will on the line. He says the will disinheriting him is invalid. Some argue that the law requires busing to integrate schools. Others deny it.

Now notice that in neither of these situations does a rule of law *by itself* solve the conflict in court. In both situations a judge or jury solves the conflict by making a *choice.* Fact X happened; fact Y did not. Legal interpretation X is better than legal interpretation Y. In a legal conflict it is the *choice* of one version of the facts over another and the *choice* of one interpretation of the law over another that resolves the conflict.

Put another way, the legal problems that lawyers handle become true legal conflicts precisely when the lawyers fail to find an interpretation of the facts or a rule of law—a statute, an administrative regulation, a constitutional clause, or a common law precedent—that provides an answer that people on all sides of the issue automatically accept. Of course, rules of law help define and narrow the conflict. Rules of law—the speed limit ordinance or the law of wills or a constitutional provision—create the issue on which the parties disagree. The motorist and the policeman, the beloved and the disinherited children, and the supporters and opponents of desegregation would not clash in court if no law created speed limits or wills or the idea that government must not classify people on the basis of their race. Laws also create courts and the procedures, like the law of evidence, that tell judges how to organize the process of resolving conflicts. My point is simply this: *when legal rules and the indisputable facts of the case make everything clear, when the parties know how the case will come out, they usually won't go to court in the first place.*

Clear rules of law solve human problems and conflicts all the time. People take problems to lawyers, and lawyers, with the help of the law, solve most of them without going to court at all. But, when cases go to court, the final decision usually depends upon a *choice* about the facts or about the meaning of the rule of law and not the rule itself.

Legal reasoning describes the ways judges make choices about rule of law. We shall see that rules of law often turn out to be ambiguous but that judges must make legal choices anyway. To study reason in law is to study how lawyers and judges make choices when rules of law do not resolve legal problems automatically.

2. Laws Cannot Be Completely Clear and Stable

Laws are a tool that government uses to govern us. But how can the government possibly govern us if we can't tell what the laws say, or if the laws keep changing? How can it be wrong to demand clarity and stability in law? The catchword above is "completely." Much of this book works toward a clear description of the circumstances in which clarity and stability in law are and are not achievable or desirable. For the moment, let me simply plant two seeds of thoughts: First, judges, being human, will occasionally create bad precedents, and the legal system should have the ability to correct such mistakes. Second, times change and laws must change with them.

3. Judges Do Not Always Know What They Are Doing

Judges, recipients of extensive legal training, engage in one of the most refined and sophisticated thinking processes we can find anywhere in public life. Compare the reasoned quality of a judicial opinion with a typically vapid and inconclusive presidential campaign speech. How can I imply that judges don't know what they're doing?

The argument I have just put in your head is a good one. Most of the time judges *do* know what they are doing. Most of the time they wisely apply the rules that define and shape the legal conflict. By stating this third point so bluntly, however, I hope to impress two other points.

First, in a real sense, none of us completely knows what he is doing. To sharpen this blunt point, nobody who makes decisions can pull out of his subconscious all the motives, values, biases, and hunches that influence his choices. We don't have time to be forever introspective. Even if we did (and judges certainly don't), dealing with our inner drives, motives, and biases can be painful. It is in our nature to avoid painful introspection. Nevertheless, these influences regularly tip the scales of justice. Judges cannot totally escape these influences, and we (and they) should not pretend they can.

Second, and more important, I assert that lawyers and judges today do not properly appreciate their own common law tradition. This chapter has introduced common law and Chapter IV will describe this tradition more fully. Here it suffices to note that in common law systems judicial opinions inevitably create law. All too often, however, judges shy away from that inevitability. Given a legal conflict properly before him for decision, a judge may decide by saying, "Let the legislature decide. That's the democratic way." Judges who defer deliberately to the legislature think they are preserving democracy when, in fact, they are more probably only making bad law or preserving bad law made by judges before them. Unlike the unavoidable ignorance discussed previously, this confusion about the proper judicial role reveals an unnecessary evil in legal reasoning that can and should occur far less often than it does.[8]

4. Judges Do Not Successfully Do Justice Most of the Time

Although you may have been initially uncomfortable with the first three "startling" statements, you may think you intuitively understand this one. After all, who knows what justice really is? But the reasons that judges cannot simply "do justice" most of the time are more complicated than that. Often judges cannot simply "do justice" because two competing ideas collide. Sometimes important ideas and principles in law collide. The Constitution contains language protecting the freedom of the press. It also contains language ensuring the fairness of criminal trials. But an unrestrained press can do much to prejudice the fairness of a trial.

In this instance, however, you will say that judges *can* do justice by reaching a fair compromise between these interests. You are right. The more difficult problem arises not when two interests collide but when two ideas of justice itself collide. Consider the occasional collision of general and particular justice. Is it just for the engineer to pull the train away from the station always exactly on time, even though a G.I. racing down

---

[8]I also mean this statement as a warning. Most of the study of law involves reading and analyzing appellate court opinions, a process described more fully in the next chapter. Judicial opinions create law, but we must constantly warn ourselves that these opinions do not necessarily reflect the judge's real reasons for choosing as he does, even when the judge can articulate to himself the unstated reasons for choice. Judges sometimes do not always tell us everything they know. Many readers will know, or know of, Woodward and Armstrong's *The Brethren.* I would prefer that you see Walter Murphy, *Elements of Judicial Strategy* (Chicago: University of Chicago Press, 1964), for a fascinating description of the ways the justices of the United States Supreme Court maneuver, negotiate, and compromise in order to create opinions with the broadest possible support. See also Walter V. Schaefer, "Precedent and Policy," 34 *University of Chicago Law Review* 3 (1966).

the platform to get home to his family for Christmas will miss it? Is it not true in the long run, to paraphrase the late Professor Zechariah Chafee, that fewer people will miss trains if everyone knows that trains always leave on the dot, that more people will miss trains if they assume that they can dally and still find the train at the station? While it is often possible to engineer compromises among competing interests, it is often impossible to compromise between different visions of justice itself. Unless he is corrupt or lazy, a judge will *strive* to do justice, but whether he succeeds often remains debatable.[9]

5. "Correct" Legal Reasoning Does Not Eliminate Bias in Law

In this book we examine a variety of ways judges ought to make legal choices, to "reason in law." The ways of making legal choices I describe and advocate here do not, however, make judges or anyone else completely "objective," because legal decisions require choices from among competing values. The problem of general versus particular justice is a good illustration. A value, a preference, or a moral "feeling" is not a concept we can prove to be right or wrong. Those who adopt values that conflict with yours will call you biased, and you may feel the same way about them.

Facts are different. Whenever we all accept a method for proving a truth, we then call whatever truth that method reveals a "fact." Because we all accept the basic rules of astronomy, we can say "for a fact" that the earth revolves around the sun, even though the sun appears to revolve around the earth.

The components of legal reasoning I describe here in part urge judges not to ignore facts. In this sense, legal reasoning can eliminate bias, for it can reveal cases in which judges make decisions based on a belief that something is true when they know, or ought to know, that it is false. But judges must also

---

[9]See Jennifer Hochschild, *What's Fair: American Beliefs about Distributive Justice.* (Cambridge: Harvard University Press, 1981). Consider more specifically whether a cutback of firemen due to budget problems was "just" if the city laid off white workers with more job seniority than black firemen hired under a recently adopted affirmative action plan.

choose among values. A discussion of legal reasoning can stress that some values are better than others, but arguments on both sides will remain. If the argument gets heated, each side will accuse the other of being biased. In the final chapter, we will examine more fully the nature of bias in law. If "biases" and "values" are identical psychological feelings or beliefs about right and wrong, then legal reasoning cannot eliminate them.

SUMMARY

In the study of law, as well as in its execution, getting the question right is always half the struggle and often all of it. Hence I summarize each chapter with a list of questions. If a question stymies you, some rereading may be in order.

- How does this book define law?
- What is legal reasoning?
- How and why do legal choices resemble everyday choices?
- How do common law, statutes, administrative law, and constitutional law differ?
- How and why do appellate judges "make" all four kinds of law?
- What problems do laws try to solve?
- What choices do laws and cases create for judges?
- Convert each of the five "startling statements" into its opposite, a "misconception of law." Why is it misleading to say that rules of law solve conflicts in court? To insist that rules always be completely clear and stable? To argue that judges know what they are doing, and so forth?

ILLUSTRATIVE CASE

At each chapter's end I give you a chance to apply some of the skills you have just learned to an actual instance of legal reasoning in a judicial opinion. At the end of the opinion I will pose questions that will help you extract the proper lessons from the opinion itself. Here I use the first case to introduce you to some case mechanics as well. I pose these "technical" questions before the case. You should be able to identify terms from the case context itself. If not, look them up in the dictionary.

1. Who are the *parties* in this lawsuit? Who sued whom in the trial court? Who lost at trial and what designation does this party have on appeal?

2. In what *jurisdiction* did this case arise: federal or state?
3. Does this case arise under a statute, the constitution, or a principle of common law?
4. Is this a *civil* or *criminal* case?
5. At what level in our court system does the following opinion arise: *trial, intermediate appellate,* or *supreme appellate?*
6. What was the *disposition* at the trial: guilty or innocent? (Note that in a civil trial the defending party is usually found *liable* or *not liable.* The terms *guilt* and *innocence* apply only to criminal trial dispositions.) What was the *disposition* on appeal: reversed or affirmed?

McBoyle v. United States
Supreme Court of the United States
283 U.S. 25 (1931)

Mr. Justice HOLMES delivered the opinion of the Court.

The petitioner was convicted of transporting from Ottawa, Illinois, to Guymon, Oklahoma, an airplane that he knew to have been stolen, and was sentenced to serve three years' imprisonment and to pay a fine of $2,000. The judgment was affirmed by the Circuit Court of Appeals for the Tenth Circuit. 43 F.(2d) 273. A writ of *certiorari* was granted by this Court on the question whether the National Motor Vehicle Theft Act applies to aircraft. Act of October 29, 1919, c. 89, 41 Stat. 324, U.S. Code, title 18, § 408. That Act provides: "Sec. 2. That when used in this Act: (a) The term 'motor vehicle' shall include an automobile, automobile truck, automobile wagon, motor cycle, or any other self-propelled vehicle not designed for running on rails.... Sec. 3. That whoever shall transport or cause to be transported in interstate or foreign commerce a motor vehicle, knowing the same to have been stolen, shall be punished by a fine of not more than $5,000, or by imprisonment of not more than five years, or both."

Section 2 defines the motor vehicles of which the transportation in interstate commerce is punished in Section 3. The question is the meaning of the word "vehicle" in the phrase "any other self-propelled vehicle not designed for running on rails." No doubt etymologically it is possible to use the word to signify a conveyance working on land, water, or air, and sometimes legislation extends the use in that direction, e.g., land and air, water being separately provided for, in the Tariff Act, September 21, 1922, c. 356, § 401 (b), 42 Stat. 858, 948. But in everyday speech "vehicle" calls up the picture of a thing moving on land. Thus in Rev. St. § 4, intended, the Government suggests, rather to enlarge than to restrict the definition, vehicle includes every contrivance capable of being used "as a means of transportation on land." And this is repeated, expressly excluding aircraft, in the Tariff Act, June 17, 1930, c. 497, § 401 (b), 46 Stat. 590, 708. So here, the phrase under discussion calls up the popular picture. For after including automobile truck, automobile wagon, and motor cycle, the words "any other self-propelled vehicle not designed for running on rails" still indicate that a vehicle in the popular sense, that is a vehicle running on land, is the theme. It is a vehicle that runs, not something, not commonly called a vehicle, that flies. Airplanes were well known in 1919 when this statute was passed, but it is admitted that they were not mentioned in the reports or in the debates in Congress. It is impossible to read words that so carefully enumerate the different forms of motor vehicles and have no reference of any kind to aircraft, as including airplanes under a term that usage more and more precisely confines to a different class. The counsel for the petitioner have shown that the phraseology of the statute as to motor vehicles follows that of earlier statutes of Connecticut, Delaware, Ohio, Michigan, and Missouri, not to mention the late Regulations of Traffic for the District of Columbia, title 6, c. 9, § 242, none of which can be supposed to leave the earth.

Although it is not likely that a criminal will carefully consider the text of the law before he murders or steals, it is reasonable that a fair warning should be given to the world in language that the common world will understand, of what the law intends to do if a certain line is passed. To make the warning fair, so far as possible the line should be clear. When a rule of conduct is laid down in words that evoke in the common mind only the picture of vehicles moving on land, the statute should not be extended to aircraft simply because it may seem to us that a similar policy applies, or upon the speculation that if the legislature had thought of it, very likely broader words would have been used. United States v. Bhagat Singh Thind, 261 U.S. 204, 209, 43 S.Ct. 338.

Judgment reversed.

QUESTIONS

1. The main lesson of Chapter I is that after you have mastered all the descriptive elements about a case, the case still seems somehow lifeless or boring. What brings the *McBoyle* case to life? Is it not that the Supreme Court must make a choice about

the meaning of an ambiguous statute? Why is the law ambiguous? What choice must the Court therefore make?

2. What are the facts, the actualities about this case? Is it a fact that the word *airplane* does not appear in the statute? That airplane theft was not a major social problem when the statute was passed? That McBoyle transported the plane, knowing it to be stolen?

3. What are the values, the beliefs about right and wrong, at work in the reasoning of this case? Is the principle that it is unfair to convict bad people under unclear statutes important here? Can you think of any other value that might lead to the opposite result? You may appreciate knowing that I think Holmes reasoned badly here and that the court wrongly decided the case because it chose to ignore some important facts and values that bore on the case. I shall describe these in the chapter on statutory interpretation, but you may be able to identify them on your own. (Hints: Is transporting an airplane, knowing it to be stolen, morally ambiguous? It may make sense to exclude airplanes from certain international trade decisions about "vehicles," and from the District of Columbia's traffic code, but does this automatically mean that it makes sense to exclude airplanes from a list of stolen vehicles it is wrong to transport under our nation's criminal statutes?)

SOME EXPLORATORY PROBLEMS*

1. When courts act as bill collectors, there may be no serious dispute between the parties either about the facts of their case or about the proper interpretation of the law. In what other circumstances might people file a lawsuit in the absence of real disagreement about both the law and the facts? Consider in this

---

*The "exploratory problems" that conclude each chapter are not simple review questions. Each problem is designed to push inquiry beyond the chapter itself, sometimes to push toward later chapters in the book, and sometimes toward problems this book does not fully address at all. The reader should not search through the chapter for "the answer" to these questions but should approach them as speculative and open-ended exercises. Readers should not hesitate to admit that they lack information necessary to determine the proper approach to these problems. The wisest people admit what they don't know. Such admissions are far preferable to blind guessing. Those who guess wildly often find it harder to appreciate a correct approach when it becomes available than do those who can identify the nature of their ignorance.

connection the fairly common situation in which one party admits he hurt the other but denies he owes as much as the other party demands. Are these conflicts about legal remedies conflicts about the law or the facts or something else? Consider also (a) the possibility that judicial incompetence makes some trial outcomes hard to predict and (b) the effect tremendous backlogs and delays in civil trial courts might have on the tendency to file lawsuits.

2. Define a fact and define a value. How do they differ? Are you satisfied that a difference actually exists?

3. Here are three brief descriptions of recent news stories. Which of the "startling statements" about law does each story illustrate? Notice that each story may illustrate more than one statement, and it is possible that you can find hints of all five statements in each story:

   - In 1981 a federal judge forbade the Boston fire department to lay off black firemen with lower job seniority (i.e., fewer years in service) than white officers who were laid off in order to maintain the required level of affirmative action. On March 23, 1983 (p. 33), the *Wall Street Journal* reported that on the day of the court decision the white firemen stated they would no longer eat with black firemen in the station house.

   - The legislature of the state of Arkansas recently passed the Balanced Treatment for Creation-Science and Evolution-Science Act after less than 30 minutes' debate. The governor reportedly signed the bill without reading it. The statute specifically forbade the teaching of religious doctrine. However, a coalition of plaintiffs including 12 clergymen, represented by the American Civil Liberties Union, established that the approved creation-science texts were identical to religious texts with the explicit religious words merely replaced. Trial judge William Overton ruled the statute unconstitutional.[10]

   - An article appeared in the *New York Times* dealing with the legal struggle to protect a person's property right to his own new ideas, ideas that inevitably are widely shared in an electronic age. It stated in part:

---

[10]"Creation Goes to Court." *Newsweek,* December 21, 1981, p. 57.

The 1976 Copyright Act gives the author of an original work—books, pantomime, music and dance are all treated the same—the exclusive right to reproduce, or perform his work for a period of years, after which it passes into the public domain, and anyone can use it.

But not every portion or germ of a work can be copyrighted. Consider the case of a young writer who sends a plot outline to a movie studio or book publisher and gets it back, rejected. He will probably feel that his story, however hackneyed, is so uniquely creative that if a similar story turns up on the screen a year later, it must be because his work has been stolen.

"No one has a right to own something like 'Boy meets girl, boy loses girl, boy gets girl,' or a set of biographical facts," said Alan Latman, who teaches intellectual property at New York University Law School. "Those are so broad that they are really just ideas, and anyone can use them. The only thing a writer can own, and protect, is a specific expression of that basic idea, a story fleshed out with so many details and characters that it becomes his special creation."

The pending lawsuit arising out of *E.T.* will involve just such a judgment. A Los Angeles woman claims she should get $750 million of the profits from Steven Spielberg's movie because she came up with the idea for it in a copyrighted one-act play, "Lokey from Maldmar," which she submitted to Universal Studios in 1979.

But Louis Petrich, the lawyer for Universal who is seeking to have the suit dismissed, said, "The problem with that is that the idea for *E.T.* was originally developed at Columbia Studios, and besides, her idea had no substantial similarity to *E.T.*

"If the claim is just 'I had an idea about a creature from outer space,' that's an idea, and it's not protectable," said Mr. Latman. "On the other hand, if you had the idea about a likable outer-space creature who was left behind on earth, and who wants to go home even after he befriends a little boy, you might have a case, assuming you can show that Steven Spielberg saw it, and knew you weren't giving him this idea as a gift. In general, though, the kinds of cases where people say their plot was stolen are pretty hard to win."[11]

---

[11]Tamar Lewin, "When Does a Creative Idea Become Intellectual Property?" *New York Times,* Sunday, March 27, 1983, section 2, pp. 1, 28.

4. Imagine yourself in a group—a family or a sorority house, for example—debating which television show to watch at a given time. Assume different people want to watch different shows on the one available set. Create hypothetical resolutions of that debate in which the following values influence the outcome: efficiency, fairness, saving face, maintaining credibility, raw power, and compassion.

5. Think more carefully about the phrase "private law," which appears several times in this chapter. Give examples of the kinds of private laws people make. Should judges and the legal system encourage the making of private laws like contracts? If so, how can judges encourage private law making most effectively?

Chapter II

ELEMENTS OF LEGAL REASONING

The problem posed by legal education in its promotion of legal thinking is not that we teach students a particular view of the world but that we fail to take proper account of it.
—James M. Elkins

The person who first said, "Ask a simple question, you get a simple answer," probably didn't ask a lawyer.
—Charles L. Knapp

The first chapter began to narrow this book's scope of inquiry. We do not in this book put ourselves in the shoes of legislators, nor do we examine how elections or lobbying efforts or presidential leadership produce new law. We look at legal problems through the eyes of judges and through the eyes of parties who bring the conflict to them: A legal conflict has started. Lawyers have failed either to prevent it or resolve it short of going to court. They have brought a case to a judge, who must in turn choose a sensible solution to the conflict from the competing arguments the lawyers make.

Chapter I introduced the inescapable truth that both judges and legislators make law. However, important differences do exist. The legislature enacts laws to handle general social problems. Its statutes try to alter the future. The judge determines whether a specific plaintiff or defendant, locked in a legal conflict that arose in the past, should win the case. (Court and legislature do touch when the judge has to decide whether the plaintiff's or the defendant's behavior exemplifies the general social problem the legislature addresses. Chapter IV returns to this problem.) The judge who resolves a legal conflict seeks primarily to impose a meaning, a legal conclusion, on the past. The law the judge makes is a product of his opinion, his justification for his conclusion that future judges may read and follow. Judges ought to care about deciding cases in ways that will promote wise solving of problems in the future. At the same time, however, they should seek a solution to the case that deals fairly with litigants' expectations *in the past*.

We have narrowed the inquiry even further. We know that people often ask courts to give them a remedy, usually money, by confirming their version of the conflict. They ask courts to determine who did or didn't do what to whom in the past, and to provide or deny a remedy based on that determination. Court trials seek primarily to answer these "historical" questions, often by deciding which witnesses seem believable and which, by comparison, do not.

Chapter I narrowed the scope of legal reasoning a final step. It stated that reason in law takes over when rules of law themselves fail to solve legal conflicts once the facts of the dispute between the parties are known. Rules fail to solve legal problems because judges and lawyers often cannot tell precisely what the words of the rule mean in their case.

This is where Chapter II takes over. The first section explains why law is so often ambiguous. The second section asserts that this uncertainty and ambiguity benefits us more than it harms us, at least as a general rule. The third section examines the other side of the uncertainty coin, the general philosophical conditions in which judges should maintain legal clarity and stability at the expense of other values. The concluding section reviews some general and inevitable characteristics of law that make it forever changing, never perfected.

UNPREDICTABILITY IN LAW

Reasoning from Words

Cases often go to courts (and particularly appellate courts) because the law does not determine the outcome. Both sides believe they have a chance to win. The legal process is in these cases *unpredictable*. Legal rules are made with words, and we can begin to understand why law is unpredictable by examining the ambiguity of words, the "disorderly conduct of words," as Professor Chafee put it.[1] Sometimes our language fails to give us precise definitions. There is, for example, no way to define the concept of "table" so as to exclude some items we call "benches" and the reverse.[2] More often, words and statements that seem clear enough in the abstract may, nevertheless, have different meanings to each of us because we have all had different experiences with the objects or events in the world that the word has come to represent. The experiences of each of us are unique in many respects, so no one word or set of words necessarily means the same thing to all of us. How many parents must reject some names for a new child because, while the mother associates a given name with a friend or hero from the past, the father once knew a villain of the same name?

Words, furthermore, are malleable: people can shape them to suit their own interests. To illustrate, in 1962, Congress, to encourage new business investment, allowed business people up to a 10 percent tax credit for investing in new personal property for their business. Investments like new machinery would qualify, but new buildings and permanent building fixtures would not. In 1982 the Justice Department sued the accounting firm of Ernst and Whinney for using words to disguise real property as personal property. What the accountants called "movable parti-

[1]Zechariah Chafee, "The Disorderly Conduct of Words," 41 *Columbia Law Review* 381 (1941).

[2]My thanks to Professor Martin Landau, University of California, Berkeley, for this example. If you don't believe it, try creating this definitional distinction paying attention to coffee tables and tool benches. Furthermore, suppose a state enacts a statute exempting from its sales tax all "food and food stuffs." What is "food"? Is chewing gum food? Is coffee? Is beer?

tions," "equipment accesses," and "decorative fixtures," were in reality doors, manholes, and windows—all real property unqualified for the tax deduction. A "freezer" was in reality an entire refrigerated warehouse, "cedar decoration" was a wood-paneled wall, and "movable partitions—privacy" described toilet stalls.[3]

The disorderly conduct of words affects legal reasoning most immediately when a judge faces the task of interpreting a statute for the first time, when no judicial precedent interpreting the statute helps the judge to find its meaning. Therefore, we shall refine the problem of disorderly words in Chapter IV, which examines judicial choices in statutory interpretation.

Reasoning from Examples of Precedents

The previous paragraph suggests that precedents help narrow the range of legal choices judges face when they resolve a case. Indeed, precedents do just that, but they never provide complete certainty. Reasoning by example also perpetuates a degree of unpredictability in law. To see why, we must proceed through six analytical stages.

Stage One: Reasoning by Example in General

Reasoning by example, in its simplest form, means accepting one choice and rejecting another because the past provides an example that the accepted choice somehow "worked." Robert,

---

[3] Jim Drinkhall, "Turnabout has IRS Accusing Taxpayers of Gobbledygook," *Wall Street Journal*, November 12, 1982, p. 1. Consider also in this context the remarks of the poet Leopardi (1798–1837):

> Like jewels in rings, ideas are enclosed in and almost bound to words. Indeed they incarnate as the soul does in the body, making one being in such a way that ideas are inseparable from words, and if they are separated they are no longer the same, they escape our intellect and conception and become unrecognizable, as would our soul if it were parted from the body.

quoted without citation in Rosanna Warren, "Magus of Language," *New Republic*, August 8, 1983, p. 32.

for example, wants to climb a tree but wonders if its branches will hold. He chooses to attempt the climb because his older sister has just climbed the tree without mishap. Robert reasons by example. His reasoning hardly guarantees success: His older sister may still be skinnier and lighter. Robert may regret a choice based on a bad example, but he still reasons that way. If he falls and survives, he will possess a much better example from which to reason in the future.

The most important characteristic of reasoning by example in any area of life is that no rules tell the decider *how* to select the facts that are similar or different. Let us therefore see how this indeterminacy occurs in legal reasoning.

Stage Two: Examples in Law

In law, precedents provide the examples for legal reasoning. For starters, a precedent contains the analysis and the conclusion reached in an earlier case in which the facts and the legal question(s) resemble the current conflict a judge has to resolve. Even where a statute or a constitutional rule is involved, a judge will look at what other judges have said about the meaning of that rule when they applied it to similar facts and answered similar legal questions. Not only might a judge resolve Chapter I's case of the rotten cantaloupe in terms of common law precedents of contract, but a judge hearing the cases of the airplane thief or of Richard Nixon's "Watergate" defense of executive privilege would look beyond the National Motor Vehicle Act and the Constitution to see how judges have interpreted these rules or rules like them in earlier precedents.

To understand more fully how precedents create examples we must return to the distinction between law and history. How does a judge know what the conclusion of a prior case was, or whether its facts really do resemble those in the case before him?

Trials themselves do *not*, as a rule, produce precedents. As we have seen, trials seek primarily to find the immediate facts of the dispute, to discover who is lying, whose memory has failed, and who can reliably speak to the truth of the matter. When a jury hears the case, the judge acts as an umpire, making sure the lawyers present the evidence properly to the jury so that it decides the "right" question. Often judges do the jury's job altogether. The law does not allow jury trials in some kinds of cases. When the law does allow jury trials, the parties may elect to go before a judge anyway, perhaps because they feel the issues are too complex for laypeople, perhaps because "bench trials" take less time. In law, time is money, a lot of money.

Of course, a trial judge must decide all the issues of law that the lawyers raise. I have provided an illustration of an unpublished trial court legal opinion at the end of Chapter III. The conscientious trial judge will explain to the parties orally for the record why and how he resolves the key legal issues in their case. In some instances he will give them a written opinion explaining his legal choices, and some of these find their way into the reported opinions. But since at trial the judge pays most attention to the historical part of the case, deciding what happened, he usually keeps his explanations at the relatively informal oral level. As a result other judges will not find these opinions reported anywhere; they cannot discover them even if they try. Hence few trial judges create precedents even though they resolve legal issues.

If one party feels the outcome of the trial was erroneous because the judge applied the wrong law to the facts, he will, if he can afford it, appeal the case to a court of appeals. Judges who hear appeals from trials concern themselves primarily with the legal issues in the case. They learn the facts in the case by reading the trial transcript, the written record of facts and conclusions produced in the oral give and take of the trial. But appellate judges then usually *assume* facts to exist as the jury or judge found them and ask whether the trial judge applied the proper law to them. Judges who review these legal questions routinely write opinions explaining their conclusions. Since appellate judges review trial judges' interpretations of all kinds of law, appellate opinions interpret and apply all kinds of law.

Thus the masses of legal precedents that fill the shelves of law libraries mostly emerge from the appellate process. The rest of this book will draw upon many appellate precedents to provide examples of legal reasoning. You should not, however, lose sight of the fact that lawyers use many of the same legal reasoning techniques when they base their recommendations to their clients on appellate precedents and when they manipulate precedents to their advantage in litigation.

Stage Three: The Three-Step
Process of Reasoning by Example

Legal reasoning often involves reasoning from the examples of precedents. Powerful legal traditions impel judges to solve problems by using solutions to similar problems reached by judges in the past. Thus a judge seeks to resolve conflicts by discovering a statement about the law in a prior case—his example—and then applying this statement or conclusion to the case before him. Lawyers who seek to anticipate problems and prevent conflicts follow much the same procedure. Professor Levi calls this a three-step process in which the judge sees a factual similarity between the current case and one or more prior cases, announces the rule of law on which the earlier case or cases rested, and applies the rule to the case before him.[4]

Sometimes precedents provide neat solutions to legal problems. If you represented the unfortunate amateur aviator described in Chapter I, for example, you would discover that in *McBoyle v. United States* (a factually similar case) the Supreme Court held that the word "vehicle" in the statute did not include airplanes.[5] If we pretend for a moment that neither Congress nor the Court itself has since 1931 changed the law, that precedent would probably settle the case. You would point out *McBoyle* to the trial judge. He would presumably see the similarity, articulate the ruling in *McBoyle,* and dismiss the charge.

If the Court had hypothetically ruled otherwise in 1931, however, your case would not be hopeless. Maybe Mr. McBoyle was a clear-eyed opportunist while your client is legally insane. Maybe your client thought the plane belonged to him. Even if the Court had said "vehicle" does include airplanes, other precedents might steer you to victory on legal grounds of mistake or insanity after all.

---

[4]Edward Levi, *An Introduction to Legal Reasoning* (Chicago: University of Chicago Press, 1949), p. 2. Please do not confuse the six analytical stages I use in this chapter with the three-step reasoning process inherent in our legal system itself.

[5]*McBoyle v. United States,* 283 U.S. 25 (1931).

Stage Four: How Reasoning by
Example Perpetuates Unpredictability in Law

To understand this stage we must return to the first step in the three-step description of the legal reasoning process, the step in which the judge decides which precedent governs. The judge must *choose* the facts in the case before him that resemble or differ from the facts in the case, or line of cases, in which prior judicial decisions first announced the rule. The judge no doubt accepts his obligation, made powerful by legal tradition, to "follow precedent," but he is under no obligation to follow any particular precedent. He completes step one *by deciding for himself* which of the many precedents are similar to the facts of the case before him and *by deciding for himself* what they mean.

No judicial opinion in a prior case can require that a judge sift the facts of his present case one way or another. He is always free to do this himself. A judge writing his opinion can influence a future user of the precedent he creates by refusing to report or consider some potentially important facts revealed in the trial transcript. But once he reports them, precedent users can use the facts in their own way. They can call a fact critical that a prior judge reported but deemed irrelevant; they can make a legal molehill out of what a prior judge called a mountain. Thus the present judge, the precedent user, retains the freedom to choose the example from which the legal conclusion follows.

I call this judicial freedom to choose the governing precedent by selectively sifting the facts "fact freedom." Our inability to predict with total accuracy how a judge will use his fact freedom is the major source of uncertainty in law. Legal reasoning explores the ways judges use and abuse this freedom. Thus we cannot say that "the law" applies known or given rules to diverse factual situations because we don't know the applicable rules until after the judge uses his fact freedom to choose the precedent.

Stage Five: An Illustration of Unpredictability in Law

Consider the following example from the rather notorious history of enforcing the Mann Act. The Mann Act, passed by Congress in 1910, provides in part that: "Any person who shall knowingly transport or cause to be transported ... in interstate or foreign commerce…any woman or girl for the purpose of prostitution or debauchery, or for any other immoral purpose… shall be deemed guilty of a felony." Think about these words for a minute. Do they say that if I take my wife to Tennessee for the purpose of drinking illegal moonshine whiskey with her I shall be deemed guilty of a felony? What if I take her to Tennessee to rob a bank? Certainly robbing a bank is an "immoral purpose." Is it "interstate commerce"? But we are jumping prematurely to Chapter IV. For the moment, you should see only that the Congress has chosen some rather ambiguous words and then move to the main problem: choosing the "right" example to decide the following case.

Mr. and Mrs. Mortensen, owners and operators of a house of prostitution in Grand Island, Nebraska, decided to take some of the employees for a well-earned vacation at Yellowstone and Salt Lake City. The girls did lay off their occupation completely during the entire duration of the trip. Upon their return they resumed their calling. Over a year later federal agents arrested the Mortensens and, on the basis of the vacation trip, charged them with violation of the Mann Act. The jury convicted the Mortensens. Their lawyer has appealed the case to you, an appellate court judge.

Unpredictability in law arises when the judge cannot automatically say that a given precedent is or isn't factually similar. To simplify matters here, let us now assume that you examine only one precedent, the decision of the U.S. Supreme Court in *Caminetti v. United States,* announced in 1917.[6] You must choose whether this example does or does not determine the result in *Mortensen.* Assume that in *Caminetti* a man from Wichita met but did not linger with a woman during a brief visit to Oklahoma City. After his return home, he sent this "mistress" a train ticket, which she used to travel to Wichita. There she did spend several nights with her friend, but not as a commercial prostitute. Assume that on these facts the Supreme Court in *Caminetti* upheld the conviction under the Mann Act. Does this case determine the Mortensen's fate? Does this precedent bind

---

[6]*Caminetti v. United States,* 242 U.S. 470 (1917). *Caminetti's* facts and holding cover noncommercial as well as commercial sexual immorality.

you? To answer these questions you must decide whether this case is factually similar to *Mortensen.* Is it?

In one sense, of course it is. In each case the defendants transported women across state lines, after which sex out of wedlock occurred. In another sense it isn't. Without her ticket and transportation the Oklahoma woman could not have slept with the defendant. But if the Mortensens had not sponsored the vacation, the women would have continued their work. The Mortensens' transportation *reduced* the frequency of prostitution. The rancher maintained or increased "illicit sex." Should this difference matter? You the judge are free to select one interpretation of the facts or the other in order to answer this question. Either way you decide you will create a new legal precedent. It is precisely this freedom to decide either way that increases unpredictability in law.

Stage Six: Reasoning by Example
Facilitates Legal Change

Why does judicial fact freedom make law change constantly? Legal rules change every time they are applied because no two cases ever have exactly the same facts. Although judges treat cases as if they were legally the same, whenever they lift the rule out of one case and drop it into another, deciding the case in terms of the rule adds to the list of cases a new and unique factual situation. To rule in the Mortensens' favor, as the Supreme Court did in 1944, gave judges new ways of looking at the Mann Act.[7] With those facts, judges after 1944 could, if they wished, read the Mann Act more narrowly than *Caminetti* did. *Mortensen* thus potentially changed the meaning of the Mann Act, thereby changing the law.

But as the situation turned out, the change did not endure. In 1946 the Court upheld the conviction, under the Mann Act, of certain Mormons, members of a branch known as Fundamentalists, who took multiple wives across state lines to Utah. No prostitution at all was involved here, and traveling to Utah did not cause them to marry bigamously. Fact freedom worked its

[7]*Mortensen v. United States,* 322 U.S. 369 (1944).

way again.[8] The Court extended *Caminetti* and by implication isolated *Mortensen*. The content of the Mann Act, then, has changed with each new decision and each new set of facts.

Is law always as confusing and unclear as these examples make it seem? In one sense certainly not. To the practicing lawyer, most legal questions the client asks possess clear and predictable answers. But in such cases—and here we return to the definition in Chapter I of legal conflicts—the problems probably do not get to court at all. Uncertainty helps convert a human problem into a legal conflict. We focus on uncertainty in law because that is where reason in law takes over.

In another sense, however, law never entirely frees itself from uncertainty. Lawyers always cope with uncertainties about what happened, uncertainties that arise in the historical part of law. If they go to trial on the facts, even if they think the law is clear, the introduction of new evidence or the unexpected testimony of a witness may raise new and uncertain legal issues the lawyers didn't consider before the trial. Lawyers know they can never fully predict the outcome of a client's case, even though much of the law is clear to them most of the time.

IS UNPREDICTABILITY IN LAW DESIRABLE?

Is it desirable that legal rules do not always produce clear and unambiguous answers to legal conflicts? Should the legal system strive to reach the point where legal rules solve problems in the way, for example, that the formula for finding square roots of numbers provides automatic answers to all square root problems?

Despite the human animal's natural discomfort in the presence of uncertainty, some unpredictablity in law is desirable. Indeed, if a rule had to provide an automatic and completely predictable outcome before courts could resolve conflicts, society would become intolerably repressive, if not altogether impossible. There are two resons why.[9]

---

[8]*Cleveland v. United States*, 329 U.S. 14 (1946).
[9]Edward Levi, *An Introduction to Legal Reasoning*, pp. 1–6.

First, since no two cases ever raise entirely identical facts, society must have some way of treating different cases *as if they were the same* in a way litigants accept as fair. Of course, judicial impartiality is an important element of fairness, and we shall return to the problem of impartiality in the final chapter. But you should also think about this fact: If the legal system resolved all conflicts automatically, people would have little incentive to *participate* in the process that resolves their disputes. If the loser knew in advance he would surely lose, he would not waste time and money on litigation. He would not have the opportunity to try to persuade the judge that his case, always somewhat factually unique, *ought* to be treated by a different rule. Citizens who lose will perceive a system that allows them to "make their best case" as fairer than a system that tells them they lose while they sit helplessly.

Only in unpredictable circumstances will each side have an incentive to present its best case. Because the law is ambiguous, each side thinks it might win.[10] This produces an even more important consequence for society as a whole, not just for the losers. The needs of society change over time. The words of common law, statutes, and constitutions must take on new meanings. The participation that ambiguity encourages constantly bombards judges with new ideas. The ambiguity inherent in reasoning by example gives the attorney the opportunity to persuade the judge that the law *ought* to say one thing rather than another. Lawyers thus keep pushing judges to make their interpretation of "the law" fit newer shared beliefs about right and wrong.

I am not encouraging legislators and judges to create or applaud legal uncertainty. Rather, I am arguing that uncertainty in law is unavoidable. This uncertainty is, however, more a blessing than a curse. The participation that uncertainty in law encourages gives the legal process and society itself a vital capacity to change its formal rules with the less formal changes in human needs and values.

---

[10]The process also has the desirable effect of encouraging negotiation and compromise. Each side has an incentive to settle because each side knows it could also lose.

THE OTHER SIDE OF THE COIN: STARE DECISIS AS A STABILIZING AND CLARIFYING ELEMENT IN LAW

I hope that this discussion of unpredictability in law has not left the impression that law is never clear at all. If rules of law amounted to nonsense—lacked any meaning—government by law could not function. If society is to work, most law must be clear much of the time. We must be able to make wills and contracts, to insure ourselves against disasters, and to plan hundreds of other decisions with the confidence that courts will back our decisions if the people we trust with our freedom and our property fail us.

There is indeed a force pushing toward stability within reasoning by example itself: Once judges determine that a given precedent is factually similar enough to determine the outcome in the case before them, then in normal circumstances they follow the precedent. We call this the doctrine of *stare decisis,* "we let the prior decision stand."

Stare decisis operates in two dimensions. Students and lawyers tend to confuse the two, so let me explain them both. Only the second really concerns us in this book. Stare decisis in the first, or "vertical," dimension acts as a marching order in the chain of judicial command. Courts in both the state and federal systems are organized in a hierarchy within their jurisdictions. Thus the supreme courts of Georgia and of the United States both sit at the top of an "organization chart" of courts. The rulings of the highest court in any jurisdiction legally control all the courts beneath it. Stare decisis stabilizes law vertically because no court should ignore a higher authoritative decision on a legal point. As long as the United States Supreme Court holds that airplanes are not "vehicles" within the NMVTA, all courts beneath it must legally honor that clear rule of law in any future airplane theft case that may arise under the Act.

There is, however, a more interesting "horizontal" dimension to stare decisis. What if a court, say a supreme court, makes a decision but then, either a few years or many decades later, develops nagging doubts about the wisdom of its precedent? When should a court follow its own precedent in the face of such doubts? As you begin to wrestle with the intricacies of horizontal stare decisis, please note that the concept applies only after a judge has reason to doubt the policy or wisdom of the precedent. Judges do not need to resort to the doctrine to justify following the example of a case they applaud. Note also that stare decisis does not substitute for reasoning by example. Judges can seek guidance from the doctrine only *after* they have used their fact freedom to conclude that a case from the past legally governs or controls the case at bar. Thomas S. Currier has stated well the values that justify the principle of stare decisis on this horizontal dimension:

1. *Stability.* It is clearly socially desirable that social relations should have a reasonable degree of continuity and cohesion, held together by a framework of reasonably stable institutional arrangements. Continuity and cohesion in the judicial application of rules [are] important to the stabilty of these institutional arrangements, and society places great value on the stability of some of them. Social institutions in which stability is recognized as particularly important include the operation of government, the family, ownership of land, commercial arrangements, and judicially created relations....

2. *Protection of Reliance.* [T]he value here is the protection of persons who have ordered their affairs in reliance upon contemporaneously announced law. It is obviously desirable that official declarations of the principles and attitudes upon which official administration of the law will be based should be capable of being taken as determinate and reliable indications of the course that such administration will in fact take in the future.... This value might be regarded as a personalized variation on the value of stability; but it is broader in that it is recognized even where no social institution is involved, and stability as such is unimportant.

3. *Efficiency in the Administration of Justice.* If every case coming before the courts had to be decided as an original proposition, without reference to precedent, the judicial work-load would obviously be intolerable. Judges must be able to ease this burden by seeking guidance from what other judges have done in similar cases.

4. *Equality.* By this is meant the equal treatment of persons similarly situated. It is a fundamental ethical requirement

that like cases should receive like treatment, that there should be no discrimination between one litigant and another except by reference to some relevant differentiating factor. This appears to be the same value that requires rationality in judicial decision-making, which in turn necessitates that the law applied by a court be consistently stated from case to case. The same value is recognized in the idea that what should govern judicial decisions are rules, or at least standards. The value of equality, in any event, appears to be at the heart of our received notions of justice.

5. *The Image of Justice.* By this phrase I do not mean that any judicial decision ought to be made on the basis of its likely impact upon the court's public relations, in the Madison Avenue sense, but merely that it is important not only that the court provide equal treatment to persons similarly situated, but that, insofar as possible, the court should appear to do so. Adherence to precedent generally tends not only to assure equality in the administration of justice, but also to project to the public the impression that courts do administer justice equally.[11]

The next chapters will describe more precisely the circumstances in which Currier's reasons for horizontal stare decisis do and do not compel a judge to follow rather than depart from a precedent. Here you should simply note the reality that, in fact, most law is clear enough to prevent litigation most of the time. Lawyers can advise us on how to make valid wills and binding contracts. We do know that if someone steals our car and takes it to another state, federal officials, under the authority of the National Motor Vehicle Theft Act, can try to track down the car and the criminal. Without a system of precedents it would be harder for us to predict judicial decisions and therefore more difficult for us to plan to avoid legal conflicts.

There is a paradox here. Because courts do exist to apply law to solve legal problems, and because we trust them in fact to do so, courts, particularly the appellate courts that concern us here, don't actually have to do this in the majority of disputes. In anticipation, private citizens who know what the law means in

[11]Thomas S. Currier, "Time and Change in Judge-Made Law: Prospective Overruling," 51 *Virginia Law Review* 201 (1965), pp. 235–238.

their case will, if for no other reason than to save money, resolve their problem without asking a court to review the law. They don't need to ask the meaning of the law; they know its meaning.

Perhaps in our legal system both clarity and unpredictability, and stability and change can benefit us, depending on the type of problem the law tries to address in a given case. You should reflect further on this possibility as you read the next and final section of this chapter.

LAW IN SOCIETY: AN OVERVIEW

This book tries to suggest new ways of thinking about legal reasoning to laymen, lawyers, and judges. So far it has adopted the tactic of emphasizing (but not yet necessarily proving) many negative aspects of law: Law is not what it seems. Law is often unclear. Legal choices are not wise or fair or just in any absolute sense. Law is not a science. But this book does state a constructive philosophy of legal reasoning. Lawyers and judges should isolate themselves less than they sometimes do from social realities. The premises of legal reasoning ought to rest on the best possible understanding of how people actually feel and act in their daily affairs. The goals of legal reasoning must serve real human needs rather than an abstract legal symmetry. Hence this overview.

To start, assume that modern governments should strive above all to create and then improve upon conditions that foster societal "health." Law should foster a social environment in which particular individuals and the citizenry collectively can develop their capacities and satisfy their needs.

In the narrow and immediate sense this means that societies must find ways to divide up their limited resources—food, clear air and water, shelter, and so forth—in a manner that most citizens can either tolerate or, more ideally, find fair.

In the broader long-term sense this means that societies must work to increase the available resources relative to the size of the population. At least societies should do so when the current level of availability leaves some citizens in conditions in which they cannot satisfy basic needs.

People often fail to appreciate, however, that, although some tangible resources or wants have limits (so that the more Peter gets the less Paul has), other wants, equally desirable, have no such limits. Hart and Sacks make this point powerfully:

> There *can* be enough freedom of thought and speech for every-body and enough freedom of worship, if society wishes to recognize and protect these freedoms. So of friendship, peace of mind, self-respect, and the sense of participation in the life of the community. So of health. So of every kind of pleasurable activity which depends upon the development and exercise of personal talent. So, for most practical purposes, of the enjoy-ment of the personal talents of others. Given a minimum of material goods, the supplies of these and other intangible satisfactions depend mainly upon people having the wit to avoid placing limits upon them by their own folly.[12]

The legal process is not the only arm of government striv-ing to achieve these basic social objectives. Our commitment to public education, for example, rests on the same philosophical ground. But the legal process, more than any part of govern-ment, affects the ability of people to work toward (or at least not against) these goals because all governmental activity—crime control and racial integration—and much private activity—business dealings—operate in a legal framework. We must judge the quality of judicial choices by asking whether they help achieve these goals. Judges who make such choices must do the same.

If we had to select one quality that societies and their legal systems should encourage to achieve these goals, would we not choose the quality of human cooperation? If so, we should judge legal choices by whether they foster some hope of encouraging or maintaining cooperation.

Cooperation doesn't necessarily mean total or perpetual agreement. Businessmen compete, husbands and wives quarrel,

---

[12]Henry M. Hart, Jr., and Albert M. Sacks, *The Legal Process* (Cambridge: Harvard Law School, 1958), p. 112. More recently the Harvard Law School has led the movement to identify and apply the techniques of negotiating mutually satisfactory solutions to conflicts rather than litigating them. See the short but potentially revolutionary book by Roger Fisher and William Ury, *Getting to Yes* (New York: Penguin, 1983).

and labor and management have bitter disputes about the conditions of work. Rather, it means that the people in conflict cannot resolve the disagreement without cooperating at a deeper level with each other by jointly agreeing to argue within the limits of disagreement that rules provide.

To illustrate, consider an extreme example of conflict. Here is a situation in which we *want* people to come to blows and hurt each other: the boxing match. You can probably think of many rules—weight classifications, weigh-in procedures, glove-weight rules, and methods for scoring rounds in the absence of a knockout—with which the fighters must cooperate. If they don't, the match loses its significance. Like sports rules, rules of law provide the cooperative framework within which disagreement works toward maintaining society's main goals. Now reflect upon the five values that support the principle of stare decisis. Does not each value appeal to us precisely to the extent that we think it fosters the kind of cooperation on which social harmony and progress depend? Later chapters return frequently to this theme.

By electing to encourage cooperation in society through the formal methods of law, as any complex human group must, we must nevertheless accept three imperfections inherent in legal systems.

1. The first imperfection economists call the problem of "opportunity costs." People who resort to law for problem solving often give up their chance to go somewhere else or to someone else for the solution. Turning to the rules of the state often draws battle lines and requires an investment of time and money so that, once started, people tend to get locked into the process. Solving a problem through law often prevents solving a problem through love or compromise. A legal solution of a conflict may be better than a shootout, but love and compromise are better still.

    Additionally, resorting to law rather than some other method means not only abiding by the state's rules but also depending upon the state's machinery for making its rules work. The problem isn't that the strangers who run the machinery don't care about deciding justly. Usually they do care, but they care simultaneously about keeping the machinery running, and this sets limits on how they decide cases. Their time is limited. Sensitive and delicate though the machinery may be, a case (someday perhaps your case) must be whittled, pounded, smoothed, and simplified to some degree to fit the machine.

Much of what appears to the casual observer as injustice in law arises from the methods lawyers and judges unavoidably adopt to keep the legal machinery moving. More important, the legal system remains distant and formal in order to maintain the appearance of impartiality. Judicial systems will not remain effective for long if losers regularly accuse the system of crumbling into an unfair power struggle in which the judge simply sides with the winner against the loser.[13] In order to retain the appearance of impartiality, judges must often make decisions by blinding themselves to some facts of the conflict and the feelings of the parties. They must often act before they have fully settled the problem in their own minds. When we choose to go to law, we choose to pay all these opportunity costs.

2. The second imperfection raises the problem of generality. If legal rules, including both statutes and the principles judges announce in their opinions, are to direct cooperation, they must direct how people should behave in the future. Since we do not know the future, and since conditions change and unique events occur in ways we cannot always predict, rules must direct behavior in general terms. But if laws are general they cannot speak with precision, certainly not to each and every human conflict. We want law to define cooperative behaviors, but the generality we need in law also means that sometimes it will fail.

3. The final imperfection deals with the problem of legal

---

[13]See Martin Shapiro, "Courts," in Fred Greenstein and Nelson Polsby, eds., *Handbook of Political Science*, Vol. 5 (Reading, Mass.: Addison-Wesley, 1975), pp. 321–371, and *Courts: A Comparative and Political Analysis* (Chicago: University of Chicago Press, 1981), also by Shapiro.

authority. Just as the boxers must believe that they *ought* to abide by boxing's rules to make the match more meaningful, so citizens should feel an obligation to law. We make law powerful in the coercive sense by backing it up ultimately with the power of armed policemen.[14] However, subjecting citizens to police force does not automatically develop a moral commitment to the rightness of law; in fact, I suspect it tends to produce the opposite psychological reaction, one of bitterness and resentment. But if the threat of force does not elicit a sense of obligation, what does?

The third imperfection arises because, I suspect, people develop a sense of obligation to law partly because they believe law is certain, free of ambiguity, and evenly applied without, as the saying goes, bias or favor. As a result, judges regularly try to hide the uncertain and changeable side of law from us, even though uncertainty and change are desirable. Judges often pretend that legal reasoning *does* resemble the process of solving an arithmetic problem, that they have "found" the right law rather than created it or chosen it, in order to bolster the authority of law. I do not think we shall completely escape the drive of judges to make the law appear more certain and hence impartial than it is. Nevertheless, judicial wisdom lies in knowing when to acknowledge the presence of uncertainty and the necessity for choice that enables law to change for the better. This book's final chapter proposes a philosophy of impartiality that permits judges to admit that they make creative choices in an uncertain world.

SUMMARY

- Although in Chapter IV, we expose more thoroughly the "disorderly conduct of words," why, generally, do the words of legal rules so often fail to resolve legal problems?

[14]Armed policemen do more than enforce the criminal laws. Any time a court rules that one person has become legally liable to another, for breaking a contract in business or negligently breaking a leg in an auto accident, for example, armed policemen, usually called deputy sheriffs or marshals, may seize the debtor or his property to enforce the judicial judgment.

- What is reasoning by example? Why do American judges resolve legal conflicts by doing so? Where do the judges' examples come from?
- Which of the steps in the three-step process of reasoning is the most crucial? Why?
- How does reasoning by example perpetuate uncertainty in law? Why is such uncertainty desirable?
- What are the stabilizing elements in law? Under what circumstances does the doctrine of stare decisis provide useful guidance to a judge?
- What are "opportunity costs" and why are they imperfections inherent in the legal process? Similarly, why is generality both a blessing and an imperfection?
- Why does judicial wisdom lie "in knowing when to acknowledge the presence of uncertainty and the necessity for choice" in law? In what circumstances should judges deny the reality of uncertainty?

ILLUSTRATIVE CASES

In the federal judicial system it is common for the intermediate appellate courts to hear cases in panels of three judges, with the outcome determined by majority vote. Here are two opinions written by Learned Hand sitting on two separate panels. The first is a precedent for the second. Notice that they were decided just a month apart. You should read the second case initially to see how Judge Hand uses his fact freedom to distinguish *Repouille* from *Francioso*, then to see how Judge Frank uses fact freedom a different way, and finally to explore the possibility that both judges in *Repouille* have used their fact freedom foolishly.

United States v. Francioso
164 F.2d 163 (Nov. 5, 1947)

L. HAND, Circuit Judge.

This is an appeal from an order admitting the appellee, Francioso, to citizenship. At the hearing the "naturalization examiner" objected to his admission upon the ground that he had married his niece and had been living incestuously with her during the five years before he filed his petition. Upon the following facts the judge held that Francioso had been "a person of good moral character" and naturalized him. Francioso was born in Italy in 1905, immigrated into the United States in 1923, and declared his intention of becoming a citizen in 1924. His wife was born in Italy in 1906, immigrated in 1911, and has remained here since then. They were married in Connecticut on February 13, 1925, and have four children, born in 1926, 1927, 1930, and 1933. Francioso was the uncle of his wife, and knew when he married her that the marriage was unlawful in Connecticut and that the magistrate would have not married them, had they not suppressed their relationship. They have always lived together in apparent concord, and at some time which the record leaves indefinite, a priest of the Catholic Church—of which both spouses are communicants—"solemnized" the marriage with the consent of his bishop.

In United States ex rel. Iorio v. Day, in speaking of crimes involving "moral turpitude" we held that the standard was, not what we personally might set, but "the commonly accepted mores": i.e., the generally accepted moral conventions current at the time, so far as we could ascertain them. The majority opinion in United States ex rel. Berlandi v. Reimer perhaps looked a little askance at that decision; but it did not overrule it, and we think that the same test applies to the statutory standard of "good moral character" in the naturalization statute. Would the moral feelings, now prevalent generally in this country, be outraged because Francioso continued to live with his wife and four children between 1938 and 1943? Anything he had done before that time does not count; for the statute does not search further back into the past.

In 1938 Francioso's children were five, eight, eleven and twelve years old, and his wife was 31; he was morally and legally responsible for their nurture and at least morally responsible for hers. Cato himself would not have demanded that he should turn all five adrift. True, he might have left the home and supported them out of his earnings; but to do so would deprive his children of the protection, guidance and solace of a father. We can think of no course open to him which would not have been regarded as more immoral than that which he followed, unless it be that he should live at home, but as a celibate. There may be purists who would insist that this alone was consistent with "good moral conduct"; but we do not believe that the conscience of the ordinary man demands that degree of ascesis; and we have for warrant the fact that the Church— least of all complaisant with sexual lapses—saw it to sanction the continuance of this union. Indeed, such a marriage would have been lawful in New York until 1893, as it was at common-law. To be sure its legality does not determine its morality; but it helps to do so, for the fact that disapproval of such marriages was so long in taking the form of law, shows that it is condemned in no such sense as marriages forbidden by "God's law." It stands between those and the marriage of first cousins which is ordinarily, though not universally, regarded as permissible.

It is especially relevant, we think, that the relationship of these spouses did not involve those factors which particularly make such marriages abhorrent. It was not as though they had earlier had those close and continuous family contacts which are usual between uncle and niece. Francioso had lived in Italy until he was eighteen years of age; his wife immigrated when she was a child of four; they could have had no acquaintance until he came here in August, 1923, only eighteen months before they married. It is to the highest degree improbable that in that short time there should have arisen between them the familial intimacy common between uncle and niece, which is properly thought to be inimical to marriage....

Order affirmed.

Repouille v. United States
165 F.2d 152 (Dec. 5, 1947)

L. HAND, Circuit Judge.

The District Attorney, on behalf of the Immigration and Naturalization Service, has appealed from an order, naturalizing the appellee, Repouille. The ground of the objection in the district court and here is that he did not show himself to have been a person of "good moral character" for the five years which preceded the filing of his petition. The facts are as follows. The petition was filed on September 22, 1944, and on October 12, 1939, he had deliberately put to death his son, a boy of thirteen, by means of chloroform. His reason for this tragic deed was that the child had "suffered from birth from a brain injury which destined him to be an idiot and a physical monstrosity malformed in all four limbs. The child was blind, mute, and deformed. He had to be fed; the movements of his bladder and bowels were involuntary, and his entire life was spent in a small crib." Repouille had four other children at the time towards whom he has always been a dutiful and responsible parent; it may be assumed that his act was to help him in their nurture, which was being compromised by the burden imposed upon him in the care of the fifth. The family was altogether dependent upon his industry for its support. He was indicted for manslaughter in the first degree; but the jury brought in a verdict of manslaughter in the second degree with a recommendation of the "utmost clemency"; and the judge sentenced him to not less than five years nor more than ten, execution to be stayed, and the defendant to be placed on probation, from which he was discharged in December, 1945. Concededly, except for this act he conducted himself as a person of "good moral · character" during the five years before he filed his petition. Indeed, if he had waited before filing his petition from September 22, to October 14, 1944, he would have had a clear record for the necessary period, and would have been admitted without question.

Very recently we had to pass upon the phrase "good moral character" in the Nationality Act; and we said that it set as a test, not those standards which we might ourselves approve, but whether "the moral feelings, now prevalent generally in this country" would "be outraged" by the conduct in question: that is, whether it conformed to "the generally accepted moral conventions current at the time."[a] In the absence of some national inquisition, like a Gallup poll, that is indeed a difficult test to apply; often questions will arise to which the answer is not ascertainable, and where the petitioner must fail only because he has the affirmative. Indeed, in the case at bar itself the answer is not wholly certain; for we all know that there are great numbers of people of the most unimpeachable virtue, who think it morally justifiable to put an end to a life so inexorably destined to be a burden on others, and—so far as any possible interest of its own is concerned—condemned to a brutish existence, lower indeed than all but the lowest forms of sentient life. Nor is it inevitably an answer to say that it must be immoral to do this, until the law provides security against the abuses which would inevitably follow, unless the practice were regulated. Many people—probably most people—do not make it a final ethical test of conduct that it shall not violate law; few of us exact of ourselves or of others the unflinching obedience of a Socrates. There being no lawful means of accomplishing an end, which they believe to be righteous in itself, there have always been conscientious persons who feel no scruple in acting in defiance of a law which is repugnant to their personal convictions, and who even regard as martyrs those who suffer by doing so. In our own history it is only necessary to recall the Abolitionists. It is reasonably clear that the jury which tried Repouille did not feel any moral repulsion at his crime. Although it was inescapably murder in the first degree, not

[a]*United States v. Francioso,* 164 F.2d 163, (2d Cir., 1947). [Footnote in original.]

only did they bring in a verdict that was flatly in the face of the facts and utterly absurd—for manslaughter in the second degree presupposes that the killing has not been deliberate—but they coupled even that with a recommendation which showed that in the substance they wished to exculpate the offender. Moreover, it is also plain, from the sentence which he imposed, that the judge could not have seriously disagreed with their recommendation.

One might be tempted to seize upon all this as a reliable measure of current morals; and no doubt it should have its place in the scale; but we should hesitate to accept it as decisive, when, for example, we compare it with the fate of a similar offender in Massachusetts, who, although he was not executed, was imprisoned for life. Left at large as we are, without means of verifying our conclusion, and without authority to substitute our individual beliefs, the outcome must needs be tentative; and not much is gained by discussion. We can say no more than that, quite independently of what may be the current moral feeling as to legally administered euthanasia, we feel reasonably secure in holding that only a minority of virtuous persons would deem the practise morally justifiable, while it remains in private hands, even when the provocation is as overwhelming as it was in this instance.

However, we wish to make it plain that a new petition would not be open to this objection; and that the pitifiable event, now long passed, will not prevent Repouille from taking his place among us as a citizen. The assertion in his brief that he did not "intend" the petition to be filed until 1945, unhappily is irrelevant; the statute makes crucial the actual date of filing.

Order reversed; petition dismissed without prejudice to the filing of a second petition.

FRANK, Circuit Judge (dissenting).

This decision may be of small practical import to this petitioner for citizenship, since perhaps, on filing a new petition, he will promptly become a citizen. But the method used by my colleagues in disposing of this case may, as a precedent, have a very serious significance for many another future petitioner whose "good moral character" may be questioned (for any one of a variety of reasons which may be unrelated to a "mercy killing") in circumstances where the necessity of filing a new petition may cause a long and injurious delay. Accordingly, I think it desirable to dissent.

The district judge found that Repouille was a person of "good moral character." Presumably, in so finding, the judge attempted to employ that statutory standard in accordance with our decisions, i.e., as measured by conduct in conformity with "the generally accepted moral conventions at the time." My colleagues, although their sources of information concerning the pertinent mores are not shown to be superior to those of the district judge, reject his finding. And they do so, too, while conceding that their own conclusion is uncertain, and (as they put it) "tentative." I incline to think that the correct statutory test (the test Congress intended) is the attitude of our ethical leaders. That attitude would not be too difficult to learn; indeed, my colleagues indicate that they think such leaders would agree with the district judge. But the precedents in this circuit constrain us to be guided by contemporary public opinion about which, cloistered as judges are, we have but vague notions. (One recalls Gibbon's remark that usually a person who talks of "the opinion of the world at large" is really referring to "the few people with whom I happened to converse.")

Seeking to apply a standard of this type, courts usually do not rely on evidence but utilize what is often called the doctrine of "judicial notice," which, in matters of this sort, properly permits informal inquiries by the judges. However, for such a purpose (as in the discharge of many other judicial duties), the courts are inadequately staffed, so that sometimes "judicial notice" actually means judicial ignorance.

But the courts are not utterly helpless; such judicial impotence has its limits. Especially when an issue importantly affecting a man's life is involved, it seems to me that we need not, and ought not, resort to our mere unchecked surmises, remaining wholly (to quote my colleagues' words) "without means of verifying our conclusions." Because court judgments are the most solemn kind of governmental acts—backed up as they are, if necessary, by the armed force of the government—they should, I think, have a more solid foundation. I see no good reason why a man's rights should be jeopardized by judges' needless lack of knowledge.

I think, therefore, that, in any case such as this, where we lack the means of determining present-day public reactions, we should remand to the district judge with these directions: The judge should give the petitioner and the government the opportunity to bring to the judge's attention reliable information on the subject, which he may supplement in any appropriate way. All the data so obtained should be put of record. On the basis thereof, the judge should reconsider his decision and arrive at a conclusion. Then, if there is another appeal, we can avoid sheer guessing, which alone is now available to us, and can reach something like an informed judgement.[b]

QUESTIONS

1. What legal questions does Judge Hand ask about Mr. Francioso's behavior? How does he answer them?
2. What facts about the *Repouille* case make *Francioso* factually similar enough to serve as a precedent?
3. It is clear, is it not, that the big problem in both cases wrestles with the method courts should use to determine whether an applicant for naturalization has the required good moral character? In *Francioso* Judge Hand uses a method that permits him to conclude that Francioso should become a citizen. What was that method?
4. Does Judge Hand use the same method in *Repouille*? If so, what facts distinguish the two cases so that, even though Francioso won, Mr. Repouille lost?
5. What method would Judge Frank use? How, if at all, does it differ from Hand's method? Which of these two do you prefer? Why?
6. What would you think of the following hypothetical solution to the *Repouille* case?

> The question in naturalization cases is always whether a *person,* never a behavior in the abstract, is of good moral character. Thus in *Francioso,* while hardly anyone would believe that incest was acceptable behavior in the abstract, the court rightly looked at the facts about the individual, Francioso, and his behaviors, and concluded that he, as an individual, possessed good moral character. In Mr. Repouille's case a criminal trial jury and two trial judges (one for the murder trial and one for the naturalization hearing) have reviewed the facts of the case and seen the applicant face to face. These 14 people appear unanimously to have concluded that this mercy killing did not reveal bad moral character. Since the legal question always concerns the character of an individual rather than an abstract act, the *Francioso* precedent requires Repouille's naturalization.

[b]Of course, we cannot thus expect to attain certainty, for certainty on such a subject as public opinion is unattainable. [Footnote in original.]

Notice that this solution would *not* set a precedent for the proposition that euthanasia in the abstract is morally good or bad. What law would this solution create for the future? Would you approve or disapprove such a precedent? Is it fair to conclude that Judges Hand and Frank both miss the whole point about the *Francioso* case, i.e., that the individual, not the abstract classification of his behavior, matters under the statute? Why or why not?

SOME EXPLORATORY PROBLEMS

1. Try to imagine another example of the ambiguous meaning of words similar to the table/bench definitional problem. Alternatively, consider the meaning of two words you shall see fairly frequently in this book, "mean(s)" and "meaning." You ought to be able to think of at least six distinguishable meanings of these words. See Reed Dickerson, *The Interpretation and Application of Statutes* (Boston: Little, Brown, 1975), Chapter 4.

2. Define stare decisis and reasoning by example carefully so as to highlight the differences between the two concepts. Then draw on this distinction to explain the apparent anomaly that, while most appellate cases raise difficult and unsettled choices for judges, most law is clear and stable the majority of the time.

3. Return to the tree-climbing youth, Robert. Suppose that in school Robert memorizes the procedures for finding square roots. On an examination he must find the square root of 15,938. Does he reason by example when he uses the memorized procedures to compute the answer? Why or why not? Does he reason by example if he copies the answer of his neighbor? (Does the answer to the last question depend on whether he copies his neighbor's answer because he has learned his neighbor always gets perfect scores on math tests?) At a deeper level is it not fair to say that even following formulas is a form of reasoning by example? We follow formulas because they have worked—produced good exam scores and smiles from the teacher—in the past, do we not? Is there in law, then, any meaningful distinction between reasoning by example and reasoning from a formula? (J.S. Mill asserted that all reasoning is from particulars to particulars.) Is there a difference in the degree of discretion you think you have if you think you ought to reason one way rather than the other? Is it fair to say that fact freedom

gives the judge the discretion to say whether a given problem is or isn't a square root problem in the first place? What other ways of reasoning can you propose in addition to reasoning by example and reasoning from a formula?

4. Recall the *Cleveland* case described briefly in this chapter. In that case several Mormons transported their multiple wives across state lines, only to suffer prosecution under the Mann Act. Assume that the case of the vacationing prostitutes, *Mortensen,* represents the most recent prior judicial interpretation of the Mann Act. In that case, as you know, the court ruled that the act did not cover this instance of interstate transportation, even though the girls were prostitutes and even though without the trip home the girls could not have resumed their trade with the Mortensens. Reread the statutory language of the Mann Act, quoted above, and then prepare arguments both for the Mormons and for the prosecution. How are reasoning by example, stare decisis, and fact freedom reflected in these arguments? As you begin to develop your own fact freedom reasoning skills, be sure to avoid a common mistake. Fact freedom does not enable a judge to contradict facts that have necessarily been proved true in the trial. A judge is never free to say black is white and white black. Rather, fact freedom allows judges to designate which facts in the case matter, which are legally relevant, and which legally unrelated to the problem at hand. Try this problem: Apply the facts of the Mann Act precedents to argue that transporting a girl across state lines solely for the purpose of taking nude photos of her for a magazine does or does not violate the Mann Act.[15]

5. One additional shortcoming that limits the capacity of courts to contribute to social well-being is that adjudication creates policy slowly and often haphazardly. Adjudicatory results take time to reach other judges, and fact freedom provides incentives to avoid new judicial trends and fight them when they are applied. The same problem has plagued many of our regulatory agencies when they have tried to accomplish their tasks through adjudication. For 50 years the Federal Trade Commission tried to promote consumer interests on a case-by-case basis, often with little success. In *Smoking and Politics,* A. Lee Fritschler defended the FTC's use of rule making to regulate cigarette advertising

---

[15]See *United States v. Mathison,* 239 F.2d 358 (7th Cir., 1956).

beginning in 1964. Comment on the potential applicability of the following passage to the judicial system as a whole:

> Ironically, the root of the Federal Trade Commission's problem was substantially the same as the government's under the Sherman Act over half a century earlier. It was a procedural difficulty as much as anything else. The commission was attempting to regulate cigarette advertising on a case-by-case basis. Each time the commission ruled a particular advertisement deceptive, the industry came up with a variation that could squeak by under the rule of the previous case. This was proving to be an endless and fruitless process. The commission needed to write general regulations for the whole industry; the case method, whether employed by an agency or by the courts, was proving to be too cumbersome a method of developing regulatory policy.[16]

[16] (Englewood Cliffs, NJ, Prentice-Hall, 1975), p. 69.

Chapter III

FACTS AND LEGAL REASONING

The first two chapters introduced the basic concepts and processes with which legal reasoning operates. One of these, the nature of facts and their relationships to legal reasoning, needs refinement before we move to the three main categories of legal analysis: statutes, common law, and constitutional law.

We have just seen that the fact freedom judges possess can steer them toward various solutions to a given legal problem, depending on the facts they think matter. The wisdom and common sense with which judges evaluate the factual issues and assumptions in a case are the most important elements in all of legal reasoning. It is essential to understand what facts are and where they come from.

There is another reason for studying facts in legal reasoning. The scientific and technical complexity of social issues today increases rapidly. The more people believe that they must master statistical and technical matters as a prerequisite for making wise and effective social policy decisions, the more they will expect judges to do so when they decide lawsuits. We must therefore evaluate the capacity of courts and legal procedures to evaluate modern factual situations effectively and efficiently.

REVIEW

In prior pages, I have provided a definition of *fact* and have mentioned three separate contexts in which facts affect legal decisions. Let us review these lessons here, starting with the definition. Facts are beliefs about the actualities of things, in contrast to values, which are beliefs about right and wrong, good and bad. (See p. 2.) Notice that both facts and values are kinds of beliefs. Both describe what people perceive. We cannot separate tangible actualities from less tangible beliefs about them because everything we perceive is processed by our brains through language, and language shapes what we think we see. This is what makes good written translation from one language and culture to another language and culture so tricky. The word for *tree* in our culture refers to a certain class of plants. The members of a culture whose word for tree means, say, *extension of earth to sky,* would think of trees as something different from our conception of trees as plants.

Still, something does differentiate a belief in an actuality from a belief in right or wrong, good or bad. The former belief asserts that something tangible exists in the physical world, something that is at least hypothetically observable, measurable, and recognizable in terms on which many people can agree. Note that the asserted thing need not be physically observed to make it a fact. I believe, as a matter of fact, that a line drawn from every point on the surface of our oceans through the center of the earth will intersect a point that our language calls an *ocean bottom,* even though I have observed such bottoms at only a few spots. And, if Smith says he believes as a matter of fact that a thunder dragon lives in every cloud in the sky, with the small puffy white clouds inhabited by baby dragons too young to cause actual rain or thunder, he is asserting a fact, that something exists in the clouds even though we can't actually observe it ourselves. Thus, when someone asserts an actuality, the assertion is susceptible to proof, to verification. Trial courts, as we have seen, are very much in business to test the parties' assertions of actualities.

But what good are facts if beliefs in thunder dragons and ocean bottoms both count as facts? Here enters the second element of our definition. The true measure of the factuality of something is the extent to which people within a culture share a belief. The greater the intersubjective agreement that something exists in the universe, the more factual that thing becomes. Since, at least in American culture, more people believe the basics of geology than believe in animal spirits in the sky, ocean bottoms are more factual than thunder dragons, even though no one will ever fully prove or disprove either phenomenon. But of course we live in a pragmatic culture, one in which most citizens believe in evidence, observation, and science. If, in a theocracy, the religious leader announced that the earth was flat, that would become a fact in that culture if the people believed it.

In common practice most statements that people make mix factual and normative beliefs together. If I say that "Bill Cosby is a great American and one of the greatest entertainers of this century" (a statement that, incidentally, I believe heartily to be true), I will combine some factual assertions (e.g., about Cosby's income, the measurable extent to which people recognize his name or laugh when they hear or see his routines) with some normative arguments about the moral questions his comedy and his career (particularly his commitment to preschool education) present to us. In thinking about any statement, in law or elsewhere, one of the important stages is to distinguish the factual elements from the nonfactual.

It is also important to identify the group that must believe a factual statement in order for it to be true and to understand the process by which those in the legal system come to believe or disbelieve a factual assertion. We shall address this point after reviewing the three contexts in which facts influence legal decisions.

First, judges and lawyers make legal choices by combining beliefs about actualities and beliefs about norms, very much as I might choose Bill Cosby as a preferred entertainer. Thus Justice McKenna dissented from the Supreme Court's interpretation of the Mann Act in the first case, *Caminetti*, because he paid close attention to Representative Mann's own statements, preserved in the written records of Congress, about what Mann thought the bill did and did not cover. McKenna's choice, his decision to dissent, combined a normative belief—that the intent of the bill's sponsor *ought* to affect the bill's legal meaning—with a factual belief—that the written record of Congress's debate of the act actually contained words expressing Mann's belief about the meaning of the bill. Note that the fact here is Justice McKenna's belief in the existence of printed words attributed to Representative Mann, not McKenna's belief in Representative Mann's actual inner reasons for uttering them; Representative Mann might, for all we know, have had his own illicit relationships to protect. (See Mann's statement, p. 102.)

Second, we referred to the presence of factual and legal questions in a single case. Most cases go to trial to resolve a specific factual dispute about who did what to whom. In these cases no one is likely to raise a major challenge to the meaning of the potentially relevant law. The law will apply to the facts depending on which facts are found to have happened. If McBoyle had been charged with transporting a Ford automobile, his case would have raised no issue of law for the Supreme Court to worry about.

Third and finally, we discussed facts in the context of fact freedom, a freedom exercised primarily at the appellate level, but which trial judges may also exercise when they resolve contested interpretations of law in a trial.

HOW ASSERTIONS BECOME FACTS IN LAW

Two very different classes of facts influence legal reasoning. You cannot master legal reasoning without mastering this difference. First, the *facts about the dispute between the parties*, introduced by testimony at trial or simply taken for granted in the case (as in the wording of the statutes in the cases at the end of Chapters I and II) influence the decisions of trial and appellate judges. But these judicial choices also rest on assumptions about actualities in society itself, beliefs in what I call *social background facts*. In the typical legal reasoning problem, both classes of facts affect the judge. For example, Justice Murphy dissented in the last Mann Act case, *Cleveland*. He concluded that the act did not cover migrating Mormons. His conclusion rested on: (1) the facts evident from the trial record—that the defendants married bigamously out of religious conviction and that the move from one state to another did not cause or allow the bigamous marriage to occur; *and* (2) the social background fact that states have laws against bigamy, adultery, prostitution, and other sex offenses. Justice Murphy combined these factual beliefs with his normative belief that states ought to have primary responsibility for criminal law enforcement. *Cleveland* from this perspective becomes legally identical to *Mortensen*.

Facts about the Dispute at Trial

This book is not the place to explore all the forces that shape case outcomes in trial courts. To name just one of many complications in this field, the bulk of civil and criminal lawsuits filed each year are settled by negotiation and agreement without a trial. In the federal courts less than 10 percent of all complaints filed actually reach the trial stage, and not all of this residue proceeds through trial to a final and formal trial court judgment.[1] These cases do not as a rule produce any appeals or formal resolution of legal ambiguities and do not concern us here. The lawsuit and threat of trial really serve to pressure the parties to settle when the facts are fairly clear or the cost of ascertaining them is higher than the benefits.

However, in order to understand how case facts affect legal reasoning, you must master two important limits our legal system imposes upon trial court fact-finding. First, rules of

[1]Austin Sarat, "The Role of Courts and the Logic of Court Reform," 64 *Judicature* 300, p. 303 (1981).

evidence prevent the decision maker, either a jury or a judge sitting without a jury, from considering certain information to which people in less formal settings would pay close attention. For example, the rules of evidence prevent juries from considering "hearsay evidence." Hearsay statements are statements made by someone who never appears in court but reported by a witness in the trial. Such statements are inadmissible before juries if the outcome of the trial could depend on the truth of the statement made by the person who never appeared and hence escaped the exposure to cross-examination. And juries may not hear "privileged" testimony: statements from the spouse, the attorney, or the priest of the accused. (Trial judges are presumed by virtue of their professional training and experience to be less easily influenced by untrustworthy evidence; hence in trials without jury some of the rules of evidence do not apply.)

Thus the first important lesson about trial court fact finding teaches that trial courts may by design fail to get all facts potentially related to the dispute between the parties when they make decisions. The "exclusionary rule," for example, forbids introduction at a murder trial of a handgun if the police located it by illegally beating a suspect until he revealed its location. The rule excludes the gun from trial even if ballistics tests show conclusively that it fired the fatal shot. Another lesson teaches that once the trial jury or judge determines a fact is true, that fact is presumed true for the remainder of the litigation, even through an appeal to the highest court in the land. No appellate court will reopen the testimony, and no appellate court should decide an issue of law inconsistent with the facts found at trial. The theory behind this practice holds that, as far as the evidence about who did what to whom, the deciders at trial, the *triers of fact* who heard the witnesses' testimony and observed their demeanor at first hand, will always be in a better position to judge the truth than will an appellate judge who is exposed to the same factual material only second-hand through trial transcripts.

How does an outsider know what facts the trial court finds to be true? In the case of a jury verdict, the judge charges the jury that, in order to find for the plaintiff, or in order to find the defendant guilty, the jury must find certain things to be true. A jury verdict of guilt or liability necessarily finds such facts to be true. A judge sitting without a jury will as a rule read into the court record his brief findings of fact and conclusions of law. In either case the only way an appellate court can overturn such findings is to hold, and it is rare, that the factual conclusions have no substantial basis in the evidence introduced at trial and are therefore "clearly erroneous."[2]

By now alert readers will have noted a serious potential discrepancy between my definition of facts and the nature of trial fact-finding. What if a trial jury or judge finds as factually true—perhaps because the rules of evidence prevented it from getting the whole picture—something central to the decision in the case, like the excluded murder weapon, that outsiders know to be false? How can we say trial courts find "false facts?" If appellate courts are "stuck" with false facts, isn't trial court fact-finding about as "scientific" as thunder dragons? If facts exist to the extent people in the relevant environment believe them, and the real world knows something the jury didn't, how can we call what goes on in the trial "fact-finding" at all?

The paradox resolves because in law the relevant environment—the *group* concerned with the fact in question—is the legal system itself, the jury and the judiciary, and no more. This condition of our legal system, has, next to proof of outright corruption, probably caused more lay hostility toward law than any other factor. The familiar lay query to lawyers, "How can you defend a guilty man?" arises from this artificial distinction between legally acceptable facts and the facts the rest of the world lives by. The legal group presumes the man innocent until proven guilty, regardless of what the larger group called society may know about the case. Some reflection, however, should reveal why the legal system must artificially limit the fact-finding environment in order to survive. If all the facts in a case were open without limit to reargument and reinterpretation, and if nothing limited the facts and arguments each side might introduce, then the bulk of trials would be endurance and bank account contests. Here we have another illustration of the distinction in Chapter I between general and particular justice.

[2]See Rule 52a, Federal Rules of Civil Procedure.

In order to make it possible to do justice at all, conditions must be set that may do injustice in particular, and we hope infrequent, circumstances.

At the beginning of this section I mentioned that trial facts also include facts that the lawyers do not bother to fight out through the presentation of evidence in the trial. Some of these facts are stipulated as true by the parties, so they become part of the officially accepted truth. On other occasions certain facts are not noticed or articulated at all until the jury deliberates or an appellate court examines the case.

In an earlier book I described an example of a fact only a jury noticed. In a criminal trial police found a small wooden matchbox containing marijuana on the floor of the defendant's car. The defendant claimed that he had seen some teenagers loitering around his car before he got in and that he believed they had left the box behind as they rushed off. Neither attorney at trial noticed that marijuana particles had leaked out of the loose-fitting halves of the box into the plastic bag in which it was presented in court. One juror, however, asked to examine the bag during deliberations, noticed the leak, and recalled testimony that no traces of the marijuana were found in the clothing of the defendant. He convinced the rest of the jury to vote to acquit on the theory that, if the defendant had been lying, some of the material would have leaked into his pockets.[3]

Such facts as these, of course, would not influence appellate judges because jurors do not report their findings of fact on the record for appellate court consideration. Of much greater significance for legal reasoning, appellate courts may rely on any fact stipulated directly in the trial transcript or less obviously implied in it. Consider, by way of illustration, the five justifications for stare decisis introduced in Chapter II. One of the most important of these, as later chapters show, is the argument that a person may actually have known and relied on the law stated in the precedent in planning his affairs. Such reliance happens more commonly in some branches of law than others. Hardly anyone chooses to have an auto accident by relying on negligence law,

[3]Lief H. Carter, *The Limits of Order* (Lexington, Mass.: Lexington Books, 1974), Chapter 2.

but businessmen may rely on their lawyers' advice regarding court-approved practices in their contractual arrangements. If a trial transcript reveals that a party relied on past law and a stare decisis issue then arises on appeal, the appellate court may lean on this fact to justify following a precedent of dubious value, even if the lawyers at trial merely accepted the assertion of reliance without contesting it. Indeed, the appellate court may find factual evidence in a trial transcript like the jurors with the marijuana box, evidence the lawyers at trial simply ignored.

Social Background Facts

And now we come to the most important, and least understood, way in which facts influence legal decisions. Each lawsuit illustrates a social problem, and each case in which the law is unclear gives courts an opportunity to rethink the sorts of policies that might best remedy the social problem illustrated by the case. In other words, since our system relies on precedent, judges resolving cases must think about the best way to solve, not only the specific case, but problems generically similar. To do so they must make decisions about the facts of the *problem* as well as the *case*. Different cases raise problems of differing degrees of factual complexity. A court that must decide how large a company's market share is large enough to constitute an illegal monopoly has a much more complex analytical task before it than did Justice Holmes in *McBoyle*. But since all cases challenge the judge to make generic policy for like cases, it is safe to say that in every case wise policy rests on facts about society in which the class of cases nests.[4]

[4]The conventional terms to distinguish case facts and social facts are, respectively, "adjudicative facts" and "legislative facts." The terms mislead because they imply that one belongs only in courts, the other only in legislatures. Yet legislative investigations of scandals such as the 1983 congressional investigations of the Environmental Protection Agency under Ronald Reagan's presidency, are fully proper yet essentially adjudicatory acts. Conversely, this book shows that courts must and do consider social facts as part of their law-making function. Donald Horowitz's *The Courts and Social Policy* (Washington, D.C.: The Brookings Institute, 1977), p. 45, uses terminology similar to mine. The various linkages between social facts and law are so immense that, in the second edition of their great reader, *Law and the Behavioral Sciences* (Indianapolis:

The reasoning in the illustrative cases at the end of this chapter rests on social background facts, as do many of the cases throughout the rest of the book. Rather than attempt to cover all this complex subject at once (and telegraph some of the solutions to the interesting mysteries that follow), let me here review briefly the main ways courts encounter social background facts in legal reasoning.

1. In both trial and appellate courts, judges may take official *judicial notice* of facts bearing on the case and the applicable law if they are notoriously or indisputably true.[5]

2. Where background information is contested (e.g., the nature of scientific evidence of the dangerousness of a substance in the environment or the economic conditions from which an antitrust accusation arose), attorneys may debate such information in the testimony and briefs developed at trial without any certainty that the issues will have any bearing on the immediate disposition of the case.

3. It is more likely that judges will learn such facts through the briefs the lawyers file in support of points of law. The attorney and later Supreme Court Justice, Louis Brandeis, introduced large quantities of social data through what became known as the *Brandeis brief*, in support of the constitutionality of maximum-hours labor legislation for women.[6] The Brandeis brief properly conceived communicates relatively well-documented and verified demographic and other back-

---

Bobbs-Merrill, 1977), Lawrence Friedman and Stewart Macaulay devote their Chapter 4 to "the impact of society on law." That single chapter is almost as long as the book you are now reading!

[5]The Model Code of Evidence permits judicial notice of "specific facts so notorious as not to be the subject of reasonable disputes, and...specific facts and propositions of generalized knowledge which are capable of immediate and accurate demonstration by resort to easily accessible sources of indisputable accuracy." See Walter Murphy and C. Herman Pritchett, *Courts, Judges and Politics,* 3d ed. (New York: Random House, 1979) p. 447.

[6]*Muller v. Oregon,* 208 U.S. 412 (1908).

ground information to the court. Usually attorneys submit such briefs at the appellate level, but they are increasingly common in complex public policy litigation, such as environmental litigation, in trial courts. The opportunity to do so of course opens up the possibility of introducing less well-verified information for courts to hang their conclusions on. The Supreme Court has been accused of doing so in the public school desegregation case.[7]

4. Finally, jurors resolving the history problem at trial as well as appellate judges often rely on their own hunches about the social background of a case when attorneys have not argued the point in briefs at all. At times the judicial opinion will confess these speculations, as Judge Hand did in *Repouille*. At other times judges will confess their factual beliefs only in private papers made available to scholars long after the judge's retirement, or not at all. Again, the greatest cause of failure in legal reasoning is the failure of judges to examine carefully the critically important social background facts on which all legal interpretations rest to some degree. Illustrations of this truth will appear throughout the book.

HOW ACCURATELY DO COURTS FIND FACTS?

When they finish this book, few readers will doubt how I answer this question. When compared to those alternative institutions and fact-finding methods in government that attempt to cope with social problems, courts are not inferior fact finders for the large majority of cases that come to them. Courts are, at least in theory, well-designed and positioned in most cases to find accurately the critical facts required for the legal decision in the case and to assess the social background facts on which wise development of legal policy depends.

[7] See Walter Murphy and C. Herman Pritchett, p. 449. See also their brief but stimulating comparison of American court fact-finding with that in some judicial jurisdictions on the other side of the Atlantic Ocean, pp. 450–451.

Unfortunately, practice and theory do not universally coincide. While much research justifies our applause for the capacity of trial courts and trial juries to find the who-did-what-to-whom facts accurately and impartially, the judicial finding and use of social background facts often leaves much to be desired. Indeed, improving judicial understanding of the manner in which background facts influence law is the greatest single improvement our legal system can make in the quality of legal reasoning.

Since the wisdom with which judges evaluate social background facts serves as grist for much of the analysis in the following pages, let me here merely clarify what readers should look for.

The background factual questions that affect legal reasoning vary along five continua.

1. Some cases rest on very specific technical facts, such as the extent to which a chemical, like dioxin, causes environmental harm; others rest on more general factual assumptions, such as, in racial discrimination cases, the general belief that overt racism does measurable psychological damage to minorities.

2. Some facts are universally believed. That is, all the groups contending in litigation agree that a given statement is true, whereas other facts are hotly contested by contending groups.

3. Some propositions in cases may be totally factual. Other statements will have varying degrees of normative beliefs mixed in with them.

4. Some facts can be fully proved through regular court procedures—testimony, cross-examination, physical evidence, and so forth at trial; Brandeis briefs and judicial research on appeal—but others will be less easily proved and will require judges to guess as intelligently as possible about the truth.

5. For some kinds of facts the immediate parties to the suit may be in the best position of anyone to prove or disprove them; for instance, the manufacturer of "Agent Orange" involved in a suit about the toxicity of such chemicals may be well suited to estimate the costs

necessary to remedy the damage. In other cases the litigating parties themselves will neither know nor possess the incentives and resources for finding out the best evidence on the factual question.[8]

This useful classification suggests a method for prescribing the circumstances in which appellate courts can take specific measures to maximize the accuracy of the social background facts. This is because appellate judges can make specific choices about the management of social background fact-finding in litigation. Through their clerks, they can conduct their own literature reviews, direct the attorneys to address certain factual questions in their briefs, order either side to respond by brief or in oral argument to the factual claims of the other, and order reargument of points when the attorneys have failed the first time.[9]

Professor Davis suggests that when background factual issues are controversial (that is, not believed by all involved to be true); when they are specific, narrow, and directly related to the main issues in the case; when they are not overly intermixed with imponderable normative beliefs; and, finally, when they are of a sort that the parties are capable of proving or disproving, then appellate courts must require the parties to deal directly with these facts through the measures described above.[10]

All too often in the pages that follow we shall see judges reasoning badly in law because they do not appreciate how much their reasoning depends on assumptions about background facts and don't appreciate that they possess measures to clarify those facts. Davis gives several illustrations. Here is one of them:

> In holding unconstitutional a New York statute because it required consent of mothers but not of fathers for adoption of an illegitimate child, the Supreme Court in *Caban v.*

[8] Kenneth C. Davis, "Facts in Lawmaking," 80 *Columbia Law Review* 931 (1980), p. 933.

[9] When courts feel they lack the capacity to decide intelligently because the facts are not yet knowable, they possess tools to avoid decisions on the merits. These rules of "justiciability"—ripeness, exhaustion, standing, and so forth—are discussed with other of the judiciary's "passive virtues" in Alexander Bickel, *The Least Dangerous Branch* (Indianapolis: Bobbs-Merrill, 1964) Chapter 4.

[10] Davis, supra, p. 933.

Mohammed, 441 U.S. 380 (1979), seemed to act on a factual impression, never clearly stated, that mothers and fathers of illegitimate children do not significantly differ from each other in their relationships with and attitudes toward their children. Yet the Court's factual assumptions almost surely would have been quite different if it had been required to spell out the main facts about such relationships and to cite its sources. Furthermore, the Court's assumed facts were never tested by allowing the losing party to challenge them before the decision was announced. Mr. Justice Stevens, speaking for three of the four dissenters, said: "I am compelled to point out that the Court marshals not one bit of evidence to bolster its empirical judgment that most natural fathers facing the adoption of their older children will have [a] relatively exemplary record with respect to admitting paternity and establishing a relationship with his [sic] children. In my mind, it is far more likely that what is true at infancy will be true thereafter—the mother will probably retain custody as well as the primary responsiblity for the care and upbringing of the child." 441 U.S. at 410-12 n 20 (1979). When the Court is nullifying state legislation, when four Justices dissent, when they assert that the Court's impression of legislative facts is erroneous, when the Court fails to state the facts with clarity or to identify their source, and when the losing party has had no pre-decision chance to challenge the asserted facts, might the dissenting protest be wholly justified and might the Court benefit by taking it seriously?[11]

I hinted at the beginning of this section that approval of judicial fact-finding rests partly on a pragmatic comparison of the fact-finding abilities of courts to those of legislatures. It is often argued that courts, since they cannot start suits on their own, are too reactive and dependent on the environment to make wise policy and that their resources are too limited and their power to enforce too feeble to carry out policies effectively. This may characterize courts in the abstract, but many of the same evils lurk equally in the corridors of legislatures.[12]

Since Chapter IV directly concerns statutory interpretation, I shall postpone until then a discussion of the weaknesses of legislative fact-finding. In the meantime, please consider that

[11]Davis, p. 933.
[12]Sarat, supra, p. 303.

the adversary method of fact-finding in courts, with its structured rules of evidence and the orderliness with which information is presented, is widely recognized as a highly accurate, if costly, method for fact-finding in many settings. Management in the private and public sectors uses various forms of this model regularly. Thus we may have reasonable confidence that courts can reach acceptably accurate findings of fact unless: (1) the information is communicable only through scientific languages that judges cannot understand; (2) judges lack the authority to compel key figures to communicate important information to the court (a frequent problem when dealing with the legality of foreign policy and military matters); (3) the resources of the litigants are badly mismatched, so that one side is in a better position to develop and present factually persuasive arguments than is the other. Unfortunately, as Professor Marc Galanter has pointed out, it is relatively common for "repeat players," frequent litigants such as insurance companies, to have a superior capacity to persuade courts when pitted against "one-shot players."[13]

On this somewhat cautionary note, I conclude the ground-laying part of this book. Many of the analytical tools described in these initial three chapters will become fully clear only as readers practice using them in the analysis of the materials to come.

SUMMARY

- State two separate reasons why attention to facts in legal reasoning is so important as to require a whole chapter devoted to the subject.
- Why must we say that both facts and values are beliefs? Why can't we say facts are simply what is true and be done with it?
- Distinguish facts that the parties may contest at trial from social background facts.
- Social background facts can influence jury trial decisions on the merits of the case, but this is not legal reasoning, especially when such facts never appear on the official trial transcript.

[13]Marc Galanter, "Why the 'Haves' Come out Ahead: Speculations on the Limits of Legal Change," 9 *Law and Society Review* 95 (1974).

Through what other mechanisms can and do social background facts affect legal reasoning itself?

- State the five continua on which social background facts can vary. Which end of each continuum is most conducive to formal judicial examination of such background facts?
- What measures can courts take to optimize the accuracy of the information they get about social background facts?
- List the reasons that judicial fact-finding is presumably as accurate as legislative fact-finding. In what circumstances should we be particularly wary of the capacity of courts to evaluate effectively the information on which wise decisions may depend?

ILLUSTRATIVE CASES

In both of the cases to follow, please distinguish the varying categories of facts the court uses in reaching a decision and evaluate the effectiveness—the wisdom, if you wish—of each result. You should know that the opinion in the second case is a relatively rare example of a written opinion by a trial court judge on a question of law. I obtained this copy directly from the judge, a personal acquaintance during my days in graduate school in Berkeley, California. It was never, to my knowledge, published. Readers will note in this opinion some curiosities in punctuation. I have reproduced the case virtually as it came from the judge's typewriter in order to expose readers to a sample of a written trial court opinion.

Prochnow v. Prochnow
Supreme Court of Wisconsin
274 Wisconsin 491 (1957)

A husband appeals from that part of a decree of divorce which adjudged him to be the father of his wife's child and ordered him to pay support money. The actual paternity is the only fact which is in dispute.

Joyce, plaintiff, and Robert, defendant, were married September 2, 1950, and have no children other than the one whose paternity is now in question. In February, 1953, Robert began his military service. When he came home on furloughs which he took frequently in 1953 he found his wife notably lacking in appreciation of his presence. Although he was home on furlough for eight days in October and ten in December, after August, 1953, the parties had no sexual intercourse except for one time, to be mentioned later. In Robert's absence Joyce had dates with a man known as Andy, with whom she danced in a tavern and went to a movie, behaving in a manner which the one witness who testified on the subject thought unduly affectionate. This witness also testified that Joyce told her that Robert was dull but that she and Andy had fun. She also said that a few days before Friday, March 12, 1954, Joyce told her she had to see her husband who was then stationed in Texas but must be back to her work in Milwaukee by Monday.

On March 12, 1954, Joyce flew to San Antonio and met Robert there. They spent the night of the 13th in a hotel where they had sex relations. The next day, before returning to Milwaukee, she told him that she did not love him and was going to divorce him. Her complaint, alleging cruel and inhuman treatment as her cause of action, was served on him April 8, 1954. On September 16, 1954, she amended the complaint to include an allegation that she was pregnant by Robert and demanded support money.

The child was born November 21, 1954. Robert's letters to Joyce are in evidence in which he refers to the child as his own. He returned to civilian life February 13, 1955, and on February 18, 1955, answered the amended complaint, among other things denying that he is the father of the child born to Joyce; and he counterclaimed for divorce alleging cruel and inhuman conduct on the part of the wife.

Before trial two blood grouping tests were made of Mr. and Mrs. Prochnow and of the child. The first was not made by court order but was ratified by the court and accepted in evidence as though so made. This test was conducted in Milwaukee on March 21, 1955. The second was had in Waukesha September 29, 1955, under court order. The experts by whom or under whose supervision the tests were conducted testified that each test eliminated Robert as a possible parent of the child. An obstetrician, called by Robert, testified that it was possible for the parties' conduct on March 13, 1954, to produce the full-term child which Mrs. Prochnow bore the next November 21st. Mrs. Prochnow testified that between December, 1953, and May, 1954, both inclusive, she had no sexual intercourse with any man but her husband....

BROWN, Justice. The trial judge found the fact to be that Robert is the father of Joyce's child. The question is not whether, on this evidence, we would have so found: what we must determine is whether that finding constituted reversible error.

Section 328.39 (1) (a), Stats., commands:

> Whenever it is established in an action or proceeding that a child was born to a woman while she was the lawful wife of a specified man, any party asserting the illegitimacy of the child in such action or proceeding shall have the burden of proving beyond all reasonable doubt that the husband was not the father of the child....

Ignoring for the moment the evidence of the blood tests and the effect claimed for them, the record shows intercourse between married people at a time appropriate to the conception of this baby. The husband's letters after the child's birth acknowledge it is his own. The wife denies intercourse with any other man during the entire period when she could have conceived this child. Unless we accept the illegitimacy of the baby as a fact while still to be proved, there is no evidence that then, or ever, did she have intercourse with anyone else. The wife's conduct with Andy on the few occasions when the witness saw them together can justly be called indiscreet for a married woman whose husband is absent, but falls far short of indicating adultery. Indeed, appellant did not assert that Andy is the real father but left that to the imagination of the court whose imagination, as it turned out, was not sufficiently lively to draw the inference. Cynics, *among whom on this occasion we must reluctantly number ourselves* [emphasis supplied], might reasonably conclude that Joyce, finding herself pregnant in February or early March, made a hasty excursion to her husband's bed and an equally abrupt withdrawal when her mission was accomplished. The subsequent birth of a full-term child a month sooner than it would usually be expected if caused by this copulation does nothing to dispel uncharitable doubts. But we must acknowledge that a trial judge, less inclined to suspect the worst, might with reason recall that at least as early as the preceding August Joyce had lost her taste for her husband's embraces. Divorce offered her freedom from them, but magnanimously she might determine to try once more to save the marriage: hence her trip to Texas. But when the night spent in Robert's arms proved no more agreeable than such nights used to be she made up her mind that they could live together no more, frankly told him so and took her departure. The medical testimony concerning the early arrival of the infant does no more than to recognize eight months of gestation as unusual. It admits the possibility that Robert begat the child that night in that San Antonio hotel. Thus, the mother swears the child is Robert's and she knew, in the Biblical sense, no other man. Robert, perforce, acknowledges that it may be his. Everything else depends on such reasonable inferences as one chooses to draw from the other admitted facts and circumstances. And such inferences are for the trier of the fact. Particularly, in view of Sec. 328.39 (1) (a), Stats., supra, we cannot agree with appellant that even with the blood tests left out of consideration, the record here proves beyond a reasonable doubt that Joyce's husband was not the father of her child.

Accordingly we turn to the tests. The expert witnesses agree that the tests excluded Mr. Prochnow from all possibility of this fatherhood. Appellant argues that this testimony is conclusive; that with the tests in evidence Joyce's testimony that she had no union except with her husband is insufficient to support a finding that her husband is the father.... But the Wisconsin statute authorizing blood tests in paternity cases pointedly refrains from directing courts to accept them as final even when they exclude the man sought to be held as father. In its material parts it reads:

> Sec. 325.23 *Blood tests in civil actions.* Whenever it shall be relevant in a civil action to determine the parentage or identity of any child,...the court...may direct any party to the action and the person involved in the controversy to submit to one or more blood tests, to be made by duly qualified physicians. Whenever such test is ordered and made the results thereof shall be receivable in evidence, but only in cases where definite exclusion is established....

This statute does no more than to admit the test and its results in evidence, there to be given weight and credibility in competition with other evidence as the trier of the fact considers it deserves. No doubt in this enactment the legislature recognized that whatever infallibility is accorded to science, scientists and laboratory technicians by whom the tests must be conducted, interpreted and reported retain the human fallibilities of other witnesses. It has been contended before this that a report on the analysis of blood is a physical fact which controls a finding of fact in opposition to lay testimony on the subject, and the contention was rejected.... When the trial judge admitted the Prochnow tests in evidence and weighed them against the testimony of Mrs. Prochnow he went as far in giving effect to them as our statute required him to do. Our opinions say too often that trial courts and juries are the judges of the credibility of witnesses and the weight to be given testimony which

conflicts with the testimony of others for us to say that in this case
the trial court does not have that function....

...The conclusion seems inescapable that the trial court's
finding must stand when the blood-test statute does not make the
result of the test conclusive but only directs its receipt in evidence
there to be weighed, as other evidence is, by the court or jury. We
hold, then, that the credibility of witnesses and the weight of all the
evidence in this action was for the trial court and error can not be
predicated upon the court's acceptance of Joyce's testimony as more
convincing than that of the expert witnesses....

Judgment affirmed.

WINGERT, Justice (dissenting). With all respect for the views of
the majority, Mr. Chief Justice FAIRCHILD, Mr. Justice CURRIE and
the writer must dissent. In our opinion the appellant, Robert
Prochnow, sustained the burden placed upon him by Sec. 328.39 (1)
(a), Stats., of proving beyond all reasonable doubt that he was not the
father of the child born to the plaintiff.

To meet that burden, appellant produced two classes of
evidence, (1) testimony of facts and circumstances, other than blood
tests, which create grave doubt that appellant is the father, and
(2) the evidence of blood tests and their significance, hereinafter
discussed. In our opinion the blood test evidence should have been
treated as conclusive in the circumstances of this case.

Among the numerous scientific achievements of recent decades
is the development of a method by which it can be definitely
established in many cases, with complete accuracy, that one of two
persons cannot possibly be the parent of the other. The nature and
significance of this discovery are summarized by the National
Conference of Commissioners on Uniform State Laws, a highly
responsible body, in the prefatory note to the Uniform Act on Blood
Tests to Determine Paternity, as follows:

> In paternity proceedings, divorce actions and other types
> of cases in which the legitimacy of a child is in issue, the
> modern developments of science have made it possible to
> determine with certainty in a large number of cases that one
> charged with being the father of a child could not be. Scientific
> methods may determine that one is not the father of the child
> by the analysis of blood samples taken from the mother, the
> child, and the alleged father in many cases, but it cannot be

shown that a man is the father of the child. If the negative fact is established it is evident that there is a great miscarriage of justice to permit juries to hold on the basis of oral testimony, passion or sympathy, that the person charged is the father and is responsible for the support of the child and other incidents of paternity.... There is no need for a dispute among the experts, and true experts will not disagree. Every test will show the same results....

[T]his is one of the few cases in which judgment of court may be absolutely right by use of science. In this kind of a situation it seems intolerable for a court to permit an opposite result to be reached when the judgment may scientifically be one of complete accuracy. For a court to permit the establishment of paternity in cases where it is scientifically impossible to arrive at that result would seem to be a great travesty on justice. (Uniform Laws Annotated, 9 Miscellaneous Acts, 1955 Pocket Part, p. 13.)

In the present case the evidence showed without dispute that the pertinent type of tests were made of the blood of the husband, the wife and the child on two separate occasions by different qualified pathologists, at separate laboratories, and that such tests yielded identical results, as follows:

	3/17/55	9/29/55
	Blood Types	
Robert Prochnow (Husband)	AB	AB
Joyce Prochnow (Wife)	O	O
David Prochnow (Child)	O	O

There is no evidence whatever that the persons who made these tests were not fully qualified experts in the field of blood testing, nor that the tests were not made properly, nor that the results were not correctly reported to the court....

Two qualified experts in the field also testified that it is a physical impossibility for a man with type AB blood to be the father of a child with type O blood, and that therefore appellant is not and could not be that father of the child David. Both testified that there are no exceptions to the rule. One stated "There is no difference of opinion regarding these factors amongst the authorities doing this particular work. None whatsoever." The evidence thus summarized was not discredited in any way and stands undisputed in the record.

Indeed, there was no attempt to discredit it except by the wife's own self-serving statement that she had not had sexual relations with any other man during the period when the child might have been conceived....

*   *   *

California v. Craig
Superior Court of the State of California
County of Alameda
Memorandum Decision on Challenge to Jury Panel, April 18, 1968

Spurgeon Avakian, Judge. By a timely challenge to the jury panel drawn for the trial of his case, Defendant questions the whole process by which trial jurors are selected in Alameda County. Four days of testimony were devoted to developing the factual basis for the challenge.

The grounds of challenge consist essentially of the following:

1. The jury selection process results in the disproportionate exclusion of identifiable groups (specifically, racial minorities and lower income citizens) and consequently produces a master panel which is not representative of the community at large, in violation of the due process and equal protection clauses of the Fourteenth Amendment;
2. The jury selection process departs from the legislative pattern by eliminating persons who possess "ordinary intelligence," particularly by use of a written test which is not geared directly to the measurement of "ordinary intelligence."...

The master panel of trial jurors is compiled by the Jury Commissioner for half-year periods at a time. The current master panel was processed during the second half of 1967. Initially, 6,336 names were selected at random from the list of registered voters of the county....

With respect to the number who were processed but either excused or found not qualified, the total of 3,420 is made up of the following groupings:

Poor health	704
Occupational exemption	542
Women with small children	454
Lack of understanding of English	112
Prior jury service	244

Poor hearing	125
Business and personal hardship	161
Travel	17
Conviction of high crime	68
Lack of transportation	34
Mental instability	19
Failed written test	940
	3,420

As indicated below, the main thrust of the contention that the master panel is not a fair cross-section of the population of the county is aimed at the written test. There is no indication in the record of any racial or socioeconomic discrimination by the Jury Commissioner's office in the other categories of elimination listed above.

The statutory qualification for jury service, insofar as the validity of the written test is concerned, is that jurors be "of ordinary intelligence" and "possessed of sufficient knowledge of the English language." C.C.P. 198. No definition of those terms is set forth in the statute, but the decisional law requires non-discretionary selection from a broad base of the community and forbids a so-called "blue ribbon" approach. *Thiel vs. Southern Pacific Co.*, 328 U.S. (1946). The use of written tests in applying this standard is neither uniform nor unusual in this state.

In Alameda County, the test currently in use was adopted by the Court in 1956, after having been prepared by a psychologist for this particular use. It consists of 25 multiple choice questions. To pass, the jurors must have at least 21 correct answers (84%) in ten minutes....

[A] special analysis was made by the Jury Commissioner of two areas designated by Defendant's attorney. One area consists of 24 contiguous precincts in West Oakland with a total voter registration of 10,862. The other consists of 27 contiguous precincts in the Montclair section of Oakland with a total voter registration of 11,070.

The residents of the West Oakland area are predominantly black and of low economic income. The residents of Montclair are predominantly white and of middle or higher economic income.

It should be noted that in the categories in which conscious or even subconscious bias could operate—namely, the excuses by the interviewers without administering the test—a substantially equal

	WEST OAKLAND AREA		MONTCLAIR AREA	
Number of Registered Voters	10,862		11,070	
Number drawn from Voter Registers	133		145	
Non-responses, deaths, moved, etc.	39		23	
Number processed	94		122	
Excused without test	40	(42.5%)	53	(43.3%)
Took written test	54		69	
Failed test*	44	(81.5%)	10	(14.5%)
Passed test	10		59	
Excused after passing test	1		7	
Qualified	9		52	
Service deferred	1		2	
Certified to current panel	8		50	

*For the two areas combined, 123 took the test and 54 persons, or 44 percent, failed it.

percentage was excused from each area. And, as already stated, Defendant disclaims any contention that there has been any intent to discriminate on the part of either the Court or the Jury Commissioner's office.

We come, then, to the test, a copy of which is attached hereto.[a] Why do 14.5% of the Montclair registered voters fail it, and why is the failure rate 81.5% in West Oakland?

A consideration of the test raises a number of questions:

(1) To what extent does it measure moral and social attitudes and level of education rather than mental capacity?
(2) Does it contain cultural, educational, or environmental biases which are not present equally in high and low income groups and in different racial groupings?
(3) Is it sufficiently comprehensive to test intelligence?
(4) Is the pass-fail cutting point placed so high as to eliminate substantial numbers of people who do possess "ordinary intelligence"?

Ten questions in the test…appear to relate primarily to vocabulary or word recognition. Nine are answered as much on the basis of personal temperament and attitude or social, political, or

[a][See Appendix to *California vs. Craig*, L.H.C.]

moral philosophy as on the basis of intelligence.... One... calls for knowledge of the law (and, incidentally, has a legally incorrect statement listed on the score sheet as the correct answer).

Only a few questions call primarily for the application of reasoning processes to situations described so as to neutralize cultural or educational differences.

The risk of built-in bias in favor of what is commonly referred to as middle-class mores and vocabulary is obvious in such a situation. The startling difference in the pass-fail rate in the two areas previously mentioned, as well as the high overall failure rate, strongly suggests that the test separates people on some basis other than "ordinary intelligence." One can well imagine how different the results might have been if half of the vocabulary questions were related to "soul" food, people and music and other terms commonly spoken in West Oakland but almost unheard and unread in Montclair.

It should be noted that the test is not a standardized test and has not been validated by comparison with standard intelligence tests administered to any sampling of the same groups of people; and, obviously, evaluating the comparative performance as jurors of those who passed and those who failed is a practical impossibility.

A psychologist with long experience in constructing and evaluating tests for different purposes testified that the test in question has the appearance of being an intelligence test but contains some items which reflect the cultural bias of the author. He also testified that at least fifty items would be needed in a well-constructed intelligence test to take into account the subcultures of a heterogenous population.

Furthermore, he expressed the opinion that ten minutes is too short a time to allow for this test, that it is not good test procedure to withhold the time limit from those taking the test, and that irrespective of time, 84% is too high a cutting point for a passing grade.

He also expressed the opinion that the test has a tendency to exclude people from the ghettoes because of "inadvertent discrimination"—that is unintended discrimination resulting from cultural factors.

In terms of the results, he also expressed the opinion that the failure rate in both of the comparison areas was much too high and indicated that a substantial number of people who possessed "ordinary intelligence" were being eliminated in both areas.

The realities of our society emphasize the importance of jury panels drawn from a representative cross-section of the community. We have significant cultural differences almost unknown in our country thirty years ago. Litigants and witnesses come into Court from all walks of life in a highly varied community. Unless jury panels represent the same walks of life and the same pattern of cultural differences they will be less likely to understand fully the implications of the testimony they hear and the situations they must evaluate, and less likely to bring into their deliberations the background of experience and wisdom required for a just result. Similarly, the narrower the cultural spectrum of our jury panels, the less confidence the under-represented groups will have in the courts as temples of justice.

The general term, "ordinary intelligence," must be interpreted and applied in this contest. The Court cannot conclude that 81.5% *of the registered voters* in a large section of Oakland are below the level of "ordinary intelligence."

Accordingly, the challenge to the panel must be sustained....

Appendix to California vs. Craig

Excerpts from Alameda County Juror Qualification Test
   6. Which of the following is a trait of character?
      1. Generosity
      2. Health
      3. Punctuality
   8. Why was Civil Service established?
      1. As a sound political move.
      2. To provide qualified workers for government jobs.
      3. To increase the number of government bureaus.
   10. The government of the United States is sound because:
      1. It follows the will of the majority.
      2. It does not allow representative government.
      3. It permits the development of dictators.
   14. A man's influence in a community *should* depend upon his:
      1. Wealth
      2. Character
      3. Ambition
   15. Of the five acts below, four are alike in a certain way. Which is the one *not* like these four?

   1. smuggle
   2. steal
   3. bribe
   4. cheat
   5. sell

16. The purpose of administering the oath to a witness is:
   1. To check his background
   2. A means taken by law to obtain true testimony
   3. To see if a person believes in God

18. What people *say* about a person makes up his:
   1. Reputation
   2. Personality
   3. Disposition

19. What is the difference between *"falsehood"* and *"perjury?"*
   1. No difference. They are the same.
   2. Perjury is a falsehood under oath.
   3. Falsehood refers to a misdemeanor; perjury refers to a felony.

20. You should not give money to beggars on the street, because:
   1. It makes it hard for the beggars to get work.
   2. It encourages living off of others.
   3. It takes away the work of organized charities.

22. The opposite of *"hope"* is:
   1. despair
   2. hate
   3. misery

25. If it rains when you are starting to go for the doctor, should you:
   1. Stay at home.
   2. Take an umbrella.
   3. Wait until it stops raining.

QUESTIONS

1. The *Prochnow* majority seems unwilling or unable to apply scientific evidence confidently. Since the judges in the majority appear to doubt Mrs. Prochnow's story, what reasons might they have for turning their backs on uncontroverted scientific evidence about blood types and paternity? Is there any good reason to reject such scientific evidence? If the police testify in an auto accident case that skid marks from the defendant's tires ran 20 feet in the lane of oncoming traffic, and if the defendant never introduces any scientific rebuttal to this evidence, but merely denies that he crossed the center line, should the trial judge tell the jury to disregard the defendant's denial and to conclude that the car was on the left side of the road? (At the time of *Prochnow,* Wisconsin law did require a judge in that circumstance to instruct the jury to disregard the defendant's denial. Isn't that an adequate precedent for the blood type issue in this case?) Do the dissent in *Prochnow* and Judge Avakian's discussion of the requisites of valid competency testing in *Craig* suggest that judges are incapable of understanding "science" intelligently? Would not such a generalization be close to downright silly?

2. In each of these cases, which facts did the winning side need to establish in order to win? Is there any difference between these cases regarding the relative importance of social background facts as opposed to official trial facts?

3. *Prochnow* gives you some flavor for the way rules of evidence work. Recall, for example, the hearsay rule. In the classic law school illustration of hearsay, a plaintiff sues a surgeon for accidentally leaving a sponge in the patient's wound. The doctor would be liable for negligence if it could be shown that a reasonable and prudent doctor would have found and removed the sponge. At trial a nurse testifies that she heard another nurse, not able to attend the trial due to illness, tell the defendant's surgeon in the operating room that "the sponge count came out wrong." Such testimony is hearsay if offered to prove that the sponge count in fact came out wrong. This is because the person who made the original statement is not available in court for cross-examination. But it is not hearsay if it is introduced to prove that somebody said the count came out wrong and that, despite this warning, the surgeon did nothing about it. The failure to respond to such a statement, whether actually true or not, could establish legal negligence. Now reread the second paragraph of the fact statement in *Prochnow.* It presents the same hearsay issue. Where? Why?

4. Of what issues do these judges take official judicial notice? Do not these judges also admit to taking unofficial notice of several important facts? For example, it seems most important to Judge Avakian that the people who flunked the test in Oakland were properly registered voters. Why? Do you agree with the factual beliefs that the judge must have had about the general competence of registered voters and their capacity to serve on juries?

5. Review the five continua derived from Professor Davis. Which facts in these two cases illustrate the two ends of each of these five continua?

6. Think about Professor Galanter's concern that "repeat players" tend to come out ahead in disproportionately large numbers in trials. Is it plausible that, based on his experience as an attorney and on the bench, Judge Avakian also believed this to be factually true? If so, should that belief influence his decision in *Craig*? Why or why not?

7. Each of the questions excerpted from the Alameda County Juror Qualification Test in the Appendix is flawed for one reason or another. None of the answers listed for Question 19 is correct, while all of the answers listed for Question 8 are correct, at least historically. The most common difficulty with these questions is, of course, their implicit cultural bias. Human beliefs and perceptions differ because they are shaped by differences in economic status, education, daily vocabulary or "street language," political, legal, and religious experiences, and, perhaps most important of all, extent of prior experience in taking tests of this sort. With this list in mind, review each question again for its potential cultural bias. Do not these culturally shaped differences in perception help explain why facts are beliefs, not simply objects?

SOME EXPLORATORY PROBLEMS

1. One of the most stimulating challenges to conventional models of judicial decision making appears in Martin Shapiro's article, "Stability and Change in Judicial Decision-Making: Incrementalism or Stare Decisis?"[14] In this article, Shapiro argues that courts decide very much as other political bodies do. That is, they react incrementally to changing social fact situations under pressure from lobby groups (litigants) much as legislatures do. In the following paragraph, Shapiro observes that Karl Llewellyn approves a similar judicial model. Do you?

> Karl Llewellyn in his great retreat from judicial realism,
> *Deciding Appeals—The Common Law Tradition*...argues
> that much of the lawyer's distress at the supposed disregard by
> American courts of stare decisis in recent years is the result of

---

[14]*Law in Transition Quarterly* 134 (1964).

excessive enchantment with logical deductive styles of decision-making, and that courts at their best do and should solve problems by evolving on-the-spot solutions that, given the practical limits of knowledge and prediction, seem best for the situation. He argues in effect that if lines of precedent are viewed not as fluctuations around a locus of principle, but as the record of a series of marginal adjustments designed to meet changing circumstances, then the legal system will regain for the viewer the coherence and predictability that are obscured when we attempt to view the work of the courts through the traditional theories of stare decisis. For Llewellyn finds in his own examination of the decisions of modern American courts that they typically seek to make incremental changes in policy in the light of feedback from earlier decisions.

2. In *Paris Adult Theater v. Slaton,* 413 U.S. 49 (1973), the U.S. Supreme Court had to determine the constitutionality of a statute forbidding the showing of "obscene" movies to consenting adults. Given the interests in freedom of expression that weighed on the side of permitting the showing of these movies, the Court then faced the factual question whether there existed "a connection between antisocial behavior and obscene material" (pp. 60–61). Using my five criteria, derived from those of Professor Davis, how susceptible is such a question to effective judicial analysis? Would it bother you to discover that the Court took no briefs on the question but instead cited a minority report of two members on the 19-member Presidential Commission on Obscenity and Pornography? Would it bother you more if the majority of the Commission found *no* established relation between obscenity and antisocial behavior but the Court ignored the majority finding? Why or why not?

3. Recall from footnote 2, Chapter II, the discussion of the uncertainty inherent in the meaning of such simple words as *food* when they are used in legal settings. In October, 1982, a federal judge ordered removed from the market a pill, commonly known as a *starch-blocker*, that purportedly inhibited the body's ingestion of calories from bread and other starches. The pill is derived entirely from an extract of kidney beans. If the pill is a food, its distribution would not require prior approval from the Food and Drug Administration, but if the substance is a drug, it would. To what extent do you think the judge's ruling, that the pill is a drug,

was based on facts? What kind of facts? On values? What values?[15]

4. A growing body of literature about courts suggests that trial and appellate courts exist not so much to find the facts and law to solve problems as to "tell stories." W. Lance Bennett and Martha S. Feldman, in *Reconstructing Reality in the Courtroom,*[16] argue that trial courts are less concerned about obtaining an accurate reconstruction of the historical reality between the litigants than they are about following the elements of a believable story. Those elements of reality that do not fit the structure of a believable story are discarded by the fact-finder. If this approach interests you, you may also want to read Milner Ball's *The Promise of American Law.*[17] Ball applies the metaphor of drama to the courtroom. He urges judges to recognize that their greatest function is not to find the technically correct law or facts of the case so much as to reinforce the deepest moral principles of our society. This they will effectively do if, according to Ball, they treat the appellate decision as if it were an old-fashioned morality play.

5. Suppose that in 1910 a state legislature passed a law requiring pregnant public school teachers to cease teaching after the third month of pregnancy. In later years, suppose the Supreme Court holds that, under the constitution, sex-based discriminations must be rationally related to a valid state purpose. Should a court consider medical data about the risks to the health of pregnant women? What if such data showed no risk to woman or child from continuing work through the eighth month of pregnancy? What if medical opinion in 1910 held that the risk was great, but current data show an increase in risk of mortality of one half of one percent for working as opposed to unworking pregnant mothers? What if this data did not control for age, wealth, or other variables that might also affect health risks of pregnant women?[18]

6. I mentioned in the text the rule of evidence known as spousal immunity. Under recent decisions the privilege to withhold tes-

---

[15]See "Starch-Blocker Pills Are a Drug, Judge Says, Backing FDA Seizure," *Wall Street Journal,* October 7, 1982, p. 47.
[16]New Brunswick, N.J.: Rutgers University Press, 1981.
[17]Athens, Ga.: University of Georgia Press, 1981.
[18]See Scott Bice, "Rationality Analysis in Constitutional Law," 65 *Minnesota Law Review* 1 (1980).

timony in criminal cases belongs to the witness spouse, not the defendant spouse. The theory is that if a person willingly testifies against his or her spouse, the marriage is in bad shape anyway. Hence the benefits to society from receiving testimony will outweigh the benefits of preserving an acrimonious marital relationship. But what if the witness spouse was indicted as a co-defendant and then received immunity from prosecution by the prosecutor in exchange for testimony against the other spouse? Does not the social background fact assumption in today's law become less believable in this light? See Richard O. Lempert, "A Right to Every Woman's Evidence," 66 *Iowa Law Review* 725 (1981), for a fascinating description of how Chief Justice Earl Warren's former experience as a prosecutor (in Alameda County, California!) led him to reject the argument, articulated by Chief Justice Burger, on which today's law of immunity rests.

7. Return, finally, to the problem of cultural bias in legal fact-finding. Is it not directly related to Professor Galanter's observation that "haves" tend to come out ahead? Do not the people who operate the legal system—judges, attorneys, reporters, and so on—tend to share with the "haves" similar backgrounds and therefore similar factual beliefs and values? If the legal process functions on an unbalanced diet of reality whenever convention, political power, economic wealth, educational attainment, and so on shape the interpretations of fact at trial, how important to the cause of justice is Judge Avakian's decision in *Craig*? Indeed, would not a class or Marxist theory of politics deny even the possibility that a judge would decide as Avakian did? Judge Avakian, an Armenian by descent, grew up on a farm near Fresno, California. He and many like him experienced hostility and rejection from "WASP" peers during their youth. Does this fact help explain his decision in *Craig*? Judge Avakian was never accepted socially by the conservative majority of the Alameda County bar when I knew him in the late 1960s and early 1970s. He was perceived as excessively liberal and potentially sympathetic to the antiwar protest centered on the campus of the University of California, Berkeley. Is it fair to say that judges like Spurgeon Avakian are heroic figures?

Chapter IV

STATUTORY INTERPRETATION

Whoever hath an absolute authority to interpret any written or spoken laws, it is he who is truly the lawgiver, to all intents and purposes, and not the person who first spoke or wrote them.

　　—Bishop Hoadly

It is of course dangerous that judges be philosophers—almost as dangerous as if they were not.

　　—Paul Freund

In some respects, legal reasoning resembles the hunt for game. This and the next two chapters examine three hunting grounds where judges seek their quarry: the resolution of the legal conflict before them on statutory, common law, and constitutional grounds.[1]

---

[1]Practicing lawyers hunt in the same places. They do so to help people plan their affairs, to make "private law" safely without litigation. They also reason like judges when they prepare their positions on the legal issues in litigation itself. To avoid the constant repetition of the phrase "judges and lawyers" in the text, you should assume that comments about how judges reason usually refer to the lawyer's search for legal answers as well.

As you cover this material, keep these points in the back of your mind:

1. Partitioning the hunting ground so neatly creates a very artificial simplification. Judges rarely settle an entire controversy by solving one isolated legal point. Many legal controversies, especially in their initial stages, *potentially* raise statutory *and* common law *and* constitutional legal points, to say nothing of the administrative law hunting ground this book omits.

2. Good lawyers and trial judges recognize that the psychological dynamics of a situation—such as the desire of a quarreling couple to compromise if each can somehow "save face" in the process—can contribute more than law can to settling controversies. We ignore that important dynamic in law here.

3. Never lose sight of the judge's objective. It always involves solving a problem, a concrete case, not merely evaluating legal questions in the abstract. The hunt for legal quarry is not a hunt for "a legal rule" in isolation but for a legal interpretation sufficient to resolve the case. Judges do not hunt always for "the one right solution," but to appear just they often pretend to do so, as the concluding paragraph of Chapter II revealed. Legal problems have a variety of defensible solutions, which makes the hunt exciting.

4. Unlike the recreational hunter, judges cannot return from the hunt empty handed. They must decide by using the best available legal reasons, even if they are weak or unsatisfying. Like the primitive man hunting for survival, the judge may set out for an elk and feel fortunate to return with a turkey or a squirrel.

5. Finally, do not forget the message of the first three chapters: Despite the hunting metaphor's initial appeal, legal reasoning is *not* fundamentally a hunt at all. One of this century's finest teachers of legal reasoning, Karl Llewellyn, was fond of the similar metaphor of "quarrying" for some stone of legal truth. But hunting and mining can be seriously misleading metaphors because they suggest that the "truth" (the animal in the

woods or the nugget in the ground) is always there somewhere and needs only to be hunted down or dug up. But the truth isn't really "there" waiting: the reasoning judge creates the truth. Maybe judges resemble artists more than hunters.[2] I suspect they do.

WHAT ARE STATUTES AND WHAT SHOULD JUDGES DO WITH THEM?

Statutes—a dusty and unromantic word! One thinks of endless rows of thick books in inadequately illuminated library stacks. The librarians have the mildew under control, but its odor remains faintly on the air.

To understand better the significance of statutory law, we must abandon our reaction to statutes as dull and musty words; we must see them as vital forces in society. Statutes are the blood of government. Statutes articulate and communicate the policies of government. People in government, when fortified by statutory authority, can take our property, our freedom, and our lives. Political campaigns and elections, indeed much in public life that does excite us, matter because they directly influence the making of laws that can dramatically affect the quality of our lives.

In the United States, the special legal meaning of statutes rests on two fundamental principles of government. First, although all officials, including judges, can and do make law, legislatures possess primary authority for doing so.[3] When legis-

[2] Jerome Frank compared legal reasoning to musical interpretation. Jerome Frank, "Words and Music: Some Remarks on Statutory Interpretation," 47 *Columbia Law Review* 1259 (1947). That metaphor doesn't work, either. See Reed Dickerson, *The Interpretation and Application of Statutes* (Boston: Little, Brown, 1975), pp. 24–26, for the explanation

[3] This familiar principle of legislative supremacy has one important exception: Courts in the United States possess the authority to reject statutory supremacy when they conclude that the enforcement of a statute would violate a legal norm expressed in or implied by the constitutions of the states or the nation. Where judges find a violation, their expression of constitutional values becomes supreme, and this political dynamic is part of the familiar set of checks and balances that American government contains.

latures make policy to address a public problem, in theory that policy controls or supersedes the policies of presidents, administrators, or judges. Second, legislatures can communicate their chosen policies in a legally binding way only by voting favorably on a written proposal. Without the vote by the legislature, no matter how forcefully legislators advocate a policy decision, they create no law. Committee reports, floor speeches, and so forth, may help us make sense of the law, but only the duly enacted statute has the force of law.

Statutes, then, are the messages from the main policy-making body of government, legislatures, that translate ideas and ideologies into law. Statutes officially say, in effect: "Society has a problem. This is how society shall cope with it." Some statutory policies are incredibly general. Early antitrust statutes said, in effect, that society has a problem preserving effective business competition, and it shall hereafter be illegal to restrain competition. In 1890 a nearly unanimous Congress passed with very little debate the Sherman Antitrust Act. Its first two sections state: (1) "Every contract, combination in the form of a trust or otherwise, or conspiracy, in restraint of trade or commerce among the several States, or with foreign nations, is hereby declared to be illegal"; and (2) "Every person who shall monopolize, or attempt to monopolize... any part of the trade or commerce among the several States, or with foreign nations, shall be deemed guilty of a misdemeanor...." Such general language leaves to judges much freedom to shape and refine law. Other statutes create extremely detailed rules. Current tax laws say that government shall raise revenues, but it takes literally thousands of pages of rules and regulations to specify how government shall do it.

In the common law chapter to come, we shall see that courts can make and have made laws to handle many problems that legislatures now address by statute. This fact does not in any way conflict with the policy-making priority we now grant to legislatures. Furthermore, many modern social problems are so complex and their effects so synergistic that legislation, which is forward-looking and susceptible to an infinite variety of pragmatic compromises, is the preferred policy-making method.

Consider the wholesale changes that we must inevitably make in our copyright laws now that we have entered the computer age. When texts of "books" are stored on our computers, we can change them. Indeed, computer programs already exist whereby the computers themselves can change texts (e.g., by correcting misspelled words). According to the *Wall Street Journal,* Professor Ithiel de Sola Pool of MIT has predicted that, once many different versions of a written work exist, we will have to change our entire way of calculating how authors get royalties for their work.[4] This is a job for legislatures, not courts. We are hardly about to return to a common law, statuteless, legal system.

A statute that states how society shall cope with business monopoly or revenue raising or any of thousands of other problems really attempts to instruct judges to settle legal conflicts in one way rather than another. The legal process that resolves case after case is the heart of the coping process, the heart that pumps statutory blood, to continue the vital metaphor. How then, should judges decide in concrete cases what statutes mean?

When judges resolve specific cases in terms of statutes, they should seek first the guidance of earlier case precedents dealing with the same interpretive problem. But what if the problem has never arisen before? Then a judge must address directly such questions as these: "What problem does this statute try to solve? Is the case before me, an example of such a problem? If so, how does this statute tell me to solve it?" The judge who approaches statutory interpretation in the first instance this way acknowledges legislative supremacy. He recognizes that it is not *his* idea of the problem that resolves the case before him. Rather, he knows that he must deal with the problem in the way the statute communicates that problem and its solutions to him.

Since he sees that statutes are a special kind of communication, the judge who approaches statutes wisely also knows that he cannot treat the words as a series of Webster's definitions strung together. He understands the difficulties of clear communication. He intuitively appreciates the saying, "The greatest difficulty with communication is the illusion that it has been

---

[4]December 17, 1982, p. 29. See also *Sony Corp. v. Universal City Studios,* 52 U.S. Law Week 4090 (1984).

achieved." He knows that words gain meaning not from dictionaries, but from their context. He knows that a blackjack player who says, "Hit me!" does not request a punch in the nose. He knows that the words of statutes become meaningful only when they are applied to the solution of public problems.

WHAT JUDGES ACTUALLY DO WITH STATUTES

We have just outlined how judges should interpret statutes. The rest of the chapter fills in the details. We must begin, however, by seeing that how judges actually interpret statutes often bears little or no resemblance to our description. As you read through the three "actualities" that follow, think critically about how each of them illustrates the blunt statement in Chapter I that judges often do not know what they are doing.

First Actuality: Sticking to the Literal Meaning of Words

In 1912 Lord Atkinson, speaking for the British House of Lords in its appellate judicial role, said:

> If the language of a statute be plain, admitting of only one meaning, the Legislature must be taken to have meant and intended what it has plainly expressed, and whatever it has in clear terms enacted must be enforced though it should lead to absurd or mischievous results.[5]

Lord Atkinson, no doubt, respected legislative powers and responsibilities, in this case, those of the House of Commons. His problem, we can safely guess, is this: If courts can go beyond the words at all, they can go anywhere they want, setting their own limits and destroying legislative supremacy in the process.

Legislative supremacy is important, but how would the good Lord react to this hypothetical statute: "A uniformed police officer may require any person driving a motor vehicle in a public place to provide a specimen of breath for a breath test if

[5]*Vacher and Sons, Ltd., v. London Society of Compositors,* A.C. 107 (1912), 121.

the officer has reasonable cause to suspect him of having alcohol in his body." Presumably Lord Atkinson would not exempt women from this law just because the last sentence reads "him" rather than "him or her." The earlier use of the word "person," even to a literalist, can cover both sexes. But how would he handle the following argument by an equally literalistic defendant? "The statute plainly says the officer may require the specimen from a person driving. I may have been slightly inebriated when the officer pulled me over, but when the officer required the specimen I was *not* 'driving a motor vehicle.' I wasn't even in my car. I was doing my imitation of a pig in the middle of the pavement when the officer requested the specimen."[6] This result is absurd, but Lord Atkinson seems willing to accept absurd results. Should he be?

American judges have also been seduced by the appeal of adhering to the words. A Virginia statute stated: "No cemetery shall be hereafter established within the corporate limits of any city or town; nor shall any cemetery be established within two hundred and fifty yards of any residence without the consent of the owner...." In 1942, after the legislature passed this statute, the town of Petersburg, Virginia, bought an acre of land within its limits on which to relocate bodies exhumed during a road-widening project. The acre adjoined and would be incorporated into a long-established cemetery. A city resident well within the proscribed distance of the added acre brought suit to prevent the expansion and cited the statute. He lost. Justice Gregory wrote for the appellate court:

> If the language of a statute is plain and unambiguous, and its meaning perfectly clear and definite, effect must be given to it regardless of what courts think of its wisdom or policy....
>
> The word, "established," is defined in Webster's New International Dictionary, second edition, 1936, thus: "To originate and secure the permanent existence of; to found; to institute; to create and regulate..."
>
> Just why the Legislature, in its wisdom, saw fit to prohibit the establishment of cemeteries in cities and towns,

---

[6]See Sir Rupert Cross, *Statutory Interpretation* (London: Butterworths, 1976), p. 59. Or imagine a city ordinance requiring all liquor stores "to cease doing business at 10:00 P.M." Does the ordinance permit them to reopen at 10:01 P.M.?

and did not see fit to prohibit enlargements or additions, is no concern of ours. Certain it is that language could not be plainer than that employed to express the legislative will. From it we can see with certainty that...a cemetery...may be added to or enlarged without running counter to the inhibition found in [the statute]....Our duty is to construe the statute as written.[7]

Judges, like Justice Gregory, who cling to the words utterly fail to appreciate that the dictionary staff did not sit in Virginia's legislature. By sticking to the words, the judges prevent themselves from asking what problem the legislature sought to address. Just why the legislature might purposely allow enlargement but not establishment of cemeteries in cities and towns *is* Justice Gregory's concern. Unless he tries to solve that puzzle, we can have no confidence that he has applied the statute to achieve its purpose.

Second Actuality: The Golden Rule

Of course, Lord Atkinson could have solved his problem another way, by sticking to the words *except* when they produce absurd results. The Golden Rule of statutory interpretation holds that judges should follow

the grammatical and ordinary sense of the words...unless that would lead to some absurdity, or some repugnance or inconsistency with the rest of the instrument, in which case the grammatical and ordinary sense of the words may be modified, so as to avoid the absurdity and inconsistency, but no farther.[8]

The Golden Rule solves the problem of the clever intoxicated driver. It would be absurd and possibly dangerous to require that the officer ride with him and collect the specimen while weaving down the road.

[7]*Temple v. City of Petersburg*, 182 Va. 418 (1944), pp. 423–424. Responding to the vague words of the Mann Act (quoted in Chapter II), Justice Day wrote in his majority opinion in *Caminetti*, "Where the language is plain and admits of no more than one meaning of the duty of interpretation does not arise...." Was the language of the Mann Act plain?

[8]*Grey v. Pearson*, 6 H.L. Cas. 61 (1857), 106, quoted in Cross, p. 15.

But the Golden Rule, unfortunately, does not solve much more because it does not tell us how to separate the absurd from the merely questionable. To test this weakness in the rule, ask yourself two questions: (1) Is it absurd to allow expansion of existing graveyards while prohibiting the creation of new ones, or only questionable? (2) Is it absurd to use the Mann Act to prevent the transportation of willing girlfriends and mistresses across state lines along with unwilling "white slaves" and prostitutes, or merely questionable? The Golden Rule provides no answer.

Both the literal approach and the superficially more sensible rejection of absurdity in the Golden Rule fail. They deceive judges into believing that words in isolation can be and usually are clear and that the words communicate by themselves. But they don't. The word "establish" in *Temple* (the graveyard case), the phrase "immoral purpose" in *Caminetti* (our first Mann Act case), and the word "vehicle" in *McBoyle* (the airplane theft case) simply are not clear, and no blunt assertion to the contrary will make them so. Even when words in isolation do seem unambiguous, the process of coordinating them with the facts of a particular case may make them unclear. The judge who simply examines the words by themselves and asserts that they are clear seeks only an easy exit. Taking Webster's definition of "establish" as an example, the responsible judge would at least have to explain why the city of Petersburg was not originating and securing "the permanent existence of" the new acre for a cemetery. Justice Gregory did not explain this. Interpreting words in isolation rather than in context, then, is a danger because it leads judges to believe that they have thought a problem through to its end when they have only thought it through to its beginning.

To summarize, words become meaningful only in context. In statutory interpretation, judges must analyze two contexts, the legislative context—what general problem exists and what kind of policy response to it the legislature has created; and the case context—what the litigants are disputing and whether their dispute involves the problem the statute addresses. To say that words are clear or unclear depending on the context really means that the words would become clear if we could imagine a *different* case or context arising under each of the same statutes this book has mentioned so far. If Mr. McBoyle had stolen a car, or if Mr. Caminetti had abducted a Mexican-American immigrant girl, judges would have had no difficulty concluding that the statutory words clearly and unambiguously determine the case. Judges would similarly not have hesitated to prohibit Petersburg from opening a brand new cemetery within the city limits.

Justice Holmes once wrote, "A word is not a crystal, transparent and unchanged, it is the skin of a living thought and may vary greatly in color and content according to the circumstances and the time in which it is used."[9] Despite his mangled metaphor, Holmes advances our understanding. The words of statutes contain ideas—policy ideas with the force of law—and judges must articulate these ideas.

Third Actuality: Legislative Intent and Legislative History

Idle Armchair Speculation

One common way in which judges try to articulate the meaning of statutes is to try to discover what the legislature "intended" its statutory words to mean. I shall try in a moment to persuade you that "legislative intent" is a most slippery and misleading concept. For now, think carefully about the following use of legislative intent. How much more comfortable are you with Chief Justice Rugg's reasoning in the next case than you were with Lord Atkinson's literal approach or Justice Gregory's reasoning in the cemetery case or Justice Day's argument in *Caminetti*?

Shortly after it became a state, and long before the Nineteenth Amendment to the United States Constitution enfranchised women, Massachusetts passed a statute providing that "a person qualified to vote for representative to the General Court [the official name of the Massachusetts legislature] shall be liable to serve as a juror." Ten years after the passage of the Nineteenth Amendment, one Genevieve Welosky, a criminal

---

[9]*Towne v. Eisner*, 245 U.S. 418 (1917), p. 425.

defendant, found herself facing a Massachusetts jury that excluded all women. Welosky protested the exclusion, appealed, and lost. Under the literal or Golden Rule approaches she would surely have won, for "person" includes women, and women were "qualified to vote." Even before the days of women's liberation, we would hardly label it absurd to allow female jurors.

But Massachusetts Chief Justice Rugg invoked the intent of the legislature:

> It is clear beyond peradventure that the words of [the statute] when originally enacted could not by any possibility have included or been intended by the General Court to include women among those liable to jury duty.... Manifestly, therefore, the intent of the Legislature must have been, in using the word "person" in statutes concerning jurors and jury lists, to confine its meaning to men.[10]

The legislature didn't intend women to become jurors when they passed the statute because at that time women could not vote. Despite the literal meaning of the words, they cannot therefore sit on juries.

The title of this section offered the hope that judges can find statutory truth by discovering legislative intent. The Massachusetts court has identified an uncontested social background fact—that women could not vote when the statute was passed—and concluded logically that the legislature did not intend women to sit on juries. This logic is straightforward enough, but the *Welosky* opinion is a virtual fraud. Rugg says the simple sequence of historical events reveals the legislature's intent; because the statute came before the amendment, the legislature did not intend to include women. But Rugg's first quoted sentence is sheer nonsense. The legislature's intent is *not* "clear beyond peradventure." Maybe the Massachusetts legislature "intended" to settle the problem of who may sit as a juror once and for all by simply gearing jury liability automatically to all future changes in the voting laws. A legislature that did so would hardly act absurdly. Rugg completely fails to show that it did not so act.

Does the hope that legislative intent will reveal the meaning of statutory language hence fail? Ultimately it does fail, but

---

[10]*Commonwealth v. Welosky*, 276 Mass. 398 (1931), pp. 402–406.

not because of poorly reasoned cases like *Welosky*. The quest for legislative intent is a search for hard evidence. It is detective work in the legal field, not Rugg's idle armchair speculations, so we should not abandon the field of legislative intent so quickly.

Judges have many sleuthing techniques for discovering "hard evidence" of intent, of which we now review three of the most prominent. What do you think of them?

Other Words in the Statute

The brief excerpt from the cemetery case may have treated Justice Gregory unfairly, for he did not simply rest his opinion on Webster's dictionary. He continued by pointing out that another section of the cemetery statute of Virginia

> affords a complete answer to the question of legislative intent in the use of the word "established" in Section 56, for the former section [Section 53] makes a distinction between "establish" and "enlarge" in these words: "If it be desired at any time to establish a cemetery, for the use of a city, town, county, or magisterial district, or to enlarge any such already established, and the title to land needed cannot be otherwise acquired, land sufficient for the purpose may be condemned. . . ."
>
> The foregoing language, taken from Section 53, completely demonstrates that the legislature did not intend the words "establish" and "enlarge" to be used interchangeably, but that the use of one excluded any idea that it embraced or meant the other.[11]

Similarly, Justice McKenna, dissenting in *Caminetti*, found support in the official title of the Mann Act:

> For the context I must refer to the statute; of the purpose of the statute Congress itself has given us illumination. It devotes a section to the declaration that the "Act shall be known and referred to as the 'White Slave Traffic Act.'" And its prominence gives it prevalence in the construction of the statute. It cannot be pushed aside or subordinated by indefinite words in other sentences, limited even there by the context.[12]

---

[11]*Temple v. City of Petersburg*, p. 424.
[12]*Caminetti v. United States*, p. 497.

The title of the statute tells Justice McKenna that Congress did not intend to police the activities of willing girlfriends. Willing girlfriends are not white slaves; the conclusion sounds sensible.

The Expressed Intent of Individual Legislators and Committee Reports

Like Justice Gregory, Justice McKenna made more than one argument to support his conclusion.[13] In fact, he went directly to the words of the bill's author and quoted extensively from Representative Mann:

> The author of the bill was Mr. Mann, and in reporting it from the House committee on interstate and foreign commerce he declared for the committee that it was not the purpose of the bill to interfere with or usurp in any way the police power of the states, and further, that it was not the intention of the bill to regulate prostitution or the places where prostitution or immorality was practiced, which were said to be matters wholly within the power of the states, and over which the Federal government had no jurisdiction.... [Mann stated]:
> "The White Slave Trade—A material portion of the legislation suggested and proposed is necessary to meet conditions which have arisen within the past few years. The legislation is needed to put a stop to the villainous interstate and international traffic in women and girls. The legislation is not needed or intended as an aid to the states in the exercise of their police powers in the suppression or regulation of immorality in general. It does not attempt to regulate the practice of voluntary prostitution, but aims solely to prevent panderers and procurers from compelling thousands of women and girls against their will and desire to enter and continue in a life of prostitution." *Congressional Record*, vol. 50, pp. 3368, 3370.
> In other words, it is vice as a business at which the law is directed, using interstate commerce as a facility to procure or distribute its victims.

---

[13]Appellate judges often give multiple arguments for the conclusions in their opinions, but they rarely articulate whether one argument, by itself, would justify the same result. They don't, in other words, spell out the relative importance of the arguments they use. This complicates the task of following precedents, which we shall explore more fully in Chapter V.

Judges rarely argue that the expressed views of any one legislator necessarily convey legislative intent, but they frequently cite committee reports and the statement of authors as proof of intent. Is there anything unsatisfactory about this practice? The answer will appear shortly.

Other Actions, Events, and Decisions in the Legislature

To establish legislative intent, judges may also look at how the legislature handled related legislation. In *Welosky*, Chief Justice Rugg noted that the Massachusetts legislature had in 1920 changed several laws relating to women in order to make them conform to the Eighteenth and Nineteenth Amendments, but said nothing about the problem of female jurors. He argued regarding the 1920 legislation:

> It is most unlikely that the Legislature should, for the first time require women to serve as jurors without making provision respecting the exemption of the considerable numbers of women who ought not to be required to serve as jurors, and without directing that changes for the convenience of women be made in court houses, some of which are notoriously overcrowded and unfit for their accommodation as jurors.

Judges may even find in the physical evidence presented to committees the key to intent. In the 1940s the postmaster general refused to grant the preferential lower postage rate to books, like workbooks and notebooks, that contained many blank pages. Congress then amended the relevant statute to grant books with space for notes the preferential rates. However, the postmaster general continued to refuse the rate to so-called looseleaf notebooks with blank pages on the basis that they were not permanently bound. A shipper of such notebooks eager for the cheaper postage rate sued for an order granting the preferential rate.

The opinion of Judge Groner concluded that Congress *did* intend to give the preferential rate to looseleaf notebooks because the many physical exhibits placed before the committee that handled the bill included some such notebooks. Groner wrote, "[I]t follows logically that textbooks of the make and quality of those of appellant were considered and purposely included by Congress in the list of publications entitled to the book rate."[14]

The list of possibilities in this category could continue for pages. For example, judges are fond of finding legislative intent by discovering that one house's version of a bill contained a clause that does not appear in the final law, approved by both houses. They conclude from this discovery that the legislature intended that the remaining words *not* mean what the dropped clause meant. But we have enough illustrations to suffice for the moment.

Superficially, these discoveries of "hard evidence" of legislative intent appeal to us because they seem to reveal the purpose of the statute. But comparing the examples of sleuthing with our "first principles" of statutory interpretation reveals that legislative intent fails as badly as our other two approaches. Only the statute, the words for which the majority of both houses of the legislature voted, has the force of law.

When Judge Groner concludes "logically" that the legislature intended to include looseleaf notebooks for the preferential rate, he is logically completely incorrect. He does not give one shred of evidence that any legislator, much less the majority, actually thought about the physical exhibits when they voted. Of course, Representative Mann's thoughts give us some clue to *his* intent, but we do not know that a majority heard or read his thoughts. Even if a majority in the House and Senate did know what Mann intended, we don't know that they agreed with him. After all, the statute uses the word "Prostitution" without Mann's qualifications. Maybe the majority voted for the act because they wanted a tougher response than did Mann. Finally, when Justice Gregory pointed out the Virginia legislature's distinction between establishing and enlarging cemeteries for condemnation purposes, he did not prove that the legislators ever thought about the distinction with respect to what is essentially a zoning problem. In *Welosky* we have no proof that the Massachusetts General Court majority ever worried about female jurors.

---

[14]*McCormick-Mathers Publishing Co. v. Hannegan*, 161 F.2d 873 (D.C. Cir. 1947), p. 875. See Arthur Phelps, "Factors Influencing Judges in Interpreting Statutes," 3 *Vanderbilt Law Review* 456 (1950).

Why then, precisely, does legislative intent fail as a tool of statutory interpretation? A legislature is an organizational unit of government. By itself a legislature can no more intend something than can a government car or office building. *People* intend things, and, because the elected representatives in a legislature are people, they may intend something when they vote. If they all intended the same thing, then that might well provide the meaning of the statute. Here three difficulties fatal to the cause of legislative intent arise.

First, intent is subjective. It is usually impossible to tell with 100 percent certainty what anyone, ourselves included, intend. Thus, if a majority of legislators were fortunate enough to intend the same thing, it is highly unlikely that judges could actually discover what that thing was.

Second, we know enough about politics to know that in all likelihood the individuals making up the voting majority do not intend the same thing. Most will not have read the statute they vote on. Some will intend to repay a debt, or to be a loyal follower of their party leaders, or to encourage a campaign contribution from a private source in the future. If we want to deduce collective intent on anything, we must take a poll, and the only poll we ever take of legislators is when the presiding officer of the house calls for the vote to enact or defeat a bill. That much intent we might presume, but no more.

The third and most serious difficulty is that if by a miracle we overcome the first two difficulties, so that we actually know that the majority intended the same thing about a statute, it is highly unlikely, if not absolutely impossible, that they intended anything about the facts of the case before the court. In all probability the precise facts of cases such as *Mortensen* or *Cleveland* arose long after the law-making legislature disbanded. Just as in the *Repouille* case, a general feeling about an issue in the abstract does not necessarily resolve concrete cases, yet legislators at best intend only such general directions. Pose for the Mann Act Congress problems of migrating Mormons or vacationing vixens and you would probably get a gruff instruction to "ask a judge about the details." And of course by the time those cases actually arose, the majority of the makers of the Mann Act were, if not in their graves, surely no longer in Congress.

We shall see later that the evidence we falsely ascribe to

legislative intent can sometimes help define the purpose of the statute, the problems the statute tries to solve. But this evidence is rarely decisive itself.

WHY DO JUDGES SO OFTEN INTERPRET STATUTES POORLY?

This chapter provides as powerful a group of illustrations of judicial confusion as any to be found in this book. Hart and Sacks have written, "The hard truth of the matter is that American courts have no intelligible, generally accepted, and consistently applied theory of statutory interpretation."[15] Three characteristics of the reasoning process help account for the problem.

The Disorderly Conduct of Words

Linguistics and the philosophy of language are abstruse and difficult subjects. Much of our knowledge of the complexity of language is quite recent. Few lawyers—hence few judges—study the disorderly conduct of words, and this is the first characteristic that helps to explain interpretive confusion. To understand this we must master some linguistic basics.

First, words are often necessarily *general*. General language allows us to think of many specific possibilities simultaneously. Advertisers often use generalities to good advantage. An advertisement that says "Dynamic Motors cars over the last

---

[15]Henry M. Hart, Jr. and Albert M. Sacks, *The Legal Process* (Cambridge: Harvard Law School, 1958), p. 1201. In a sense the problem is even worse, for scholars of legal reasoning are themselves confused about the confusion. Many writers discuss at length the "plain meaning rule" of interpretation. But each scholar (as well as each judge) tends to define this "rule" of statutory interpretation his own way, so that the plain meaning rule has no plain judicial or scholarly meaning. See Dickerson, pp. 229–233. And see Arthur Murphy, "Old Maxims Never Die: The 'Plain Meaning Rule' and Statutory Interpretation in the 'Modern' Federal Courts," 75 *Columbia Law Review* 1299 (1975), p. 1308. Murphy asserts, "[T]he courts have no clear idea about what the plain meaning rule is and, what is more,...they really do not care."

five years have needed fewer repairs than Universal Motors cars," wants us to believe that all Dynamic Motors (DM) cars perform more reliably than all Universal Motors (UM) cars. Of course, even if the ad is completely true, it does not mean that. It certainly does not mean that DM's bottom line models perform more reliably than UM's top line models. But this is a helpful generalization, especially if you are debating whether to invest in DM or UM stock. Statutes necessarily speak in general language in order to control the wide variety of specific cases that are part of the social problem with which the statute copes, but judges must take care to discover what the generalization does *not* mean.

Second, language can be *vague*. The Dynamic Motors ad may be general (it may also be factually wrong!), but it is not vague because we can easily tell DM-built cars from UM-built cars. But consider this statement: "Bigger cars are safer than little cars." Vagueness in language refers to uncertainty about how much or of what degree of something a statement encompasses. We do not know how much car is enough to make it big, and we don't know whether bigness is size, weight, or both.

Third, and most important, words turn out to communicate *ambiguous* ideas; that is, words allow us to think of two simultaneously inconsistent concepts. Sometimes ambiguity in language arises when one or just a few words have mutually inconsistent meanings, because the dictionary itself permits such a clash of meanings. What does this statute mean? "It shall be a misdemeanor to sleep at a railway station." Does the word "at" include those comfortably asleep in their upper berths while their train rests at the station? Sleep can mean (1) being in a state of unconscious repose or (2) deliberately bedding down and spending the night. The first definition would cover both the hobo sprawled on a bench and the tired commuter dozing upright while waiting for the delayed train. The second meaning would spare the commuter but not the hobo.[16]

[16]Linguists call this semantic ambiguity. See Dickerson, pp. 45–46. It may help you to understand these distinctions if you figure out why the general and vague statements about cars are not semantically ambiguous, or syntactically or contextually ambiguous either, as the next few paragraphs define these concepts.

Language may also possess syntactic ambiguity. In this case, it is the ordering of the words, not varying dictionary definitions, that causes a problem. A statute regulating bank loans might say, "The banker shall require the borrower promptly to repay the loan." Does this mean the banker shall require the borrower to repay as soon as the law permits the banker to do so, or does this mean that the borrower must repay quickly once the banker begins requiring repayment, whenever that might be? Relocating the position of the word "promptly" in the sentence would have avoided the ambiguity.[17]

This chapter has emphasized the importance of interpreting the meaning of words by examining their context.[18] If the sentence proscribing sleeping in train stations augments a statute controlling vagrancy, the context of vagrancy solves the problem. If the neighboring language in the bank statute governs bankers on one hand or borrowers on the other, that ambiguity would disappear. But, despite this chapter's lecture about the importance of context, context can create as well as eliminate ambiguity. This was one of the problems created by the wording of the Mann Act. While "prostitution" normally carries a fairly clear meaning, placing it in the context of the "White Slave" act potentially changes the word's interpretation. While prostitutes as a rule need not be unwilling, maybe *these* prostitutes must be unwilling before the statute applies.

Once we realize that the context of statutes can render them ambiguous, we must face this reality: The linguistically honest judge will, from time to time, have to admit that the statute does not, through its words, communicate any clear-cut solution to

[17]Dickerson, pp. 46–47. The meaning of "ambiguity" here is much narrower than in Chapter II, where it encompassed all sources of imprecision in law.

[18]The classical illustration in the literature is from Wittgenstein, one I have modernized here. Suppose a father takes his child to Las Vegas, hires a croupier, and says "Teach the kid some games." Would the father be disappointed to find the croupier taught the boy the fine points of Monopoly? If the father had uttered the same sentence to a baby sitter at home, he could be equally disappointed to discover the child gambling his college savings on the chance of drawing to an inside straight in seven-card stud. The context—Las Vegas versus living room—makes all the difference. Readers with backgrounds in philosophy may want to consult also Hans-Georg Gadamer, *Truth and Method* (New York: Seaburg Press, 1975), pp. 345–498.

the case and context before him. We'll see later what this judge must then do.

The Booming Canons of Statutory Construction

In the past, judges have defended themselves against the imprecision of words by arming themselves with interpretive weapons called "canons of construction." Judges have often used these weapons unwisely, and this unwise use of the canons is another source of confusion in statutory interpretation.

A canon of construction or interpretation (they are, for our purposes, the same), is really a rule for interpreting rules, a device designed to make vague or ambiguous words appear precise. Here is an example:

> It is a general rule of construction that where general words follow an enumeration they are to be held as applying only to persons and things of the same general kind or class of thing to which the specifically mentioned things belong.

This canon may not mean much to you until you apply it in the context of a specific case. Fortunately, we have already covered two legal problems to which this canon could apply.

In the first, *McBoyle,* which involved the theft of an airplane, the relevant statute forbade transportation across state lines of a stolen "automobile, automobile truck, automobile wagon, motorcycle or any other self-propelled vehicle not designed for running on rails." Is an airplane such a vehicle? By invoking the above canon—judges usually use the shorthand phrase *ejusdem generis,* "of the same kind"—a judge could conclude that the general words "or any other self-propelled vehicle..." refer only to items *like* (in the same genus as) the objects the statute specifically mentions (the species). In this case, all the specific items run on land. Therefore, an airplane is not a vehicle.

Similarly, Justice Day invoked the ejusdem generis canon in reaching the conclusion that the Mann Act did cover concubines. He said that the general words "other immoral purposes" refer only to sexual immorality because all the specific examples fit that genus. Therefore, you will no doubt be relieved to know that you *can* take your mother or your wife across a state line to gamble illegally or rob a bank without violating the Mann Act.

Before we consider why the canons represent a vice rather than a virtue in statutory intepretation, it will help to review a few more examples from among dozens of canons that judges utilize. One frequently cited canon instructs judges to interpret criminal statutes narrowly. This means that, when a judge finds that the statute does not clearly resolve his case, he should resolve it in favor of the defendant. Again *McBoyle* can illustrate. Justice Holmes wrote for the Supreme Court in that case:

> [I]t is reasonable that a fair warning should be given to the world in language that the common world will understand of what the law intends to do if a certain line is passed. To make the warning fair, so far as possible the line should be clear.

Holmes argues, in other words, that unless judges interpret criminal statutes narrowly, judges will send to jail people who had no clear notice that they had committed a crime.[19]

Holmes's concern for fairness in *McBoyle* reminds us that the canons are not totally ineffective or undesirable weapons. Felix Frankfurter said that "even generalized restatements from time to time may not be wholly wasteful. Out of them may come a sharper rephrasing of the conscious factors of interpretation; new instances may make more vivid but also disclose their limitations."[20] Nearly every canon that judges have created contains at least a small charge of sensibility. Canons exist to support each of the principles of proper interpretation that this chapter covers. For example, the canon *noscitur a sociis* ("it is known by its associates") states that words are affected by their context. One British court used this canon to confine a statute regulating houses "for public refreshment, resort and enter-

---

[19]*McBoyle v. United States*, p. 27. A narrow interpretation may produce a very different decision from that of a literal interpretation. A literal interpretation of the words "other immoral purposes" in the Mann Act *would* make the act cover my taking my wife to another state to rob a bank. A narrow interpretation would not.

[20]Felix Frankfurter, "Some Reflections on the Reading of Statutes," 2 *Record of the Association of the Bar of the City of New York* 213 (1947), p. 236.

tainment" only to places where people received food and drink and excluded musical and other theatrical places, refreshing though their shows might be. The statute bore the title Refreshment House Act.[21]

Again we must ask why the canons are part of the problem rather than part of the solution.

By making disorderly words appear orderly, canons deceive judges into thinking they have found a sensible and purposeful application of the statute to the case. In fact, the canons often allow judges to evade the difficult task of untangling statutory purpose. The best (actually the worst) example of this judicial evasion of purpose concerned the interpretation of an act of Congress in 1893 designed to promote railway safety.[22] In part, Section 2 of the statute stated:

> [I]t shall be unlawful for any...common carrier [engaged in interstate commerce] to haul or permit to be hauled or used on its line any car...not equipped with couplers coupling automatically by impact, and which can be uncoupled without the necessity of men going between the ends of the cars.

Section 8 of the Act placed the right to sue for damages into the hands of "any employee of any such common carrier who may be injured by any locomotive, car or train in use contrary to the provisions of this act...." At common law, the injured employee often had no right of action against his employer; Section 8 created that right. Additionally, the act imposed criminal penalties on railroads that failed to comply.

A workman was injured while positioned between a locomotive and a car. He had tried to couple them by hand because the locomotive did not possess a coupler that coupled automatically with that on the car. He sued for damages and lost both in the trial court and in the U.S. Court of Appeals, the latter holding that the statute did not require locomotives to possess the same automotive couplers. Judge Sanborn fired canon after

---

[21]Cross, p. 118. The list of canons is lengthy. Karl Llewellyn cites and provides judicial citations for 56 canons in "Remarks on the Theory of Appellate Decision and the Rules or Canons about How Statutes Are to Be Construed," 3 *Vanderbilt Law Review* 395 (1950), pp. 401–406.

[22]27 Stat. c. 196, p. 531.

canon in defense of his conclusion that the statutory word "cars" did not include locomotives:

- "The familiar rule that the expression of one thing is the exclusion of the others leads to [this] conclusion."
- "A statute which thus changes the common law must be strictly construed."
- "This is a penal statute, and it may not be so broadened by judicial construction as to make it cover and permit the punishment of an act which is not denounced by the fair import of its terms."
- "The intention of the legislature and the meaning of a penal statute must be found in the language actually used."[23]

Do any of these canons convince you that this statute does not require locomotives to have automatic couplers? Again, the canons are not themselves absurd; the damage occurs when they seduce judges so easily into applying them simplistically and into thinking the canon gives *the* answer when the canon only justifies *an* answer. Does not Judge Sanborn's reasoning at least create the suspicion in your mind that he wanted, for whatever reasons, to rule for the railroads, and that the easy availability of canons only provided convenient justification for him to enact his own beliefs? We hardly want to encourage legal reasoning that only camouflages personal preferences.

The vice of the canons resembles the familiar law of mechanics. For each and every canon there is an equal and opposite canon. Llewellyn organizes his 56 canons noted in footnote 21 into 28 sets of opposing canons: "THRUST BUT PARRY," he calls them. The judge who, for whatever reason, reaches any conclusion can find a canon to defend it.

Consider this example of Llewellyn's point: A federal statute prohibits the interstate shipment of any "obscene... book, pamphlet, picture, motion-picture film, paper, letter, writing, print or other matter of indecent character." One Mr. Alpers shipped interstate some phonograph records that, ad-

---

[23]*Johnson v. Southern Pacific Co.*, 117 Fed. 462 (C.C.A. 8th 1902). Fortunately the United States Supreme Court reversed, 196 U.S. 1 (1904).

mitted for the sake of argument, were obscene. On the basis of ejusdem generis and "strict construction of criminal statutes," two canons, we might expect Mr. Alpers to win his case. After all, the genus to which all the species belong to is "things comprehended through sight." Instead, Justice Minton, for the Supreme Court, alluded to noscitur a sociis, another canon, and upheld the conviction.[24]

In short, the canons themselves are at war. In *Caminetti*, ejusdem generis pushes toward conviction, but "narrow construction" pushes toward acquittal. Shall judges flip coins?

Judicial Naiveté about the Legislative Process

The last and most serious source of judicial confusion in statutory interpretation involves the naive, if not simply wrong, assumptions judges often make about how legislatures make laws. Former Representative Wayne Hays once remarked, "There are two things that the public should never see being made: sausages and laws." Judges often ignore the mundane realities of legislative life. The frequent judicial discoveries of the intent of the legislature, when in all probability the legislature intended nothing with respect to the unique factual situation before the court, best illustrates the problem.

Much can be (and has been) said for abandoning the concept of legislative intent permanently. The ever-skeptical Holmes wrote, "I don't care what their intention was, I only want to know what the words mean." And Frankfurter added, "You may have observed that I have not yet used the word 'intention.' All these years I have avoided speaking of the 'legislative intent' and I shall continue to be on my guard against using it."[25] A few pages back I introduced the reasons that the concept of intent fails. Let me expand those observations in three directions here.

First, legislatures respond to public problems by creating general public policies. The problem is nearly always an accumulation of many different specific instances, like vehicle

---

[24]*United States v. Alpers,* 338 U.S. 680 (1950).
[25]Frankfurter, pp. 227–228.

thefts, white slavery, juror selection, or controlling of the location of cemeteries. Legislatures simply do not confront the concrete and always somewhat unique factual case. In this sense, as former Attorney General Levi once said, "Despite much gospel to the contrary, a legislature is not a fact-finding body. There is no mechanism, as there is with a court, to require the legislature to sift facts and to make a decision about specific situations."[26] In all probability no one in the legislature foresaw the precise problem facing the judge, and it is even less likely that the legislature consciously intended to resolve the case one way or another.

The candid judge looking for firm evidence of intent often won't find it. A candid Rugg would, for example, have concluded, "I simply can't say whether the Massachusetts legislature thought about women becoming jurors or not." The names Holmes and Frankfurter endure more prominently than Rugg because they were especially able to make such candid judgments.[27]

For further illustration of this point, consider one final problem. A federal immigration statute requires that immigrants receive an immigration permit prior to leaving their home country and that they present the permit on arrival before being allowed to enter and move about the United States. Imagine that in a voyage of immigrants from China a woman with a permit gives birth to a child. While the mother can present her permit and enter, her new infant cannot. There is no shred of evidence in the legislative history of the immigration law that Congress ever once thought about this problem. Must the infant (and presumably its mother) return to China?[28]

Second, although the United States government prints reams of information about legislation in Congress—committee

---

[26]Edward H. Levi, *An Introduction to Legal Reasoning* (Chicago: University of Chicago Press, 1949), p. 31.

[27]The eminent jurisprudent John Gray wrote, "The fact is that the difficulties of so-called interpretation arise when the Legislature has had no meaning at all; when the question which is raised on the statute never occurred to it...." *The Nature and Sources of the Law* (New York: Macmillan, 1927), p. 173.

[28]Charles Curtis, "A Better Theory of Legal Interpretation," 3 *Vanderbilt Law Review* 407 (1950), p. 413.

hearings, committee reports, speeches, and so forth—judges often have no access to this kind of information about how state legislatures operate. Even if we could count on this information to reveal the true intent of legislators (which we can't), much of the time judges won't get the information in the first place.

The *third* and most important set of reasons that judges misunderstand the legislative process is that they hide from the mundane facts of political life; legislatures are very practical and political places. Consider:

- We saw earlier (on p. 104) that Judge Groner could not logically conclude that the Congress intended to include looseleaf notebooks in the preferential rate just because one committee's exhibits contained samples of them. The conclusion appears even shakier once we acknowledge that a lobbyist, with or without conscious help from a busy committee chairman, might have deliberately planted that evidence before the committee. The lobbyist may not aggressively try to influence the committee, but he would hope to persuade the judge later in litigation that the planted evidence proves legislative intent and thereby win a favorable judicial ruling for the lobbyist's client. As long ago as 1947, Archibald Cox wrote that "it is becoming increasingly common to manufacturer 'legislative history' during the course of legislation."[29]

- Both houses of a bicameral legislature must approve the identically worded bill before it becomes law. Often when the two houses disagree, special joint committees form to negotiate the compromise. Whatever force committee reports and speeches might have had on the passage of the original bill in each house, it is difficult, if not impossible, to discern the grounds on which the two houses jointly compromise. Often the compromise package includes a decision to leave a question deliberately unanswered simply to avoid stalemate. The pro-

[29]Archibald Cox, "Some Aspects of the Labor Management Relations Act, 1947," 61 *Harvard Law Review* 1 (1947), p. 44.

cess of deciding on a compromise also often means, in practice, that one house may ratify without debate a bill containing provisions it never considered one way or another when it debated and passed its own bill.

- Judges often claim to distill congressional intent from the formal speeches and remarks of legislators printed in the *Congressional Record,* as if the entire body of legislators sat in rapt attention, devouring and ultimately approving the tenor of the remarks. But the bulk of the *Record*'s comments simply appear there at the request of the legislator. Even when debate precedes the vote, the floor usually contains virtually no one but debaters and a very few listeners. The *Record* tells nothing about how many rushed in to record their votes without hearing the floor debate.

- Most voting legislators never read the bill on which they vote at all; more likely, they hurriedly glance at the committee report. Most often, the voting legislator relies on party leadership, or on the advice of an aide who has reviewed the problem, or on the record of public opinion, or on the private urging of a lobbyist. They may do any or all of these without giving any detailed thought to the bulk of the words and sentences in the act (drafted most likely by administrators, aides, and lobbyists in combination—not by legislators) that lawyers piously debate later in court.

- Finally, judges often ignore the possibility that the lawmaking process might purposely create unclear law because legislators *want* the courts to fill in the details. This may amount to buck-passing in the hope that the courts will take the pressure for an unpopular result. But legislators may also believe that case-by-case judicial action is the best way to decide precisely what the statute should include and exclude. The judge who fails to look for that purpose evades his own judicial responsibilities.

These examples of legislative realities should make judges wary of concluding that the legislature ever intended anything. "Legislative intention," Professor Horack wrote,

is useful as a symbol to express the gloss which surrounds the
enacting process—the pre-legislative history, the circumstances
and motivations which induced enactment.... Society cannot
act effectively on subjectivity of intent; and, therefore, legislative intention becomes not what the legislature in fact
intended but rather what reliable evidences there are to satisfy
the [judicial] need for further understanding of the legislative
action.[30]

The ultimate danger in all of these methods of statutory interpretation—the literal and Golden Rule approaches, the use of
canons, and the search for legislative intent in legislative history—is that each allows the judge to reach a conclusion without
ever struggling with the fundamental question whether one
interpretation or another actually copes with social problems
effectively. These methods, in other words, perpetuate decisions
that may not promote law's basic goal, that of social cooperation. The next section describes a better way for judges to interpret statutes.

HOW JUDGES SHOULD INTERPRET
STATUTES IN THE FIRST INSTANCE

The preceding section was not particularly kind to judges. In
statutory interpretation, judicial elk hunters often return with
turkeys. But condemnation accomplishes little more than relative self-aggrandizement. Let us try to grapple with the basic
difficulty and then offer improvements.

Statutory interpretation so frequently seems inadequate
because judges face an unavoidable necessity. Judges must say
what the law "is" in order to resolve the case before them. I call
this a necessity for judges because our society, our culture,
believes that judges act unfairly when they do not decide on the
basis of what the law says and is. Judges cannot hear a case and
then refuse to render a decision because they cannot determine

[30] Frank E. Horack, Jr., "The Disintegration of Statutory Construction," 24
Indiana Law Journal 335 (1949), pp. 340–341.

the legal answer.[31] We do not pay judges to say, "Maybe the law is X. Maybe the law is Y. I'll guess Y. You lose!" (Or worse, "I don't care if it's X or Y. You still lose!") In order to render justice in our culture, justices must make certain that which is inherently uncertain.

Making the uncertain appear certain is particularly difficult in statutory interpretation. In common law and in constitutional law, the courts know that they have authority to make law. In these realms judges can say, "The law ought to be X, not Y. Therefore the law is X." But legislative supremacy bars judges from interpreting statutes so boldly. They must try to find the "oughts" somewhere in the legislative process, an uncertain and distant process in which judges themselves play little part. It is like sending forth a knight with orders to find the Holy Grail, requiring him to return in a week with anything he finds as long as he can prove that what he found is the Grail, and repeating this order week after week.

Judges will continue to make uncertain statutes certain in their application by creating and asserting that certainty can and does emerge from the generality, the vagueness, and the ambiguity in words, and from the disorderly world of politics. How can judges create certainty out of uncertainty wisely?

The Centrality of Statutory Purpose

Judges should believe, almost as an article of faith, that words by themselves *never* possess a plain or clear or literal meaning. Statutes become meaningful only to the extent that their words fit some intelligible purpose. The problem the statute addresses always gives direction to the search for purpose. A dictionary never does.

Judges must satisfy themselves that their application of a statute to the case before them serves statutory purpose. Sometimes a statute seems automatically to determine a case. We saw that this would occur if McBoyle had transported a stolen auto-

---

[31]This is true of most formal legal systems. For example, the French Civil Code dating from 1804 states, "A judge who refuses to enter judgement on the pretext of silence, obscurity, or inadequacy of the statute is subject to prosecution for the denial of justice."

mobile instead of an airplane. But judges must understand that no conclusion is totally automatic. We can imagine that a particular individual could transport an automobile across state lines, knowing the car to be stolen, and yet not violate the act. This individual would be the FBI agent driving the car back to its owner. The agent does not violate the act, because he is not part of the problem the act tries to solve—he is part of the solution.

Let me explain this a slightly different way. The questions people ask determine the answers they receive. The key to legal reasoning is asking the right question. The right answer to the wrong question should never satisfy a judge. In statutory interpretation, the right questions always begin with a question about statutory purpose. Think of the difference it can make in *Johnson* (the locomotive coupling case) to ask (1) "Is a locomotive a railroad car?" versus (2) "Is protecting the safety of workers coupling locomotives to cars as well as cars to cars a sensible part of the problem this law tries to cope with?" Notice that whenever a judge inquires into the purpose of the legislation he must *inevitably* inquire into the background facts that reveal the nature of the social problems involved in the case and how the statute tries to cope with it.

Determining Purpose: Words Can Help

It is the language of a statute that alone has the force of law. Nothing else that individual legislators or legislative bodies say or do legally binds a judge. Some legislation includes specific definitions of key words. These definitions in statutes may or may not agree with a dictionary definition, but they are law and they bind the judge. Legislation, though lacking an internal dictionary, always contain words whose ordinary definitions unambiguously shape its purpose. By including the word *prostitution,* the Mann Act unambiguously covers more than white slavery because by no ordinary definition are prostitutes necessarily enslaved in that occupation. Judges must never give words a meaning that the words, in their context, cannot bear. Except for its euphemistic title, the "White Slave Act" contains not one word to indicate that the women whose transportation it forbids must be unwilling. It is in this context that the word *prostitution* unambiguously shapes the Mann Act's meaning.

Context is always crucial. Some contexts require courts to decide precisely the opposite of the literal command of words. If, through some printing error, the officially published version of a statute omits a key word, judges properly include the word if the context makes such a purpose clear. Suppose that a statute prohibiting some very undesirable behavior omits in its official version the key prohibitory word "not." Although the statute would then literally permit or even require the unwarranted behavior, judges may apply the statute as if it contained the missing and critical "not."

Canons of interpretation may help reassure judges that a given word, phrase, or sentence has a certain meaning in a specific context. They may serve as shorthand reminders of ways of thinking about purpose. But a canon should never dictate to a judge that words must have one meaning regardless of context. The canons of ejusdem generis and of narrow construction of criminal statutes may help a judge exclude airplanes and obscene records from the reach of those two statutes, but they do not compel that conclusion, as the next section illustrates.

Noscitur a sociis can also be a helpful reminder for a way of thinking about purpose. The context of neighboring words may crystallize the meaning of an ambiguous phrase. What, for example, is "indecent conduct"? In the abstract, we might agree that it depends on individual perceptions and moralities and that we can't really tell what it is. But consider two statutes, one that prohibits "indecent conduct at a divine service of worship" and another that prohibits "indecent conduct at a public beach or bathing place." The contexts of worship and beach would both classify total nudity as indecent conduct, but only one context would classify playing a game of volleyball in bikini bathing suits as indecent.

Determining Purpose: The Audience

Legislatures direct different statutes to different kinds of audiences. Some statutes, especially criminal statutes, communicate to the community at large. Criminal statutes thus have the purpose of communicating general standards of conduct to large populations containing people of widely varying degrees of literacy and local customs and habits. Judges properly interpret such words according to the common meanings they may expect these words to convey to this diverse population. Other perhaps highly technical laws may communicate only to special classes of people, such as commercial television broadcasters or insurance underwriters. Here the words may assume unusual and technical meanings that only the special audience understands. Similarly, judges should hold that a statute purposely changes a long-held principle of common law or the legality of a behavior widely believed proper in the past only when they think a statute makes that purpose unambiguously clear.

Determining Purpose: Generality in Statutes

Many statutes, in effect, direct courts, administrative agencies, or both to develop specific policies within very broad and general limits set by statute. The antitrust statutes provide the archetype. When judges apply general statutes, they must accept the fact that purpose may emerge clearly only from the facts and problems revealed in litigation itself. Here courts possess the responsibility for shaping purpose. When judges assume this responsibility, they should assume that changes in technology, attitudes, scientific information, or private customs may require changes in the specific meaning and application of statutes.

Determining Purpose: The Assumption of Legislative Rationality and the Uses of Legislative History

In determining whether an issue in a lawsuit is part of the problem that a statute purposely tries to address, judges should treat the people who make laws and the process of lawmaking as rational and sensible, "reasonable persons pursuing reasonable purposes reasonably," as Hart and Sacks put it.[32] This assumption helps judges determine purpose because it forces them to

[32] Hart and Sacks, p. 1415.

determine what portion of the law, prior to the enactment of the statute, worked so poorly that a rational legislature wanted to change it.[33] Again, think about how the result in the locomotive coupling case would differ if the court had approached the problem this way. Finally, what purposes would a rational legislator have for inserting the "good moral character" test in our nationalization laws? Is such a purpose well served by making moral judgments about incest or mercy-killing in the abstract?

The judge who thinks about lawmaking as a logical process also recognizes that no statute exists in isolation, for rational lawmakers understand that no one act can completely define where its policy stops and another competing policy ought, instead, to govern. Congressmen realize (and the courts grasp that they know) that state law, not federal law, assumes the major responsibility for defining and policing criminal behavior. Knowing that state laws purposely define and prohibit sexual immorality should have limited the purpose the Court attributed to the Mann Act in *Caminetti* and in *Cleveland*.

Courts can generate sensible conclusions about the purpose of statutes from the statements of legislative committees, sponsors of the bill, and so forth. This history may allow a judge to understand what aspects or consequences of prior law failed to cope with a social problem so that the legislature needed to create a new law. Legislative history may also clarify where one policy should give way to another. Legislative history relating to specific applications of the statute, as in the looseleaf notebook case, only helps the judge to the extent that it provides good evidence of the legislation's general purpose. (You should recall that the physical presence of looseleaf notebooks bore virtually no relationship to the purpose of that statute—the statute did not attempt to create a standard definition of the word *book* for postage purposes. Judge Groner should therefore have ignored that evidence.) In sum, where isolated examples of legislative

---

[33]Lord Coke originated this helpful approach, sometimes labeled the *mischief rule*, in 1584. Occasional judicial attention to history can prove surprisingly profitable. For a lucid discussion of the concept of statutory purpose and its modern applications see Julian B. McDonnell, "Purposive Interpretation of the Uniform Commercial Code: Some Implications for Jurisprudence," 126 *Pennsylvania Law Review* 796 (1978).

intent don't mesh with sensible statutory purpose, judges should ignore them.

Illustrations

Three Easy Cases

You should now have little difficulty resolving comfortably some of this chapter's cases. Despite the ambiguities in the statutory language, you should not hesitate (1) to allow the officer to collect the breath specimen from a driver standing on the shoulder of the road, not merely from a driver while he is weaving down a highway; (2) to prohibit the liquor store from reopening at 10:01 (see footnote 6); and (3) to allow the sleepy commuter to doze upright on the bench while prohibiting the hobo from encamping in a corner. The words don't require these conclusions and judges probably lack any legislative history for these state and local laws, but judges can still reach sensible results. The words can bear these interpretations, and our knowledge of social problems and purposes compels these conclusions. Notice, by the way, how the wise solution to each of these three cases hinges on the judge's realistic assessment of social background facts as discussed in Chapter III.

Of course, other cases could arise under these same statutes in which the words themselves would not bear the interpretation claimed for them. Our officer cannot collect breath specimens in parking lots and driveways outside cocktail parties at midnight, even if he safely assumes that many will soon drive home and even if we believe it a highly wise social policy to prevent intoxicated drivers from driving in the first place. This action might be an effective preventive, but it is not found in the meaning or purpose of this law because the words make "driving" a prerequisite for demanding the specimen.

The Case of the Lady Jurors, or Why Legislative Intent Does Not Necessarily Determine Statutory Purpose

Recall briefly Chief Justice Rugg's justification for excluding women from jury liability despite the fact that they could vote and despite the fact that the statute required jury duty of "persons" (not "men") qualified to vote. The legislature did not intend "person" to include females because females could not then vote.

Like the case of the automatic couplers, *Welosky* offers a classic example of a judge reaching the right answer to the wrong question. Of course the legislature did not intend to include women, but that doesn't answer the right question. The proper question is, "What purpose does legislation serve that gears jury liability to voter eligibility?"

Efficiency is one possible answer because this policy spares the legislature from repeatedly rehashing the issue. Quality is another, for this policy provides a test of qualifications that will insure at least the same degree of responsibility, competence, education, and permanence of residence for both jurors and voters. Both voting and jury duty are general civic functions of citizens. Gearing the right to practice medicine, for instance, to voting eligibility would not make much sense, but gearing these two similar civic functions sounds reasonable. But where does turning the problem around leave us? Does it serve a good public purpose to pass a statute saying, in effect, "If you are qualified to vote, you are qualified to serve as a juror; however, any changes in voter eligibility hereafter enacted won't count because we haven't thought of them yet"? If the legislation had this purpose, why didn't it simply list the desirable qualifications for jurors? Read the statute as Rugg did and the gearing loses purpose. Rugg did not treat the policy process as rational and sensible. He did not admit that juror qualifications could have been purposely designed to change with the times.

The difference between a search for legislative intent and a search for purpose, then, is the difference in the evidence judges seek. A judge who believes he must show intent will examine reports, speeches, and prior drafts of bills. This evidence probably won't give clear meaning to the statute because it will contain internal inconsistencies or raise issues only in general terms. Moreover, the judge who thinks he must find intent to do his work can fool himself into believing that he has found it in the evidence. On the other hand, the judge who feels he must articulate a sensible statement of purpose will necessarily search much further, into dictionaries, canons, verbal contexts, and competing social policies as well as history itself. He will coordinate the materials in order to reach a confident articulation of purpose. He will perform the judicial function as Benjamin Cardozo described it. (See the epigraph that opens this book.) He will work harder than will the judge who stops when he has found a nugget of legislative history, which is why so many judges, possessing the all-too-human tendency to laziness, are satisfied with the nugget.

Statutory Purpose in the Cases of Criminal Commerce: Caminetti, McBoyle, and Alpers

In each of these three cases, Congress, under the authority of the commerce clause of the U.S. Constitution, forbade citizens from moving what Congress deemed evil from one state to another. Let us assume that every state had laws to deal with each of the evil things—stolen vehicles, women on whom evil designs were made, and pornography. What purpose, therefore, does additional *federal* legislation on these matters serve? For each of the federal statutes we possess records of committee reports, floor speeches, and other legislative history. In no case, however, does the solid data of legislative history reveal whether the purpose of the statute does or does not include the cases of our defendants. Levi (after a delightfully detailed review of the House and Senate reports on the Mann Act and of the discussions reported in the *Congressional Record* showing, if not total confusion about the act, at least much disagreement about its specific meaning) concludes, "The Mann Act was passed after there had been many extensive governmental investigations. Yet there was no common understanding of the facts, and whatever understanding seems to have been achieved concerning the white-slave trade seems incorrectly based. The words used were broad and ambiguous."[34]

These cases resemble each other not only in their constitutional origins but also because the canons of construction could resolve each of them. The canon dictating narrow construction

[34]Levi, p. 40, and see pp. 33–40.

of criminal statutes could allow a judge to reverse the three convictions, since the law does not unambiguously apply to any of these special factual situations. A judge who adopted Holmes's belief that criminal laws must communicate to a general lay audience with a clarity the average man can understand would reach the same result. Following ejusdem generis, the boyfriend, however, might go to jail, but McBoyle, the airplane thief, and Alpers, the seller of obscene records, would still go free.

Despite these similarities, these cases do not come out this way. The smut peddler and the boyfriend go to jail. McBoyle went free. The three judicial opinions together articulate no coherent linkages between purposes and outcomes. To link purposes and outcomes, we must begin with the right question: Why would Congress, "reasonable persons pursuing reasonable purposes reasonably," pass laws making actions crimes when all the states already have, through their criminal laws, expressed a policy? Does not the purpose lie in the fact that movement from state to state makes it difficult for the states to detect or enforce the violation? A car owner who has his car stolen may have trouble tracking it in another state. The prosecutor in the state where citizens receive wanted or unwanted pornography cannot reach the man who peddles by mail from another state. Men who hustle girls far from home may make both detection and social pressure to resist prostitution impossible. Movement has consequences. It makes objects and behaviors physically harder to locate. It makes apprehension and prosecution more difficult because police and prosecutors in one jurisdiction don't have authority in another. The presence of physical movement thus helps to reveal purpose.

In *McBoyle*, then, the proper questions ought to look something like this: (1) Do airplanes, because they are movable, complicate the task of catching people who steal them? (2) Does it, secondarily, serve any purpose to assume that McBoyle thought of flying a stolen airplane to another state was legal because of the ambiguities in the word *vehicle*? Is it, in other words, unfair to McBoyle to convict him under this act because the act does not unambiguously include airplanes? You should reach your own conclusion, but I would answer the first question with a yes, the second with a no, and respectfully dissent from Justice Holmes.

You should ask one other question about *McBoyle*. Suppose McBoyle's lawyer had argued that when the Motor Vehicle Theft Act was passed air travel was in such infancy that Congress probably did not intend to include airplanes. Notice that this argument should matter to you only if you think it important to ask what Congress intended. If you instead consider legislation as policy designed to adjust to technological and other changes, and if you ask instead what kind of crimes call for the kind of law enforcement help that this act provides, you would find McBoyle's lawyer's argument trivial.

Is *Alpers* any different? It might be, particularly if you see the case as presenting a constitutional problem of free expression. The purpose of this statute might be said to prevent exposing children or unwilling people, people who open mail or see magazines left around, to visual pornography. Is this purpose served by prohibiting the shipment of obscene records?

Again, you should reach your own conclusion. I would argue that, unlike Mr. Boyle, Mr. Alpers could reasonably have interpreted the act as not banning records for two reasons. First, the competing principle of free expression does set limits on government interference with the communication of ideas. No such principle limits governmental interference with the movement of property known to be stolen. Second, the purposes of the Motor Vehicle Theft Act specifically seem to apply to airplanes. They are very transportable. The act's purposes may therefore especially apply to airplanes. But one reading of the purpose of the statute in *Alpers*—visual pornography left around may offend—reduces its applicability to *Alpers*. But, although it reduces it, it doesn't eliminate it. The recipient might play the dirty record to an unwilling wife or child and cause them great offense. On balance, I lean toward exempting *Alpers*. The moral ambiguity of obscenity calls for clarity in criminal statutes. Theft of property, in our time anyway, is less morally ambiguous.

Finally, consider the man who brings in a willing girlfriend from out of state for a night or for the big game weekend. Conceivably, the Mann Act could purposely try to police all forms of sexual immorality, involving, somehow, interstate transportation. But what are the probabilities that this legislation has such purpose in light of: (1) The title of the act; (2) The canons of narrow construction of and clear communication in criminal statutes; (3) The problem arousing public concern at the time; (4) The fact that states are just as able, if they so choose, to discover and crackdown on noncommercial illegal sex as the FBI; (5) Representative Mann's report and the widespread belief that the general police powers reside in state and not federal hands?

Notice how only by using many different techniques of interpretation together do we begin to develop confidence about the purpose of the Mann Act.

A Final Complication

This summary of sensible judicial approaches to statutes may, I fear, have misled you in one critical respect. You may now feel that in every case the "right-thinking" judge will find the one "right" solution simply by uncovering a single purpose of the statute. This chapter's illustrations all make sense when we analyze them in terms of purpose. *We may, however, still honestly disagree about purpose.* Justice does not reside in judges who find the one right solution as much as it resides in judges who do their best to discern purpose and decide cases in terms of purpose. The task of judging is choosing among plausible alternative possibilities, not solving an algebra problem. Even judges who work to discover purpose may disagree about the resolution of a specific case.

To illustrate, suppose Holmes had said in *McBoyle,*

> The purpose of this act is to permit federal assistance to states in finding easily moved and hidden vehicles. But airplanes, while easily moved, are really like trains, which the act expressly excludes, because, like trains, they are tied to places where they cannot be hidden—airports. What goes up must come down, and only in certain places. One black Ford may look like a thousand other black Fords almost anywhere, but an airplane is much more like a train in this respect. Therefore, since we believe states, not the federal government, possess primary police powers, this act does not cover airplanes.

Finally, suppose Justice Gregory argued,

Establishment and expansion of cemeteries differ because the people near an expanded cemetery are already used to its presence, but to create a new cemetery in a place where residents had not planned on seeing funeral processions and graves and other unwanted reminders of life's transience is another matter.

Whether we agree or disagree with these analyses, at least these analyses rest on purpose. We should prefer them to the automatic citation of a canon, a quotation from a dictionary, or to any technique of interpretation that allows judges to evade the difficult task of determining statutory purpose.

STARE DECISIS IN STATUTORY INTERPRETATION

This chapter has reviewed some of the most enticing problems in legal reasoning. These problems and their solutions appeal to our instinctive quest for sensibility, not just in law but in all our affairs. They shw us that reason, our reason, can give us the confidence to assert that some judicial choices are wiser than others. The discovery that we can make sense of important and apparently complex legal issues can give us, more generally, a feeling of independence and competence in an increasingly complex society. Democracy will not survive in conditions of high complexity if most citizens conclude that government and politics have become too complicated for them to understand and influence.

Having thus spoken for democracy, sincerely if a bit piously, let me hasten to add that these problems also appeal to a less noble instinct. It is deliciously rewarding to point to the failings and errors of those in power. We should, however, try to push beyond intellectual titillations. These materials illustrate a serious error in the way many judges think they should do their jobs. It is an erroneous view of the role of courts with respect to legislative institutions and to government generally. Worse, it is an error based on a false view of law, of language, and of the nature of man himself. It is an error that should not simply titillate us; it should worry us.

To bring this error and its remedy into sharper focus, we must start by recognizing that in nearly all of this chapter, we have thus far studied an atypical occurrence in statutory interpretation, interpretation *in the first instance*. This may already have puzzled you, for in Chapter II I stated that reasoning by example—using precedents as guides for resolving legal conflicts—is central to legal reasoning. So far, however, this chapter has not mentioned reasoning by example at all. In the interpretation of statutes in the first instance, courts by definition have no precedents with which to work. In this chapter, we have examined some methods for interpreting statutes in the first instance, but these methods do not resolve the more typical problem: Once a court has given direction and meaning to a statute by interpreting it in the first instance, when should courts in the future follow that interpretation? When, conversely, should courts prefer a different interpretation and ignore or overrule an earlier court's first effort to make sense of the statute's meaning?

Let me make this point more sharply. Assume that the *McBoyle* decision wrongly interpreted the National Motor Vehicle Theft Act because its purpose does cover the theft of airplanes. Or assume that *Caminetti* wrongly applied the Mann Act to include the transportation of girlfriends. Should a court facing a new airplane or girlfriend case feel bound to accept that interpretation? Once a precedent or series of precedents gives a clear answer on a point of law, should courts leave it to legislatures to change that questionable interpretation by statutory amendment? In what circumstances should judges adhere to stare decisis in statutory interpretation?

It might seem sensible to you to answer these questions by referring to the justifications for stare decisis that appeared near the end of Chapter II. When adherence to a prior interpretation or series of cases interpreting a statute promotes stability in law and this stability in turn allows citizens to plan their affairs on the basis of certain and stable law—in short, when stability promotes the paramount social goal of cooperation—courts should not abandon stare decisis. Similarly, if a citizen now deserves to receive the same treatment a citizen in a precedent did, or if we feel stare decisis would preserve efficient judicial administration or a positive public image of justice, then courts should honor it. When stare decisis does not promote these goals, courts should freely ignore it.

I hope this approach sounds sensible to you. It is the way I think that courts should approach stare decisis in all areas of law. Thus it may surprise you to learn that some judges and legal scholars believe that judges should invariably follow the first judicial attempt to find statutory meaning even when they have doubts about the wisdom of the first attempt and, worse, when none of the characteristics of the problem call for stare decisis.

We shall first review an example of this "one-shot theory" of statutory interpretation in action. Then we shall evaluate its shortcomings. We shall see that, in part, it fails because it depicts judges once again misunderstanding how legislatures operate and how courts should reason from legislative action and inaction. We shall also see in this example considerable judicial ignorance about stare decisis itself.

Major League Baseball, Haviland's Dog and Pony Show, and Government Regulation of Business

The power of the federal government to regulate business derives from the constitutional clause empowering Congress to make laws that regulate commerce "among the several States." Armed with this authority Congress has passed many statutes regulating wages, hours of work, safety and health standards, and so forth in businesses. Such laws apply not only to businesses and businessmen that physically cross state lines or transact business among states. They also apply to businesses operating within one state entirely, on the theory that these businesses nevertheless may compete with and affect businesses operating from other states.[35] Modern economic and political theory also suggest that the collective health of small businesses and of labor can and does affect the national welfare.

[35]*United States v. Darby*, 312 U.S. 100 (1941), and *Wickard v. Filburn*, 317 U.S. 111 (1942).

Among the many such statutes regulating business, we shall consider only two. The more substantial of the two, the federal antitrust laws, responded to the huge cartels and monopolies that emerged in the nineteenth century by prohibiting certain activities that restrain competition in business. (See page 93.) They authorize criminal and civil proceedings by government and by citizens privately when they feel they are damaged by anticompetitive business practices. The Animal Welfare Act of 1970, our second statutory example, specifies a variety of requirements for handling animals in a humane manner.[36] The statute requires "exhibitors" of animals "purchased in commerce or the intended distribution of which affects commerce or will affect commerce..." to obtain an exhibitor's license. The statute explicitly includes carnivals, circuses, and zoos. It empowers the Agriculture Department to administer its regulatory provisions.

Within the context of these two statutes, we shall now observe a truly wondrous phenomenon in contemporary law. Within the past twenty years courts have held: (1) that the multimillion-dollar industry of professional baseball, with all its national commercial television coverage and travel from state to state and to foreign countries, *is not* a business in interstate commerce such that the antitrust laws govern the owners of baseball clubs; and (2) that "Haviland's Dog and Pony Show," consisting of a maximum of two ponies and five dogs traveling the rural byways of the American Midwest and earning a handful of dollars weekly, *is* a business in interstate commerce that must therefore meet the requirements of the Animal Welfare Act.[37]

We need say little more about the *Haviland* case. Haviland refused to obtain an exhibitor's license. The court held that he was wrong to refuse. Given the current legal definition of commerce, the interpretation is entirely defensible constitutionally. This interpretation and result also make sense in terms of the presumed purpose of the statute. Owners of dog-and-pony shows, we can assume, are no less likely to abuse their animals

---

[36] 15 U.S.C. 1 et seq. and 7 U.S.C. 2131 et seq.

[37] *Flood v. Kuhn*, 407 U.S. 258 (1972); *Haviland v. Butz*, 543 F.2d 169 (D.C. Circuit 1976).

than is the staff of the San Diego Zoo; rather more likely, I should think.

But why don't antitrust statutes regulate major league baseball? Rigid adherence to stare decisis in statutory interpretation provides the answer, as the following chronology of decisions illustrates.

1922   The "Federal Baseball Club of Baltimore," a member of a short-lived third major league, sued the National and American Leagues claiming that the two leagues had, in violation of the antitrust laws, bought out some Federal League clubs and induced other owners not to join the league at all. The Baltimore franchise found itself frozen out and sued to recover the financial losses caused by the anticompetitive practices of the other leagues. The case reached the United States Supreme Court, where Justice Holmes's opinion held that the essence of baseball, playing games, did not involve interstate commerce. The travel from city to city by the teams, Holmes thought, was so incidental that it did not bring baseball within the scope of the act. Thus, without reaching the question whether the defendants did behave anticompetitively within the meaning of the statute, Holmes ruled that the act did not apply to professional baseball any more than it would apply to a Chautauqua lecturer traveling the circuit.[38]

Comment: We should not hastily condemn Holmes's reasoning. His opinion predated by 20 years the final shift in the legal meaning of commerce that solidified in the holding of *Wickard v. Filburn,* so we cannot blame him for an antiquated definition. Also, to his credit, Holmes did not try to discover whether Congress intended to include baseball within the scope of the antitrust laws. There is nothing in the opinion that stamps its results with

[38]*Federal Baseball Club of Baltimore v. National League of Professional Baseball Clubs,* 259 U.S. 200 (1922).

indelibility, nothing that says if the commercial character of baseball changes, baseball club owners would nevertheless remain free to behave monopolistically. For its time, *Federal Baseball* rested on defensible if not indisputable reasoning.

1923   A year later Justice Holmes addressed the applicability of the antitrust laws in the field of public entertainment. In this case, the plaintiff, a Mr. Hart, acted as a booking agent and manager for a variety of actors. He specialized in negotiating contracts between vaudeville performers, on one hand, and large theater chains sponsoring vaudeville shows on the other. Hart sued the Keith Circuit, the Orpheum Circuit, and other theatrical chains, claiming that, in violation of the antitrust laws, they colluded to prevent any of his actors from obtaining contracts in their theaters unless Hart granted them what we would today call kickbacks. Holmes noted that some of these contracts called for the transportation of performers, scenery, music, and costumes. Distinguishing *Federal Baseball,* he held that "in the transportation of vaudeville acts the apparatus sometimes is more important than the performers and... the defendant's conduct is within the [antitrust] statute to that extent at least."[39]

Comment: Note fact freedom at work here. Holmes does not, despite vaudeville's obvious resemblance to baseball, find that the two are factually similar enough to govern vaudeville by baseball's precedent. There was, he said, a difference. Some of the disputed contracts did involve transportation itself. Holmes could have chosen to follow the previous year's precedent. The travel is still incidental to local performance of either baseball or vaudeville. Compare this with what happened 30 years later.

1953   Baseball again, but not an alleged attempt to prevent the formation of a third league. Now it was the

---

[39]*Hart v. B.F. Keith Vaudeville Exchange,* 262 U.S. 271 (1923), p. 273.

players' turn to allege violation of the antitrust laws. The violation took the form of the well-publicized reserve clause,[40] or so players claimed. The players contended that the clause prevented open competition for better salaries. In *Toolson v. New York Yankees* the Supreme Court ruled in an unsigned *(per curiam)* opinion that baseball still did not fall under the coverage of the antitrust laws. It so held despite the efforts of Justice Burton and Reed, who dissented, to marshall extensive evidence of baseball's dramatic growth since 1922. The majority opinion stated:

> Congress has had the [*Federal Baseball*] ruling under consideration but has not seen fit to bring such business under these laws by legislation having prospective effect. The business has thus been left for thirty years to develop, on the understanding that it was not subject to existing antitrust legislation. The present cases ask us to overrule the prior decision and, with retrospective effect,

---

[40]*Toolson v. New York Yankees*, 346 U.S. 356 (1953), pp. 362–363. The reserve clause, quoted by the dissenters, began by stating:

[Major-Minor League Agreement, December 6, 1946]

1. All players' contracts in the Major League shall be of one form and that all players' contracts in the Minor Leagues shall be of one form.
2. That all players' contracts in any league must provide that the Club or any assignee thereof shall have the option to renew the player's contract each year and that the player shall not play for any other club but the club with which he has a contract or the assignee thereof.
3. That each club shall, on or before a certain date each year, designate a reserve list of active and eligible players which it desires to reserve for the ensuing year. That no player on such a reserve list may thereafter be eligible to play for any other club until his contract has been assigned or until he has been released.
4. That the player shall be bound by any assignment of his contract by the club, and that his remuneration shall be the same as that usually paid by the assignee to other players of like ability.
5. That there shall be no negotiations between a player and any other club from the one which he is under contract or reservation respecting employment either present or prospective unless the Club with which the player is connected shall have in writing expressly authorized such negotiations prior to their commencement....

hold the legislation applicable.... Without re-
examination of the underlying issues, the judgments
below are affirmed on the authority of *Federal
Baseball* ... so far as that decision determines that
Congress had no intention of including the business of
baseball within the scope of the federal antitrust laws.

Questions: Did Justice Holmes conclude in 1922
that "Congress had no intention of including the
business of baseball within the scope of the federal
antitrust laws"? Do you believe that, because Congress has not legislated on the subject of baseball and
the antitrust laws, therefore professional baseball
does not fall within the act? Remember that not only
had baseball become more businesslike since 1922,
but the definition of commerce had also changed so
that travel or movement from state to state did not
have to be an essential part of a business's activities
in order to put it under the act. Why is it necessary to
follow the 1922 precedent? Why could not the *Toolson* opinion simply say that both the law and the
sport have changed and the owners have no justified
expectation to rely on an outdated judicial ruling?
Do you think, in other words, that because in 1922
the Court told the established leagues they could try
to prevent the formation of a third league, they
therefore rightly planned in 1946 to deal with their
players by contracts that prevented free competition
in that business?

1955 In *United States v. Shubert,* Chief Justice Warren,
speaking for the Supreme Court, upheld the government's claim that theater owners who monopol-
ized the booking of theater attractions violated the
antitrust laws.[41] The Court acknowledged *Hart,*
though only in passing. It refused to follow *Toolson,*
calling it "a narrow application of the rule of *stare
decisis.*"

Question: One purpose of stare decisis is to
promote equality. On what basis should the law

---

[41]*United States v. Shubert,* 348 U.S. 222 (1955).

treat actors and baseball players unequally, as this case concludes the law must?

Chief Justice Warren, in a companion case to *Shubert*, held that professional boxing did fall within the scope of the antitrust laws.[42] He distinguished *Toolson* for the same reasons he gave in *Shubert*.

Questions: How equally do you think baseball players felt the courts applied the law in 1955? If you had managed the Boxing Club, would you have relied on the *Toolson* decision? Would you think of boxing as any more of a business than baseball? Would the new boxing decision possibly surprise you?

1957 In *Radovich v. National Football League,* the lower appellate court, mystified by the distinction between baseball and boxing, the Supreme Court had created, decided that football did not fall under the antitrust laws because football, like baseball but unlike boxing, was a team sport. The Supreme Court reversed.[43]

Comment: "Foolish consistency is the hobgoblin of little minds."

1971 The Supreme Court held that the antitrust laws did govern professional basketball.[44]

Question: By now do you think the Court could safely overrule *Federal Baseball*?

1972 Fifty years after *Federal Baseball,* Curt Flood's challenge to the reserve clause reached the Supreme Court. Justice Blackmun, after a panegyrical review of baseball's history, replete with references to Thayer's "Casey at the Bat," and a long and curious list of baseball's greats (the list includes such immortals as Three-Finger Brown and Hans Lobert but omits Stan Musial, Joe DiMaggio, Ted Williams, and Hank Aaron), refused to abandon *Toolson* or stare decisis. Flood lost. Blackmun wrote:

---

[42]*United States v. International Boxing Club of New York, Inc.,* 348 U.S. 236 (1955).

[43]*Radovich v. National Football League,* 352 U.S. 445 (1957).

[44]*Heywood v. National Basketball Association,* 401 U.S. 1204 (1971).

> [W]e adhere once again to *Federal Baseball* and *Toolson*
> and to their application to professional baseball. We
> adhere also to *International Boxing* and *Radovich* and
> to their respective applications to professional boxing
> and professional football. If there is any inconsistency or
> illogic in all this, it is an inconsistency and illogic of
> long-standing that is to be remedied by the Congress
> and not by this Court. If we were to act otherwise, we
> would be withdrawing from the conclusion as to
> congressional intent made in *Toolson* and from the
> concerns as to retrospectivity therein expressed. Under
> these circumstances, there is merit in consistency even
> though some might claim that beneath that consistency
> is a layer of inconsistency.[45]

> Justice Douglas dissented. He wrote, "The unbroken
> silence of Congress should not prevent us from correcting
> our own mistakes."[46]

That's enough of the chronology of judicial decisions. In
the wake of judicial and Congressional failure to deal with the
reserve clause, the baseball players struck in the early 1970s. The
strike successfully freed the players from the clause, and recent
increases in players' salaries can be credited to this change.

What went wrong here? In the immediate case of sports
and the antitrust laws, *Toolson's* utterly inaccurate insistence
that *Federal Baseball* means that Congress did not intend to
include baseball wreaked the most havoc. *Toolson*, to paraphrase, says, "The highest lawmaking body in the country,
Congress, has determined that the antitrust laws should not
apply to professional baseball. Therefore the owners of baseball
teams have made many business arrangements in reliance on
this state of the law. It would be wrong to upset these expecta-

---

[45]*Flood v. Kuhn*, p. 284.

[46]In mid-September, 1982, federal District Court Judge Juan Burciaga ruled
that the National Collegiate Athletic Association's television contracts for
member schools violate the antitrust laws, and in November of the same year the
Justice Department approved Judge Burciaga's position. See "Justice Agency
Backs Ruling against NCAA over Football on TV," *Wall Street Journal*,
November 18, 1982, p. 18. The Court of Appeals in Denver upheld Burciaga's
ruling in May, 1983.

tions legitimized by the intent of Congress." This position is pure nonsense. Congress did not intend to exclude baseball. Holmes in *Federal Baseball* never said Congress so intended. As my questions at the end of the *Toolson* excerpt imply, the baseball owners had no reason to rely on *Federal Baseball,* at least not in 1953, given intervening precedents. Stability and reliance do *not* in this instance require the Court to invoke stare decisis and follow *Federal Baseball.* Note, however, that if Congress had legally commanded the exclusion of baseball, you would reach a different result.[47] *Toolson* reached that different result by merely saying, without supporting evidence, that Congress so commanded.

Unfortunately, the Supreme Court's reasoning in these cases is worse than that. At least, you might say, baseball owners probably did honestly believe that they had a good chance of escaping the antitrust laws and acted on that basis. There is some merit in the reliance argument. But if stare decisis seeks to assist people in making plans of reliance on stable law, then surely owners of football, basketball, and boxing franchises and athletes had every bit as much reason for relying on *Federal Baseball* or *Toolson* as did the baseball owners. After all, in terms of the antitrust laws, there is no difference among these sports that ought to induce baseball owners to rely on the original precedent while preventing those in the other sports from doing so.

In the name of stare decisis, then, we have a series of decisions that hardly seems stable, that violates reliance expectations to the extent that there are any, and that does not treat equals equally. To complete the list of justifications for adhering to precedent, do these decisions strike you as efficient judicial administration? What image of justice do these cases flash in your mind? Oafish, perhaps?

---

[47] Professor Guido Calabresi has recently taken the opposite approach. In *A Common Law for the Age of Statutes* (Cambridge: Harvard University Press, 1982), he argues that statutes can become hopelessly obsolete and that legislative inertia is so great that we have no guarantee of timely legislative updating of obsolete provisions. He believes that courts should openly update statutes to restore the achievement of their original statutory purposes, even in express disregard of explicit prior "definitive" interpretations of statutory purpose.

Fortunately, I have deliberately chosen an extreme example. Faced with statutory precedents, courts do not invariably invoke stare decisis in order to wreak havoc on the very justifications for stare decisis. Nevertheless, this critical question remains: *If* a judge feels that an existing judicial interpretation of a statute is erroneous and *if* the judge also feels that he may overrule it without doing violence to the five justifications of stare decisis, do *any* aspects of the court's relationship to the legislature nevertheless compel adherence to the questionable interpretation? I believe the proper answer to this question is no. However, on two analytical levels, judges and legal scholars have at times reached a different conclusion. Let us review their reasons for doing so on both levels.

The Case Against Increased Adherence to Precedent in Statutory Interpretation

The first, and more superficial, analytical level holds that the legislature may take certain actions that compel the courts to adhere to precedent. In *Toolson,* for example, the Supreme Court seemed to say that, since Congress had not passed a statute to cover baseball by the antitrust laws, Congress had somehow converted *Federal Baseball* into statutory law. Would any of the following events in Congress, or in any legislature, strengthen such a conclusion?

- Many bills were introduced to cover baseball, but none of them passed.
- Many bills were introduced to exempt baseball, but none of them passed.
- Congress re-enacted the relevant antitrust provisions, with some modifications, none of which attempted to cover or exempt baseball specifically.
- Congress passed a statute explicitly placing, say professional boxing prior to 1955, under the antitrust laws but makes no mention of baseball's status.
- Congress passed a joint resolution that officially states that baseball is hereinafter to be considered "The National Pastime of the United States."

Judges often buttress their adherence to precedents on such grounds, but these grounds are insufficient. Congress possesses no power to make law other than by passing statutes. Statutes are, among other items, subject to presidential veto power. Not even joint resolutions, which escape presidential veto, therefore create law. To say that any of the legislative acts I just listed create law is to give Congress a law-making power not found in the Constitution.

Furthermore, consider these reasons that a legislature might not, in fact, directly respond to a judicial interpretation by law:[48]

- Legislators never learn of the judicial interpretation in the first place.
- Legislators don't care about the issue the interpretation raises.
- Legislators care but feel they must spend their limited time and political resources on the other more important matters.
- Legislators like the proposed new statute or amendment but feel it politically unwise to vote for it.
- Legislators decide to vote against the bill because they do not like another unrelated provision of the bill.
- Legislators feel the bill does not go far enough and vote against it in hopes of promulgating more comprehensive law later.
- Legislators don't like the bill's sponsor personally and therefore vote negatively.
- Legislators believe, in the words of Hart and Sacks, "that the matter should be left to be handled by the normal process of judicial development of decisional law, including the overruling of outstanding decisions to the extent that the sound growth of the law requires...."[49]

Do not all these possibilities, especially the last, convince you that courts should not speculate about the meaning of a statutory

---

[48]Hart and Sacks, pp. 1395–1396.
[49]*Ibid*, p. 1396.

interpretation by guessing at why the legislature didn't pass a law affecting the interpretation?

The second analytical level is more complex. Sophisticated proponents of the "one-shot" theory of statutory interpretation admit that legislative silence is meaningless.[50] They worry instead about the proper apportionment of legislative and judicial responsibilities. Their argument goes this way: Legislatures deliberately use ambiguous language in statutes, not simply to bring many somewhat different specific events under one policy roof but also to allow room for the compromises necessary to generate a majority vote. Once written, the words of a statute will not change, but, because they are general, vague, and ambiguous, courts will cerainly have the opportunity to interpret those same words in many different ways.

If, the argument continues, words have different meanings at different times and places, the legislature's power to make law becomes pointless, or at least quite subordinated to judicial power of interpretation. Courts must find one meaning. They do so by determining legislative intent. The judiciary insults the legislature if it says that at one time the legislature intended the words to carry one meaning and at another time another meaning. To say this is to say of the legislature that it had no intent and that it did not understand its actions. That assertion would embarrass the legislature, to say the least.

The argument thus holds that part of the judicial responsibility to the legislature is to reinforce the concept that the legislature did in fact have a specific intention because that is what the public expects of legislatures. The first half of this chapter has, I trust, revealed why this argument fails.

Fortunately, the argument does not stop there. Levi asserts:

> Legislatures and courts are cooperative law-making bodies. It is important to know where the responsibility lies. If legislation which is disfavored can be interpreted away from time to time, then it is not to be expected, particularly if controversy is high, that the legislature will ever act. It will always be possible to say that new legislation is not needed because the court in the future will make a more appropriate interpretation. If

[50]See especially Levi, pp. 31–33.

the court is to have freedom to reinterpret legislation, the result will be to relieve the legislature from pressure. The legislation needs judicial consistency. Moreover, the court's own behavior in the face of pressure is likely to be indecisive. In all likelihood it will do enough to prevent legislative revision and not much more. Therefore it seems better to say that once a decisive interpretation of legislative intent has been made, and in that sense a direction has been fixed within the gap of ambiguity, the court should take that direction as given. In this sense a court's interpretaton of legislation is not dictum. The words it uses do more than decide the case. They give broad direction to the statute.[51]

Levi's argument cuts too deeply. Indeed, there are instances in which legislators breathe sighs of relief that courts have taken delicate political problems from them. (Curiously enough, courts most often do so by applying constitutional standards to legislation, and in this area Levi does not demand similarly strict stare decisis.) But Levi's position is simply inaccurate in its assumption that most questions of interpretation raise highly charged public issues that legislatures ought to deal with but won't if the court does it for them. For the most part, judicial errors in statutory intepretation involve borderline application of statutes. The interpretations may do considerable injustice to the parties who find themselves in borderline situations without, in any significant way, damaging the central purposes of the statutory policy as a whole. In the large bulk of cases, then, it is wholly unrealistic to assume that either overruling or adherence will affect how legislators perform. Try to imagine, for example, how Congess would have reacted had the Supreme Court held in 1946 that the traveling bigamous Mormons did not violate the Mann Act. I suspect with a yawn.

To conclude, notice how many of the problems that courts have created for themselves regarding the place of stare decisis in statutory interpretations would evaporate if only judges convinced themselves to seek the purpose of a statute and not to speculate about legislative intent from inconclusive legislative evidence. The inadequate conclusions that judges reach when

[51]*Ibid.*, p. 32.

they reason on the first and more superficial analytical level would disappear altogether. At the more sophisticated level, the concept that the courts embarrass legislatures by implying the rather obvious truth that the legislators probably had no intent with respect to the precise issue before the court would also disappear. Is this truth so awful? Of course not. That statutes speak in general terms is a simple necessity in political life. Such generality explains and justifies the existence of courts.

A SUMMARY STATEMENT OF THE APPROPRIATE JUDICIAL APPROACH TO STATUTORY INTERPRETATION

Judges should follow precedents when the justifications of stare decisis so dictate. Their primary obligation to the legislature is to apply the statutes it creates so as to achieve, as best judges can determine it, the intelligible purposes for which the statute exists. Judges should try to determine purpose accurately, but they will err from time to time. It is no embarrassment to the legislature for judges to admit that they erred in determining statutory purpose and applying it to cases properly before them. They should therefore give stare decisis no special weight in statutory interpretation. They should do so with the confidence that, to the extent that they can predict legislative behavior at all, they can predict that the legislature is no less likely to correct them if they err today than if they erred yesterday. Of course, legislation needs judicial consistency. The attainment of consistency and thereby the affixing of proper legislative responsibility will occcur only when courts seek, in all cases, to discern sensible statutory purposes.

SUMMARY

- What are statutes?
- What is statutory interpretation "in the first instance"?
- What characteristics of words prevent statutes from resolving all legal cases arising under them?
- What are the strengths and weaknesses of the canons of statutory interpretation?

- In what ways does the statute-making process in legislatures differ fom judicial assumptions about it?
- How and why do legislative intent and statutory purpose differ?
- Do reasoning by example, fact freedom, and stare decisis operate in unique ways in statutory interpretation? Should they? Why have some judges and scholars insisted that judges should follow precedents more rigidly in statutory interpretation than in other areas of law? Does not this point of view rest on essentially the same naive assumptions about politics and law-making that infect the search for legislative intent?

ILLUSTRATIVE CASE

The next opinion's format will seem unfamiliar to you because the case comes from England over a century ago. Note that this report summarizes the positions of the attorneys as well as the opinions of each of the judges. The reference at the very beginning is the citation to the statute that the court must interpret. Also, the word "personate" is the same as our modern "impersonate." Hart and Sacks used this case to good advantage in their materials, cited frequently in this book. I still remember the lessons I learned from it in law school with great fondness.

Whiteley v. Chappell
L.R. 4 Queen's Bench 147 (1868)

The following is the substance of the case:—

By 14 & 15 Vict. c. 105, s. 3, if any person, pending or after the election of any guardian [of the poor], shall wilfully, fraudulently, and with intent to affect the result of such election.... "personate any person entitled to vote at such election," he is made liable on conviction to imprisonment for not exceeding three months.

The appellant was charged with having personated one J. Marston, a person entitled to vote at an election of guardians for the township of Bradford; and it was proved that Marston was duly qualified as a ratepayer on the rate book to have voted at the election, but that he had died before the election. The appellant delivered to the person appointed to collect the voting papers a voting paper apparently duly signed by Marston.

The magistrate convicted the appellant.

The question for the Court was, whether the appellant was rightly convicted.

Mellish, Q.C. (with him *McIntyre*), for the appellant. A dead person cannot be said to be "a person entitled to vote;" and the appellant therefore could not be guilty of personation under 14 & 15 Vict. c. 105, s. 3. Very possibly he was within the spirit, but he was not within the letter, of the enactment, and in order to bring a person within a penal enactment, both must concur. In Russell on Crimes...under a former statute, in which the words were similar to those of 2 Wm. 4, c. 53, s. 49, which makes it a misdemeanor to personate "a person entitled or supposed to be entitled to any prize money," &c., *Brown's Case* (1) is cited, in which it was held that the personation must be of some person primâ facie entitled to prize money. In the Parliamentary Registration Act...the words are "any person who shall knowingly personate...any person whose name appears on the register of voters, whether such person be alive or dead;" but under the present enactment the person must be entitled, that is, could have voted himself.

Crompton, for the respondent. *Brown's Case* is, in effect, overruled by the later cases of *Rex v. Martin,* and *Rex v. Cramp,* in which the judges decided that the offence of personating a person "supposed to be entitled" could be committed, although the person, to the knowledge or belief of the authorities, was dead. Those cases are directly in point. The gist of the offence is the fraudulently voting under another's name; the mischief is the same, whether the supposed voter be alive or dead; and the Court will put a liberal construction on such an enactment; *Reg. v. Hague.*

Mellish, Q.C., in reply. "Supposed to be entitled" must have been held by the judges in the cases cited to mean supposed by the person personating.

LUSH, J. I do not think we can, without straining them, bring the case within the words of the enactment. The legislature has not used words wide enough to make the personation of a dead person an offence. The words "a person entitled to vote" can only mean, without a forced construction, a person who is entitled to vote at the time at which the personation takes place; in the present case, therefore, I feel bound to say the offence has not been committed. In the cases of *Rex v. Martin,* and *Rex v. Cramp,* the judges gave no reason for their decision; they probably held that "supposed to be entitled" meant supposed by the person personating.

HANNEN, J. I regret that we are obliged to come to the conclusion that the offence charged was not proved; but it would be wrong to strain words to meet the justice of the present case, because it might make a precedent, and lead to dangerous consequences in other cases.

HAYES, J., concurred.

Judgment for the appellant.

QUESTIONS

1. If a student attends class one day dressed in a 10-gallon hat, Western boots, and chaps, is it linguistically possible to say that he is "impersonating" a cowboy? If I go out on Halloween wearing light blue long underwear, red briefs, a red and yellow "S" on my chest, and a red cape, is it linguistically possible to say that I am "impersonating" Superman? Is it linguistically possible to define "impersonation" as any act in which someone pretends to be someone other than his or her real self?

2. If it is possible to impersonate a general type of character, or a fictitious character, is it not linguistically possible to violate the statute simply by pretending to be a voter entitled to vote?

3. Does not the question in *Whiteley* inescapably boil down to what purpose it would serve, if any, for the legislature to make it a crime to impersonate a live person but not a dead person at an election?

4. What important background facts does your determination of the purpose of this statute depend on? Is it not true that impersonating a live registered voter might deprive such a person of his right to vote, whereas this plaintiff did not so deprive anyone? But the statute does not distinguish between an attempt to vote in the name of a living person before, rather than after, that person successfully votes. Or does it? Do we not suspect that the main purpose is to protect the integrity of the voting system, rather than an individual right to vote? If so, what conclusion should the court have reached in this case?

5. If you were a member of the legislature making the statute in this case, how carefully do you think you could anticipate all of the situations that might arise under this law? In what spirit would you want a judge to interpret your law? Would you want a judge to appreciate that you were trying to state general policy to solve a problem at the polls and that you would not be able to anticipate and cover in statutory language every quirky factual situation that might arise under it? You should be able to think of at least a half-dozen other quirky situations that might or

might not be covered under this statute, depending on the technique you choose to use to interpret it.

SOME EXPLORATORY PROBLEMS

1. Starting with the phenomenon of logrolling, wherein a legislator agrees to vote for another's bill in exchange for the other's promise to vote for his own legislation, list as many reasons as you can that a legislator would vote for or against a bill without understanding the legal meaning of the act or caring about the alternative ways a judge might interpret its words.

2. The interpretation of a statute that rests on an analysis of the plausible purposes of the statute does not necessarily produce only one correct legal solution to the case. What argument derived from the purpose of the railroad safety act in *Johnson* might the attorneys for the railroad have made to support the position that the act did not require locomotives to couple with cars automatically? You should speculate on the process of coupling cars and also on the possible costs involved in using locomotives equipped with the proper couplers. At what point would you expect a judge to find your hypothetical argument convincing?

3. Read Felix Frankfurter's "Some Reflections on the Reading of Statutes" cited on page 110. In what respects do his views and the views in this chapter differ? Do the same analysis after reading William R. Bishin, "The Law Finders: An Essay in Statutory Interpretation," 38 *Southern California Law Review* 1 (1965).

4. Congress does not always ignore judicial interpetations of statutes. For examples of legislative responses to judicial interpretations of statutes, see "Congressional Reversal of Supreme Court Decisions: 1945–1957," 71 *Harvard Law Review* 1324 (1958).

5. Between interpretation in the first instance and questions of stare decisis in statutory interpretation, fact freedom, and reasoning by example work just as I have described them in earlier chapters. Thus the Supreme Court in *Alpers* could have chosen *McBoyle* as a precedent relevant to that case. Why? In fact the Court did not do so, but what result do you think it would have reached in *Alpers* if it had?

6. On July 6, 1983, the United States Supreme Court announced, in *Arizona v. Norris,* 103 S. Ct. 57, that employer-sponsored pension plans cannot pay lower monthly benefits to a female than a male upon retirement merely because women statistically outlive men. The ruling interpreted Title VII of the 1964 Civil Rights Act, which forbids employers to discriminate against employees on the basis of gender. Four of the nine justices dissented. Since women as a class actually do live longer than men, isn't it possible that the Court's decision creates a discrimination against men rather than eradicating one against women? If so, on what reading of the statute's purpose do you think the majority's decision must have rested? Do note that the insurance industry has plenty of muscle in Congress and that Congress can amend the act if it chooses.

7. Suppose, in order to reverse a judicial ruling that the government cannot be held liable for harm done to citizens by negligent public employees, Congress passes a statute that says, "The U.S. government shall be liable in tort in the same manner and to the same extent as a private citizen under like circumstances." Suppose that an Air Force pilot gets drunk and negligently flies a military jet plane so that it crashes into a farmer's barn. The farmer sues the government. Suppose a court rules for the government, saying that "since private citizens do not fly military jets, the statute does not allow recovery for this damage." Criticize this reasoning. See *Feres v. United States,* 340 U.S. 135 (1950).

8. In 1971 the Internal Revenue Service issued a ruling interpreting the Internal Revenue Code, Section 501(c)(3) (which grants tax exemptions to organizations for religious or educational purposes) as inapplicable to schools practicing racial discrimination. Bob Jones University refuses to admit black students who are interracially married or who advocate interracial dating or marriage. In 1983 the Supreme Court upheld the IRS's denial of the tax exemption to Bob Jones University. To what extent, if any, should the Court rely on Congressional silence about the IRS ruling since 1971? Should legislative silence play a greater role here than it should have in the sports and antitrust cases? Why or why not? Is it relevant that 13 bills were introduced to overrule the IRS position, but none of them even made it to the floor of Congress? See *Bob Jones University v. United States,* 103 S. Ct. 2017 (1983).

9. Assume for the sake of argument that both the *McBoyle* and *Cleveland* cases were wrongly decided. Construct an argument that, on the basis of the stare decisis theory introduced in Chapter II, it would be perfectly permissible for the Court to overrule *Cleveland* but not permissible to overrule *McBoyle*.

10. The Immigration and Nationality Act, Section 244, allows either House of Congress by resolution to reverse an order suspending deportation of aliens. Similar provisions exist in nearly 200 other statutes. By these "legislative vetoes" Congress can change decisions by executive bodies, including, for example, presidential decisions to commit troops to combat in undeclared wars.

    In *Immigration and Naturalization Service v. Chadha,* 103 S. Ct. 715 (1983), the Supreme Court agreed with the argument of defendant Chadha, whose suspended deportation the House had reinstated, that the legislative veto violated Article I of the Constitution. In essence, the Court voided such provisions because they never present a bill to the president for his signature or veto. They make law by circumventing this constitutional requirement.

    Based on the material in this chapter, comment on Justice White's statement near the beginning of his dissenting opinion:

    > Without the legislative veto, Congress is faced with a Hobson's choice: either to refrain from delegating the necessary authority, leaving itself with the hopeless task of writing laws with the requisite specificity to cover endless special circumstances across the entire policy landscape, or in the alternative, to abdicate its lawmaking function to the executive branch and independent agencies. (p. 4921)

Chapter V

COMMON LAW

The life of the law has not been logic; it has been experience. The felt necessities of the time, the prevalent moral and political theories, intuitions of public policy, avowed or unconscious, even the prejudices which judges share with their fellow-men, have had a good deal more to do than the syllogism in determining the rules by which men should be governed.
—Oliver Wendell Holmes, Jr.

Near its beginning this book urged you to treat reason in law as a puzzle that may achieve its full significance only as the last pieces fit into place. One of the sections of the still-incomplete picture that may now puzzle you is the large group of pieces called common law. Common law is judge-made law, a process distinct from statutory interpretation and constitutional law. However, the examination of reason in statutory interpretation reveals that judges inevitably make law when they interpret statutes. Chapter VI will explain how courts inevitably exercise even broader constitutional lawmaking power. How then is common law any more judge-made than any other kind of law?

The short, and therefore inadequate, answer lies in our legal tradition, which empowers judges to resolve conflicts when no statute or constitutional provision addresses the problem. When a statute speaks to the issue, the judge must look to the statute for his solution. But, when no statute speaks, the judge resolves the conflict by reasoning from common law cases that judges have decided in the past and from the principles that emerge from them.

The origins of a better answer come from the complex history of English law.[1] To make sense of this history, let me ask you to start by joining in a role play.

ORIGINS OF COMMON LAW

Put yourself in the position of William the Conqueror. You are, like many of your Norman kin, a superb administrator, which is to say you are a shrewd politician. You have just managed the remarkable political feat, at least for the eleventh century, of assembling thousands of men and the necessary supporting equipment to cross the English Channel and to win title to England in battle. In these feudal days title means ownership, and in a real sense you own England as a result of the Battle of Hastings.

However, your administrative headaches have just begun. On the one hand you must reward your supporters—and your supporters must reward their supporters—with grants of your land. On the other hand, you don't want to give up any of the land completely. You deserve to and shall collect rents—taxes are the modern equivalent—from the landholders beneath you. You must give away with one hand but keep a legal hold with the other.

---

[1] Plucknett's "concise" history of the subject is over 700 pages long. Theodore F.T. Plucknett, *A Concise History of the Common Law*, 5th ed. (Boston: Little, Brown, 1956). For real conciseness try Frederick G. Kempin, *Historical Introduction to Anglo-American Law in a Nutshell*, 2nd ed. (St. Paul: West, 1973). To contrast common law systems with the deductive or "code-based" systems of law on the European continent I recommend John Henry Merryman, *The Civil Law Tradition* (Stanford: Stanford University Press, 1969).

Furthermore, you must keep the peace, not only among the naturally restless and resentful natives but also among your supporters. As time goes on and their personal loyalty to you dwindles, they will no doubt tend increasingly to fight over exactly who owns which lands. And, of course, you have a notion that you and your successors will clash with that other group claiming a sort of sovereignty, the Church.

You must, in short, develop machinery for collecting rents, tracking ownership, and settling disputes.

Fortunately, you have conquered a relatively civilized land. At the local level some degree of government already exists on which you can build. In what we might call counties, but which the natives call shires, a hereditary *shire reeve* (our sheriff) cooperates with a bishop representing the Church to handle many of the problems of daily governance. These shires have courts, as do the smaller villages within them. You hope that, in the next century at least, your successors will be able to take control of them.

Meanwhile you take the action of any good politician. You undertake a survey, a sort of census, of who owns what lands— the *Domesday Book*. You organize all the lords, to whom you granted large amounts of land, church leaders, and many of the major native landlords who swear allegiance to you, into a Great Council. They advise you (and you thus co-opt their support) on the important policy questions before you. You start appointing the local sheriffs yourself. You also create a permanent staff of bureaucrats, personal advisors who handle and resolve smaller problems as they arise.

You succeed in creating a new political reality, one in which it soon becomes somehow right to govern in the name of the ultimate landlord, the king.

So much for the role play.

William in no sense developed the contemporary common law system, but he did create the political reality in which that development had to happen: Governing in the king's name— settling land disputes, collecting rents, and keeping the peace— meant rendering justice in the king's name. William's personal advisors, his staff, often traveled about the country administering *ad hoc* justice in the king's name. Additionally, many of the more serious offenses, what we would today call crimes, came directly to the Great Council for decision because they were offenses against the king's peace.

One hundred years later, the second great English king, Henry II, began the actual takeover of the lower local courts. Initially, the king insisted on giving permission to the local courts before they could hear any case involving title to his land. A litigant would have to obtain from London a writ, the *writ of right*, they called it, and then produce it in court before the court could hear the case. Shortly thereafter the king's council began to bypass the local courts altogether on matters of land title. Certain council members heard these cases at first, but, as they became more and more specialized and experienced, they split off from the council to form the king's Court of Common Pleas.

Similarly, the council members assigned to criminal matters transformed into the Court of the King's Bench. The Court of the Exchequer, which handled rent and tax collections, evolved in similar fashion.

Only three problems remained. The first concerned the law these judges should use. One solution, ultimately adopted in many continental jurisdictions, was simply to use the old Roman codes. In England, however, partly because it was easy and partly because it possessed considerable local political appeal, the king's judges adopted as far as possible the practice of the pre-Conquest local courts. This practice of the lower courts consisted of adopting as far as possible the local customs of the place and time and applying to daily events what people felt was fair. We might call this the custom of following custom.

The custom of following custom, however, produced the second problem. In a sparsely populated area, a primitive area by today's standards of commerce and transportation, customs about crimes, about land use, and about debts and so forth varied considerably from shire to shire, village to village, and manor to manor. But the king's judges could hardly decide each case on the basis of whatever local custom or belief happened to capture the fancy of those living where the dispute arose. To judge that way would amount to judging on shifting and inconsistent grounds. It would not judge in the king's name but only in the name of the location where the dispute arose. It would undercut William's long-range objective.

Hence the royal courts slowly adopted some customs and rejected others in an attempt to rule consistently in the king's name. Because justice in England rested on the custom of customs, the customs that the royal courts adopted and attempted to apply uniformly became the customs *common* to all the king's land. Thus the royal courts did not just follow custom. They created new common customs by following some and rejecting others and combining yet others into new customs.

Of course, by doing this the courts no longer ruled by custom, strictly speaking. Because they sought to rule in the king's name, they sought to rule consistently. In doing so, the courts rejected some customs. Although judges no doubt felt that what they decided was right because it had its roots in some customs, it would be wiser to say they created not common custom but common law, law common throughout England. We might call this creation of law in the King's name the crowning touch.

With the solution of the third problem as follows, the story of the origins of common law ends. If judges adopt today a custom by which to govern other similar cases before the royal courts tomorrow, then tomorrow the judges must have some way of remembering what they said today. By the year 1250, the problem of faulty judicial memory so bothered one judge, Henri de Bracton, that he wrote a huge treatise attempting to solve it. Plucknett describes the work this way:

> [Bracton] procured, for his own private use, complete transcripts of the pleadings in selected cases, and even referred to the cases in the course of his treatise. This great innovation gives to his work in several places a curiously modern air, for like modern law writers he sometimes praises and sometimes criticises his cases. At the beginning of his book he explains, however, that the contemporary bench is not distinguished by ability or learning, and that his treatise is, to some extent, a protest against modern tendencies. He endeavours to set forth the sound principles laid down by those whom he calls "his masters" who were on the bench nearly a generation ago; hence it is that his cases are on the average about twenty years older than his book. Of really recent cases he used very few. It must not, therefore, be assumed that we have in Bracton the modern conception of case law. He never gives us any

discussion of the authority of cases and clearly would not understand the modern implications of *stare decisis*. Indeed, his cases are carefully selected because they illustrate what he believes the law ought to be, and not because they have any binding authority; he freely admits that at the present moment decisions are apt to be on different lines. Bracton's use of cases, therefore, is not based upon their authority as sources of law, but upon his personal respect for the judges who decided them, and his belief that they raise and discuss questions upon lines which he considers sound. Although it is true that the use of cases as a source of law in the modern sense was still far in the future, nevertheless Bracton's use of cases is very significant. He accustomed lawyers of the thirteenth and early fourteenth centuries to read and to discuss the cases which he put in his book, and this was a great step towards the modern point of view.[2]

Bracton's great work, together with smaller pamphlets of other judges and lawyers, were followed within half a century by "year-books," annual reports of court proceedings and decisions that heavily emphasized procedure. Procedure in England, the correct way and the incorrect way to proceed in court, had rapidly become rigid, and lawyers who could not master it and who could not remember all the strict technicalities lost their cases. They needed to write the technicalities down to remember them. Bracton and his successors, of necessity, began the tradition, very much expanded today, of writing down the essential conclusions of the courts and using these writings as guides for future judicial choices.

As Plucknett reminds us, however, Bracton and his followers did not create the practices of reasoning by example and stare decisis as we know them. Indeed, until the American Revolution, men actively rejected the notion that judges actually made law as they decided cases. Men believed rather in natural law, if not God's law at least nature's own. To them the proper judicial decision rested on true law. The decision that rested elsewhere was in a sense unlawful. This was, after all, the problem facing Bracton. Prior to and throughout most of the eighteenth century, lawyers and judges thought of common law

[2] Plucknett, pp. 259–260.

as a collected body of correct legal doctrine, not the process of growth and change that reasoning by example makes inevitable. The true principles of common law guided judicial choices, not the examples of specific precedents.

Additional reasons explain why common law only rather recently began to emphasize reasoning from precedents. Bracton's treatise and the many that followed it did not reliably report the factual details of each and every case. These were unofficial, incomplete, and often critical commentaries. Not even a judge who wanted to follow the examples of precedents could use them with confidence. Only the radical and recent change in viewpoint and the recognition that law comes from politicians and not from God or nature, coupled with accurate court reporting, permitted reasoning by example and stare decisis to flourish.[3]

It is time to close this historical circle. In calling common law judge-made law we mean that, for a variety of historical reasons, a large body of legal rules and principles exist because judges without legislative help have created them. As long as judges continue to apply them, they continue to recreate them with each application. The fact that judges for most of this history thought they simply restated divine or natural law matters relatively little to us today. What matters is that the twentieth-century United States has inherited a political system in which, despite legislative supremacy, judges constantly and inevitably make law. How they do so—how they reason, in other words—thus becomes an important question in the study of politics and government themselves; one of the central questions in this book is not *whether* courts should make law but *when* and *how* they should make law.

COMMON LAW REASONING ILLUSTRATED

Much of the everyday law around us falls into the category of common law. Although modern statutes have supplanted some of it, particularly in the important area of business contracts, even these statutes for the most part preserve basic definitions,

---

[3]Kempin, p. 85, suggests that as late as 1825 in the United States and 1865 in England stare decisis rested on very shaky ground.

principles, and values articulated first in common law. One of the most important common law categories, also probably the one least touched by statute today, concerns the law of tort. Tort law wrestles with this problem: What limits a person's liability to compensate those he hurts? When does law impose liability on me if I threaten someone with a blow (assault)? If I strike the blow (battery)? If I publicly insult another (libel and slander)? If I do careless things that injure other people (negligence)? These questions may sound like questions of criminal law to you, but they are not, for the law of torts does not expose the lawbreaker to punishment by the state. The law of torts, while much of it overlaps criminal law, defines at what times people who hurt other people's bodies, their property, their reputations, or their freedom must compensate them for their hurt.

In this section, indeed for the bulk of the chapter, we illustrate common law in action with problems of tort law, mostly of negligence. But we do not discuss tort law in its entirety, of course, for it would take books triple the size of this one to review all the subtleties and uncertainties in the law of tort. We shall instead focus in some detail on an important and perennial problem in the law of tort: To what extent may we hurt other people without incurring a legal liability to compensate those we hurt *because we hurt them on our own land?*

Let us begin with a review of the basic rules of common law that seemed to govern this situation in the middle of the last century. First, the common law of negligence required one to act in a way a reasonable and prudent person would act and to refrain from acting in a way a reasonable and prudent person would refrain. Lawyers would say that a "standard of care" and a "duty to conform" to it existed. Second, law imposed liability upon those who in fact carelessly violated the "reasonable man" standard. Whether a person in fact acted negligently in a specific case is one of those legal history questions juries often decide. Third, someone must actually suffer an injury as a result of the hurt. In lawyers' language, the violation of the standard caused a hurt. Juries often make this factual decision also. Thus the critical *legal* questions in negligence cases involve the definition of the standard and the duty.

Similarly, the law of battery commands us not to strike another deliberately unless a reasonable person would do so, as in self-defense. If we strike another unreasonably, then we become liable as long as we owe a duty to the injured person not to strike.

As you may already suspect, the last element in these two torts, the requirement of a duty before liability attaches, can make a great difference. One of the common law principles of the last century quite plainly said that people do not owe a duty to avoid injuring, carelessly or deliberately, people who trespass on their property.

We shall examine three common law cases to illustrate some of the main features of reasoning in common law. These cases provide evidence, clues, that support some basic truths about the common law process:

- General principles, including the rules of negligence and battery just described, do not neatly resolve legal problems.
- Precedents do not neatly resolve legal problems, either.
- In reasoning from precedents, judges do make choices, do exercise fact freedom, and it is this exercise that best describes how and why they decide as they do.
- Social background facts often influence case outcomes more powerfully than the facts in the litigation itself.
- The beliefs and values of individual judges do influence law.
- The precise meaning of common law rules changes as judges decide each new case.
- Over time, as fundamental social values change, common law also changes in a fundamental way to reflect these changes in social values.
- Judges have shifted their conception of their role, have shifted from a belief that their role requires them to apply divine or natural law toward a recognition of the inevitability of judicial lawmaking and its consequences.

Here are the three cases.

The Cherry Tree

It is summer in rural New York. The year is 1865. The heat of midday has passed. Sarah Hoffman, a spinster living with her brother, a country doctor, sets out at her brother's request to pick ripe cherries for dinner.

The cherry tree stands on her brother's land about two feet from the fence separating his land from that of his neighbor, Abner Armstrong. Sarah's previous cullings have left few cherries on Hoffman's side of the fence. Hence, nimbly enough for her age, Sarah climbs the fence and from her perch upon it begins to take cherries from the untouched branches overhanging Abner's yard.

Angered by this intrusion, Abner runs from his house and orders her to stop picking his cherries. She persists. Enraged, he grabs her wrist and strongarms her down from the fence. Ligaments in the wrist tear. She cries from the pain and humiliation. She sues at common law for battery. The trial jury awards her $1,000 damages.

Abner appealed. He claimed that *he*, not Sarah or her brother, owned the cherries overhanging his land. Because he owned the cherries, he had every right to protect them, just as he could prevent Sarah from pulling onions in his garden with a long-handled picker from her perch. In other words, Sarah was not a person to whom Abner owed a duty. By her trespassing and her interference with Abner's property, Sarah exposed herself to Abner's legal battery committed in defense of his property.

Abner's lawyer cited many legal sources in support of his argument. He began with the maxim, *cujus est solum, ejus est usque ad coelum et ad inferos,* sometimes translated as "he who has the soil, has it even to the sky and the lowest depths." He then referred the appellate judge to the great English commentator, Blackstone, quoting: "Upwards, therefore, no man may erect any building, or the like to overhang another's land." He also cited *Kent's Commentaries,* the Bouvier *Institutes, Crabbe's Text on Real Property,* and seven cases in support of his position. One of these, an English case titled *Waterman v. Soper,* held "that if A plants a tree upon the extremest limits of his land and the tree growing extends its roots into the land of B next adjoining," then A and B jointly own the tree.[4]

Sarah's lawyer responded that, in law, title to the tree depends on who owns title to the land from which the tree

---

[4] *Waterman v. Soper,* 1 Ld Raymond 737 (opinion undated).

grows. Sarah did not trespass; therefore, Abner owed her the duty not to batter her. In support he cited several commentaries, Hilliard's treatise on real property, and four cases. Sarah's lawyer relied especially on a case, *Lyman v. Hale*, decided in Connecticut in 1836.[5] In *Lyman* the defendant picked and refused to return pears from branches overhanging his yard from a tree the plaintiff had planted four feet from the line. The *Lyman* opinion explicitly rejected the reasoning of the English precedent, *Waterman*. Despite the antiquated language, *Lyman* is a remarkably sensible, unlegalistic opinion. The court held that *Waterman's* "roots" principle is unsound because of the practical difficulties in applying it:

> How it may be asked, is the principle to be reduced to practice? And here, it should be remembered, that nothing depends on the question whether the branches do or do not overhang the lands of the adjoining proprietor. All is made to depend solely on the enquiry, whether any portion of the roots extend into his land. It is this fact alone, which creates the [joint ownership]. And how is the fact to be ascertained?
>
> Again; if such [joint ownership] exist, it is diffused over the whole tree. Each owns a certain proportion of the whole. In what proportion do the respective parties hold? And how are these proportions to be determined? How is it to be ascertained what part of its nourishment the tree derives from the soil of the adjoining proprietor? If one joint owner appropriate...all the products, on what principle is the account to be settled between the parties?
>
> Again; suppose the line between adjoining proprietors to run through a forest or grove. Is a new rule of property to be introduced, in regard to those trees growing so near the line as to extend some portions of their roots across it? How is a man to know whether he is the exclusive owner of trees, growing, indeed, on his own land, but near the line; and whether he can safely cut them, without subjecting himself to an action?
>
> And again; on the principle claimed, a man may be the exclusive owner of a tree, one year, and the next, a [joint owner] with another; and the proportion in which he owns may be varying from year to year, as the tree progresses in its growth.

[5]*Lyman v. Hale,* 11 *Conn. Rep.* 177 (1836).

> It is not seen how these consequences are to be obviated, if
> the principle contended for be once admitted. We think they
> are such as to furnish the most conclusive objections against
> the adoption of the principle. We are not prepared to adopt it,
> unless compelled to do so, by the controuling force of
> authority. The cases relied upon for its support, have been
> examined. We do not think them decisive.[6]

In effect the *Lyman* opinion says property titles must be clear to help us plan our affairs, to help us know whether we can or can't cut down a tree for winter firewood, for example. Given the inescapable background facts about trees, the roots rule introduces inevitable uncertainty. We must therefore reject it.

Sarah won.[7] The appellate court in New York found *Lyman* most persuasive and followed it.

Abner appealed again, to the state's highest court of appeals. In 1872 (court delays are not a uniquely modern phenomenon) Abner lost again. The attorneys presented the same arguments. Perhaps surprisingly, however, the highest court did not mention *Lyman*. Instead it seemed to say that *Waterman* does correctly state the law, but Abner's lawyer forgot to prove that the cherry tree's roots actually extended across the property line:

> We have not been referred to any case showing that where no
> part of a tree stood on the land of a party, and it did not
> receive any nourishment therefrom, that he had any right
> therein, and it is laid down in Bouvier's Institutes...that if the
> branches of a tree only overshadow the adjoining land and the
> roots do not enter into it, the tree wholly belongs to the estate
> where the roots grow.[8]

Therefore Abner lost.

This simple case, occupying only a few pages in the reports of the two New York appellate courts, richly illustrates many essential features of common law:

> 1. Note first that none of the judges either in *Hoffman* or
>   in *Lyman* questioned their authority to decide these

---

[6]*Lyman v. Hale,* pp. 183–184.
[7]*Hoffman v. Armstrong,* 46 Barbour 337 (1866).
[8]*Hoffman v. Armstrong,* 48 N.Y. 201 (1872), pp. 203–204.

cases without reference to statutes. The laws, both of assault and battery and of the more fundamental problem of ownership, come from the common law heritage of cases, commentaries, and treatises. The judges automatically assumed the power to make law governing a very common human conflict, overlapping claims to physical space on this planet. Surely a legislature could legislate on the subject, but judges have no guilt feeling about doing so themselves in the face of legislative silence.

In this connection, recall that legislatures pass statutes addressing general problems. How likely is it that a legislature would ever pass a statute regulating tree ownership on or near property lines? Is it not better that our government contains a mechanism, the courts, that must create some law on this subject once the problem turns out to be a real one?

2. The general common law definitions of battery and of property ownership do not resolve this case. Neither do specific precedents. Instead, both sides cite conflicting principles and inconsistent precedents and urge from them contradictory conclusions. The judge must find some justification, some reason, for choosing, but nothing in either side's argument, at least in this case, compels the judge to choose one way rather than another. Judges possess the freedom to say that either *Lyman* or *Waterman* expresses the right law for resolving this problem.

Consider specifically the matter of the Connecticut precedent, *Lyman*. Judges possess the freedom to say, as the first appellate court said, "We find the facts of *Lyman* much like those in Abner's conflict with Sarah. We also find *Lyman*'s reasoning persuasive, therefore we apply the rule of *Lyman* to this case and rule for Sarah." But judges also possess the freedom to say, as did the second court, "Connecticut precedents do not govern New York. Older common law precedents and principles from England conflict with Connecticut's law. We choose the older tradition. Abner would win if only he could show that the roots really grew on his property."

The New York courts in *Hoffman* had other options. The second court could have easily assumed that, since roots underground grow about the same distances as do branches above ground, that the roots did cross the line and that their nourishment probably supported the cherries Sarah tried to pick. Or they could take judicial notice of the fact that any reasonably sized tree grows roots in all directions more than two feet from its base. But they didn't.

Judges must decide which facts in the case before them matter and what they mean. They must simultaneously decide what the facts in the known and often inconsistent precedents mean in order to reach their legal conclusion. The two appellate courts reached the same conclusion but by emphasizing different facts. The first court found that roots shouldn't matter. Even though legal authorities sometimes mention them, the court believed the location of roots should have no legal significance. To give root location legal significance suddenly makes our knowledge of what we own more uncertain. Before we can cut down a tree we must enter our neighbor's land and dig a series of holes in his yard looking for roots. And what if the neighbor has flowers growing in a bed that he doesn't want dug up? The root rule leaves us out on a limb.

3. To understand how these two courts choose differently to reach the same result, examine the difference in their basic approach to the problem. The first appellate court seems eager to assume the responsibility to shape law, to acknowledge relevant background facts and hence to make laws that promote human cooperation in daily affairs. The second court approaches the problem much more cautiously. It seems to say: "We admit the precedents conflict. Fortunately we do not really need to choose between them. As long as Abner failed to prove the roots grow on his side of the fence, he loses either way. Therefore we choose the path that disturbs com-

mon law the least. The lower appellate court explicitly chose to reject *Waterman*, but we don't have to do that, so we won't.''

This judicial caution is very common, but it is not particularly wise. Without realizing it, the highest New York court (whose opinion therefore overrides the precedential value of the better opinion of the court below) has made new law. Now we have New York precedent endorsing *Waterman*. Future courts will have to wrestle with the problem of overruling it or blindly follow it and produce all the practical problems against which *Lyman* rightly warned.

The reason these two sets of judges ruled differently, therefore, rests precisely on the fact that they are different people with different values and beliefs about what judges ought to do. Their values help determine the law they create.

4. At a deeper level, the difference reflects much more than a difference in judicial beliefs and styles. These two approaches illustrate two common law traditions. The final higher court opinion in *Hoffman* views common law as fixed, stable, and true. It wants to avoid upsetting Bouvier's *Institutes* and Blackstone's maxims if it possibly can. The court thinks these are the common law. The lower court's *Lyman* approach, though it predates *Hoffman* by nearly 40 years, observes the spirit rather than the letter of common law. It views common law as a tradition in which judges seek to adapt law so that it improves our capacity to live together peacefully and to plan our affairs more effectively. It retains the capacity to change with changing conditions. Do you have any difficulty preferring the spirit to the letter?

5. Finally, the case of the cherry tree illustrates a fundamental difference between statutory interpretation and common law. In statutory interpretation we saw that many judges often try to determine the intent of the legislature. Since in practice legislative intent proves slippery at best, we prefer interpretation based on determinations of statutory purpose. In either case of

statutory interpretation, however, we saw that judges must attempt to see the legal problem through the eye of the lawgiver. Once the court determines a statute's purpose, it has no need to second-guess the wisdom of that purpose.

In common law, on the other hand, the judge who reasons from a precedent does not care about what the prior judge intended or about the purpose of the announced rule of law. In common law, the judge is always free to decide on his own what the law ought to say. The prior judge's intent or purpose does not dictate how his opinion will bind as precedent. Put another way, the legislature's classification of what does and does not belong in its legal category, a classification created by the words of the statute, does bind the judge. In common law, the judge deciding the case creates the classification. He sets his own goals.

This goal-setting occurred in both the first and second *Hoffman* opinions. The first court wanted to make workable and practical law, not because *Lyman* or any other precedent commanded it to but because the court wanted to achieve that goal. The second court ruled as it did not because Bouvier's *Institutes* or *Waterman* commanded it to do so but because that court preferred the goal of changing past formal statements of law as little as possible.[9]

The Pit

Five years after Sarah's final victory, New York's highest court faced a related common law problem. A Mr. Carter, along with several other citizens of the town of Bath, maintained an alley running between their properties: "Exchange Alley," people called it. The public had used the alley for 20 years as a convenient way to travel from one long block to another, but the town never acknowledged Exchange Alley as a public street nor

---

[9] By contrast, the words of the Mann Act do command the courts to include at least the transportation of willing prostitutes, and the courts could not properly ignore that command.

attempted to maintain it. In May 1872, Carter began excavating to erect a building on his land. The construction went slowly, so slowly in fact that on a gloomy night the next November an open pit still remained on Carter's property. That night a Mr. Beck passed through the alley on his customary way to supper when, rather suddenly, a carriage turned down the alley and rushed toward him. Beck stepped rapidly to his left to avoid the carriage, tripped, and fell headlong into the pit, injuring himself. Although the evidence was never totally clear, since the alley had no marked border, it appeared that the pit began no less than seven feet away from the outermost possible edge of the alley.

The lawsuit that followed brought much the same kind of problem to the court as had Sarah's problem. Lawyers for Carter cited the common law rule that landowners have the right to use their property as they please. They have no duty to avoid harming trespassers negligently. The lawyers cited English cases to show that travelers who were hurt falling into pits 5, 20, and 30 feet from a public way could not recover damages because the danger must "adjoin" the public way.

Despite these arguments the court held for Beck. It had no difficulty whatsoever determining that, even though Carter and others together privately owned Exchange Alley, allowing the public to use the property over time created a duty to the users not to hurt them negligently.[10]

But the pit excavated truly private property. Is a seven-foot distance from a public alley sufficient to exempt the owner from liability to the public, or does the pit legally "adjoin" the alley, thereby creating a duty of care?

The court ruled that the alley did adjoin. It approved the idea that if the hole was "so situated that a person lawfully using the thoroughfare, and, in a reasonable manner, was liable to fall into it, the defendant was liable."[11]

---

[10] As an aside, you might try at this point to define property. You should observe from this example that, legally speaking, property is not so much what people hold title to as it is what the law says you can and cannot do with it. The owners of Exchange Alley cannot do anything they wish with it just because they hold the deed.

[11] *Beck v. Carter*, 68 N.Y. 283 [six] (1876), p. 293.

The court did not have to rule this way. It could have defined adjoining pits as pits that literally border on public land. Or it could have said that seven feet was simply too far away to make a landowner liable. But the court offered a better decision. As in *Lyman*, it relied on common sense to produce a workable distinction between injuries to deliberate trespassers and to those who reasonably attempt to use either their own space or the public's space. Just as in the *Lyman* and *Hoffman* decisions, the judges in *Beck v. Carter* chose as they did because their values, their beliefs about desirable and undesirable social relations, led them to this conclusion. If they deeply believed in the absolute sanctity of private property, ambiguity in common law would certainly have given them freedom to say, "Land owners must be free to do what they wish with their land. Carter's pit was entirely on his private land, separated from the thoroughfare. Therefore Carter owed Beck no duty of care."

Think about the difference between this result and the real outcome in *Beck*. If judicial values determine choices, if legal choices are partly ethical choices, then ultimately we must, at least in a democracy, ask whether the political and legal systems work to preserve some correspondence between judicial and popular values. Later chapters return to this problem. For now it may suffice to recall one of the lessons of Chapter II. Precisely the same ambiguity in law that makes personal judgment inevitable also allows law to change to correspond to popular values over time.

The Diving Board

Before you proceed, note how these two principal cases, reduced to their simplest terms, combine to form a seemingly comprehensive statement of law: When the plaintiff's deliberate act is not proved a trespass on the defendant's property, then the defendant owes the plaintiff a duty of care *(Hoffman)*. Furthermore, when the plaintiff accidentally but conclusively does trespass on the defendant's property, but the defendant should have forseen the injury from such accidental trespass, the defendant is also liable *(Beck)*. Thus arises the final question: What result should a court reach when the plaintiff deliberately and unambiguously trespasses on the defendant's property and is injured?

On another summer day in New York, July 8, 1916, Harvey Hynes and two friends had gone swimming at a favorite spot along the Bronx bank of the then relatively unpolluted Harlem River. For five years they and other swimmers had dived from a makeshift plank nailed to the wooden bulkhead along the river.

The electrified line of the New York Central Railroad ran along the river. The power line was suspended over the track between poles, half of which ran between the track and the river. Legally the railroad owned the strip of river bank containing track, poles, wires, and bulkhead. Hence, about half of the 16-foot diving board touched or extended over the railroad's land while the rest reached out, at a height of about three feet, over the surface of the public river.

As Harvey prepared to dive, one of the railroad's overhead supports for the power line suddenly broke loose from the pole, bringing down with it the writhing electric line that powered the trains. The wires struck Harvey, throwing him from the board. His friends pulled him dead from the waters of the Harlem River.

Harvey's mother sued the railroad for the damages caused by its alleged negligence in maintaining the supports for the wire. Conceding that the New York Central's maintenance of the supports failed to meet the "reasonable man" standard of care, the trial court and the intermediate appellate court nevertheless denied her claim. Harvey was a trespasser, a deliberate trespasser, and property owners have no duty to protect such trespassers from harm.

Before proceeding further, reflect on the cases of the cherry tree and the pit because you are about to see these rather distantly related cases, two cases among thousands that had tried to thrash out the borderline between property and tort, merge as key precedents in the final *Hynes* decision. They merge because the author of the final opinion in *Hynes*, Benjamin Cardozo, chose to cite them from among the available thousands.

The lawyers for the railroad presented a battery of cases in their favor. they cited *Hoffman* to show that, while perched on the board, even if he was over the river, Harvey trespassed, because the board was attached to the railroad's land. They also cited cases, *Beck* among them, to establish the point that the trespass was not a temporary and involuntary move from a public space but a sustained series of deliberate trespasses onto the defendant's land.

Three of the justices on New York's highest court agreed. The railroad had no duty of care to this trespasser. But a majority of four, led by Cardozo, supported Harvey's mother and reversed.

Cardozo cited relatively few precedents. He did, however, cite *Hoffman* and *Beck*, but not in the way the railroad's lawyers had hoped. The lawyers tried to convince the judges that a mechanical rule commanded a decision for the railroad. Anything, a cherry tree or a diving board, belongs to the railroad if it is affixed to the railroad's land, regardless of what it overhangs. Therefore, Harvey, at the time the wires struck him, trespassed. Since the trespass was deliberate, *Beck* commands a decision for the railroad.

Cardozo, however, appealed to the deeper spirit of these cases, a spirit that rejects mechanical rules like the root rule for determining ownership of cherry trees. He cited *Hoffman* not for its reasoning but for its result: There was no real trespass. The spirit requires enunciating policy—law—that corresponds to a deeper sense of how society ought to regulate rights and responsibilities in this legal, as well as physical, borderland. He wrote:

> This case is a striking instance of the dangers of "a jurisprudence of conceptions" (Pound, "Mechanical Jurisprudence," 8 *Columbia Law Review,* 605, 608, 610), the extension of a maxim or a definition with relentless disregard of consequences to... "a dryly logical extreme." The approximate and relative become the definite and absolute. Landowners are not bound to regulate their conduct in contemplation of the presence of trespassers intruding upon private structures. Landowners *are* bound to regulate their conduct in contemplation of the presence of travelers upon the adjacent public ways. There are times when there is little trouble in marking off the field of exemption and immunity from that of liability and duty. Here structures and ways are so united and commingled, superimposed upon each other, that

the fields are brought together. In such circumstances, there is little help in pursuing general maxims to ultimate conclusions. They have been framed *alio intuitu*. They must be reformulated and readapted to meet exceptional conditions. Rules appropriate to spheres which are conceived of as separate and distinct cannot, both, be enforced when the spheres become concentric. There must then be readjustment or collision. In one sense, and that a highly technical and artificial one, the diver at the end of the springboard is an intruder on the adjoining lands. In another sense, and one that realists will accept more readily, he is still on public waters in the exercise of public rights. The law must say whether it will subject him to the rule of the one field or of the other, of this sphere or of that. We think that considerations of analogy, of convenience, of policy, and of justice, exclude him from the field of the defendant's immunity and exemption, and place him in the field of liability and duty....[12]

Note again the effect of fact freedom on judicial choices. Although they wrote no dissenting opinion, we can make an intelligent guess that the dissenters in *Hynes* reasoned from *Hoffman* this way: "The fact is that the diving board grew from the railroad's land. If the cherry tree growing from Hoffman's land belongs to him, then the board belongs to the railroad." But Cardozo in effect responds, "No! The important fact is that Sarah didn't really trespass. Just as she used what didn't clearly belong to Abner, so these boys diving into the river from a board over the river didn't really interfere with the railroad's property." Reason in law does not allow us to call one approach legally right and the other legally wrong. After all, with a switch in one vote, *Hynes* would produce a very different legal precedent. However, by recognizing that ethics and values determine choices, we do free ourselves to say that one choice is better, another worse, and to justify why we feel that way.

These cases reveal the inevitability of ambiguity, fact freedom, and choice in the legal process. They teach at least three additional lessons about the analysis of cases, about changing judicial styles, and about the way law itself changes.

---

[12]*Hynes v. New York Central R.R.*, 231 N.Y. 229 (1921), pp. 235–236.

Analyzing Cases

For the better part of a century, students of law, both in law schools and in college courses, have paid special attention to the opinions of appellate courts. In 1930 Professor Arthur L. Goodhart published what has turned out to be one of the more popular methods for reading an opinion and discerning its meaning. I shall paraphrase his statement of the method for locating what he calls the principle or *ratio decidendi* of the case. Think about the preceding cases as you read, and you will see why Goodhart's well-known method gives a very misleading view of legal reasoning. I shall explain why in a moment. Here is the paraphrase of Goodhart:[13]

1. We cannot determine the principle, the essential legal meaning of a case, simply by examining the reasons the judge gives in the opinion. Sometimes judges state reasons that don't logically relate on close examination to the legal issue; sometimes judges never state the reasons that produce the result.

2. We cannot determine the principle only by articulating the rule of law set forth in the case. This is because judges often state legal rules in very general terms—landowners have no duty to trespassers—when the facts of the case raise a much more precise and delimited question.

3. We cannot, moreover, find the principle by looking at all the facts in the case, for some of the facts have no legal significance. Had Sarah Hoffman's parents instead christened her Griselda or if Harvey had been a girl, the result, we devoutly hope, would not have been different.

4. We *can* find the principle of a case by examining the facts that the deciding judge treats as material and his rulings of law based on these material facts.

5. In doing so we must also take account of the facts the judge determines do not matter, facts the judge determines to be immaterial.

---

[13] Arthur L. Goodhart, "Determining the *Ratio Decidenci* of a Case," 40 *Yale Law Journal* 161 (1930).

Think about how Cardozo treated *Hoffman* and *Beck*. Does Goodhart's method accurately describe how Cardozo found the meaning, the precedential value, in these cases? The basic problem with Goodhart's method is that it asks us to determine the principle of a case in the abstract, by reading it. But a judge starts from a very different place. The judge starts always with a new case, a legal conflict he must resolve. He inevitably looks at any precedent from the frame of reference provided by the new facts before him. By Goodhart's method the principle of the final *Hoffman* opinion would look something like this: To collect the fruit of a tree overhanging your property you must introduce evidence that the roots also intrude into your land. Neither Cardozo nor the dissenters, confronted with the problem of liability for Harvey's death, saw the case that way at all. The meaning of cases, then, emerges only as judges compare them and use them.

Professor Julius Stone has, crisply if rather primly, criticized the Goodhart method this way:

> The assumption that "the material facts" will thus yield only one *ratio* would imply, if true, that there is only one set of such "material facts" which is to be related to the holding. And this immediately confronts the theory with a main difficulty. This is that, apart from any explicit or implicit assertion of materiality by the precedent court, there will always be more than one, and indeed many, competing versions of "the material facts"; and there will therefore not be merely one but many *rationes*, any of which will explain the holding on those facts, and no one of which therefore is strictly *necessary* to explain it. For apart from any selection by the precedent court, all the logical possibilities remain open; and in the logician's sense it is possible to draw as many general propositions from a given decision (each of which will "explain" it) as there are possible combinations of distinguishable facts in it. It is in these terms that, it has been said, the question—What single principle does a particular case establish? is "strictly nonsensical, that is, inherently incapable of being answered." ...
>
> Yet these are not the most crucial difficulties with Professor Goodhart's system. The crucial ones arise rather from the several alternative *levels of statement* of each "material fact" of the precedent case, ranging from the full

unique concreteness of that actual case, through a series of
widening generalisations. In this series only the unique
concreteness is *firmly* anchored to the precedent court's view
that a given Fact A is "material"; and *ex hypothesi* that level
of unique concreteness can scarcely figure as a part of the
binding *ratio* for other cases. By the same token the reach of
the *ratio,* even after each "material fact" seen by the original
court is identified, will vary with the level of generalisation at
which "the fact-element" is stated. How then is the "correct"
level of statement of each fact-element to be ascertained by the
later court?[14]

The distinction between letter and spirit that separates Cardozo
from his dissenters in *Hynes* perfectly illustrates Stone's point
about indeterminate levels of factual meaning.

How, then, does one analyze cases? One analyzes them only
on an incremental, comparative basis, only through reasoning
by example.

Changing Judicial Styles

In earlier chapters you have been exposed to many examples of
poorly reasoned judicial opinions. Perhaps to compensate, to
avoid the impression that judges usually err but Professor

---

[14] Julius Stone, *Legal System and Lawyers' Reasonings* (Stanford: Stanford
University Press, 1964), pp. 269, 272. On page 268, Stone adds this footnote:

See A.L. Goodhart, "Determining the Ratio..." to which we also offer
certain additional comments. One is that even the learned author could
not claim that his rules for finding the "binding" *ratio* were supported by
uniform English judicial practice. It is notorious that reasons given and
propositions of law formulated are, for instance, no less influential, even
if they are no more conclusive, than the facts. Moreover, for the reasons
given in the text, the facts of time, place and person could not be excluded
with the cleanness which Professor Goodhart attempts. Further his rules
for determining *the* "material" facts are artificial and, in part, indeterminate, requiring guesses as to what facts the courts tacitly took as
material. They would thus leave the *ratio* in many, if not in most
appellate cases, a matter for variable judgment even if they were accepted.
Finally, his rules would result in a serious restriction on the scope of
"binding" precedents issuing from appellate courts with several members. The increased area thus left for "persuasive" authorities would be
subject to the processes analysed in the text.

Carter is always right, I stress the positive in this chapter. *Lyman,* the first *Hoffman* (if not the second), *Beck,* and *Hynes* reach convincing results.

We could, if we choose, uncover many "dryly logical" examples of mechanical jurisprudence in common law, just as, in Chapter IV, we could have uncovered many more examples of wise ascertainments of statutory purpose. You should not assume that the common law tradition assures the best results. Precisely because men so often find it painful to live with uncertainty, judges have a natural tendency to slip into mechanical jurisprudence, to pretend away the uncertainty and the need for choice in life.

We can, however, detect a style in these cases that seems to strengthen over time. We might label this style change with the question, "Whatever happened to Bouvier's *Institutes*?" Judges are today more conscious of their discretion and of the importance of social background facts. They are less likely to hide behind a formal statement of law in a treatise, a commentary, or a common law principle. Do they indeed carry this style too far in the discretionary direction? We shall return to this question in the final section of this chapter.

Change in Law Itself

Before reading further in this subsection, stop to ask this question: What general change in the borderline law of property and tort do all the preceding cases suggest?

Do they not reflect a narrowing of the freedom one has for doing as one pleases with one's land and an expansion of our obligation to avoid hurting others? Make no mistake about it. The shift in the last 50 years from a legal philosophy whose principles emphasize property rights and individualism to a system that promotes social caring and cooperation is as major a change as our legal system has ever experienced, at least in so short a time. The case at the end of this chapter will illustrate the trend further. Do you believe that, if such a change is occurring in our law, it corresponds to a more fundamental shift in public sentiments recognizing interdependence and acknowledging our collective obligation to share and help rather than compete?

If so, then common law here has passed at least the minimal test of changing to reflect changing social values.

But how, over a period of time, does change in law occur? Some legal scholars say that law changes in a circular way. Basic concepts, much less crisp and precise than legal rules, build up in law as cases accumulate, but then disappear when, as they become rigid, they prove too inflexible to accommodate new ideas. Levi describes it this way:

> In the long run a circular motion can be seen. The first stage is the creation of the legal concept which is built up as cases are compared. The period is one in which the court fumbles for a phrase. Several phrases may be tried out; the misuse or misunderstanding of words itself may have an effect. The concept sounds like another, and the jump to the second is made. The second stage is the period when the concept is more or less fixed, although reasoning by example continues to classify items inside and out of the concept. The third stage is the breakdown of the concept, as reasoning by example has moved so far ahead as to make it clear that the suggestive influence of the word is no longer desired.[15]

Levi illustrates the point by describing the emergence and later decay of the legal concept known as the "inherently dangerous" rule. The courts had, for several decades in the beginning of this century, held manufacturers of products legally liable to people who were hurt by *negligently* manufactured items only if (1) the injured person was the one who actually contracted the purchase of the product or (2) the product was "inherently dangerous."

No doubt, legal concepts do move in and out of law in much the way Levi describes. The history of the inherently dangerous rule, studied carefully, makes fascinating reading.[16] Many texts in legal process have reprinted it. I must, however, voice two related cautionary notes.

---

[15] Edward H. Levi, *An Introduction to Legal Reasoning* (Chicago: University of Chicago Press, 1949), pp. 8–9.

[16] Not too surprisingly, the hero in the dispatch of the inherently dangerous rule was Benjamin Cardozo, writing in *MacPherson v. Buick*, decided in the year of Harvey's death, 217 N.Y. 382 (1916). Cardozo's principal tactic for discrediting the concept was to deny that it ever really existed in the first place.

First, the neatness of Levi's thesis and illustration that makes it such an appealing addition to textbooks also makes the model seem universal when it is not. The more typical model of legal change must accommodate the fact that common law can evolve by a process of fumbling from one half-formed concept to another without ever moving through Levi's crystallized stage. The second *Hoffman* opinion's deliberate ignoring of *Lyman* and Cardozo's creative use of *Hoffman* in *Hynes* to recover the spirit of *Lyman* illustrate my point.

Second, do not lose sight of Levi's own qualification of the model. Even when concepts in law do crystallize, they do not automatically resolve cases. The facts of the case, as we have seen, may permit the judge to invoke a variety of different concepts, some of them crystallized and some of them created spontaneously. Which one he chooses, and hence the impact of his decision on change in law, is still very much a function of fact freedom.

In summary, concepts do exist in law. Often they turn out to be sufficiently fixed and stable so that lawyers can engineer from them secure plans for their clients. At any given time for any given problem, however, lawyers must initially be prepared to contend with changing, uncertain, or competing concepts rather than fixed law.

KEEPING THE TRADITION ALIVE: WHAT COURTS SHOULD DO WITH NO LAW AND WITH CERTAIN BUT QUESTIONABLE LAW

The preceding section introduces the most typical common law judicial problem, one in which precedents provide some guidance but do not automatically resolve problems. In the typical situation, the judge faces an array of precedents, some of which may seen inconsistent, some of which seem imaginative, and others wedded to the past "truths" in common law. None of them necessarily control, so the judge must make a choice. Sometimes the precedent or principle he chooses gives him no more than a point of departure from which to justify the unexpressed beliefs and values that determine the result. Precedents in many cases are vehicles for rationalizations.

Sometimes, however, a genuinely new problem arises, one to which precedents prove so remote, so factually different, that the judge cannot build his rationalizations on them. He must then realize that a decision for either party in the case will create not a new variation on older law but a new and different law, a new and different definition of how people should relate to one another. In other situations, the reverse happens. The judge faces a precedent so factually similar to the one before him that he cannot distinguish or ignore it. If he chooses to reach a new result, he must overrule the precedent.

This section answers two questions involving these less typical judicial problems: How should judges proceed when they cannot find any common law principles or cases that seem to apply to the case before them? In what circumstances should courts choose deliberately to reject a case or principle that controls the case before it?

Answers to these questions depend, as did much of the analysis in Chapter IV, on what we think about the proper balance between judicial and legislative lawmaking. What kinds of problems require the kind of fact-gathering and value-balancing techniques available to legislatures but not courts? What types of problems require, for their solution, the creation of complex administrative planning and enforcement apparatus that only legislatures can create, fund, and supervise?

You may have already discerned my own general approach to the problem of judicial-legislative balance. Let me make it explicit here. Courts and legislatures have much in common. They both gather facts in a systematic way, courts through witnesses at trial and through the briefs of the parties on appeal and legislatures through committee hearings and the many other efforts of lobbyists. Both institutions do so, at least formally, in an open-minded way. Courts hear both sides. Our adversary system requires it. Legislatures also hear competing arguments in committee hearings and in the vying efforts of lobbies. Furthermore, we acknowledge that both courts and legislatures possess lawmaking power. People who look to law to plan their affairs know they should look to both institutions to find final answers. Finally, politics influences both branches of government. Many state judges win office by election. Politicians appoint federal judges and those state judges in nonelective posts, so political restraints affect both.

In Chapter VI, we will address some important political differences. Nevertheless, *judges should always presume themselves competent to take the lawmaking initiative when the legislature has not spoken clearly to them.* In other words, because as a general matter courts and legislatures have a similar authority and competence, the burden of proof always rests on the party that argues for the court to remain silent because the legislature is better qualified to speak.

As you think about my assertion and about the material in this chapter, bear in mind that judicial activity does not seek primarily to divide people into ethical categories. The legal process attempts to reduce as far as possible the uncertainties inherent in our daily relations with each other. Simply by existing, by being there, and costing us money, time, and trouble if we decide to use them, courts encourage us to resolve our problems on our own. They cannot encourage this autonomy, however, if they regularly refuse to try to clarify law because they think the legislature should do so. Even when courts reach controversial or erroneous results, they reduce uncertainties. Does not society benefit from machinery that constantly attempts to reduce these uncertainties? Would not society suffer if its judges refused to attempt to solve problems because they felt the law wasn't clear?

Keeping the Tradition Alive: Making New Common Law

In early March 1928, two seagoing tug boats towing barges of coal set out in good weather from Norfolk, Virginia, bound for New York. About midnight on March 8, under fair skies but with the barometer falling slightly, the tugs passed the Delaware Breakwater, a safe haven for tugs and barges caught in bad weather. The next morning, however, the wind began to freshen. By noon, gale force winds blew up heavy seas. Early in the afternoon two barges sprung leaks. Their crews signaled the tugs that they would proceed to anchor the barges and ride out the storm. They did so, but conditions steadily worsened. The

Coast Guard heroically rescued the crews of both barges late in the day. The dawn light on March 10 revealed no trace of the barges. By then, both the barges and their cargoes rested on the ocean floor.

The coal owners sued the barge company alleging both that the company had breached its contract of carriage and that the unseaworthiness of the barges made it liable for the loss of the coal. The barge company in turn sued the tug boat owners for the loss of both the coal and the two barges. The barge owners claimed that the two tugs had not properly handled the cargo. More precisely, they claimed that the tug owners should bear the total loss because they had not provided their tugs with conventional AM radio receivers.

At trial, the barge owners established several critical facts. On March 8 the Arlington weather bureau broadcast a 10:00 a.m. prediction calling for shifting and increasing winds the following day. Another ship in the vicinity of the tugs and barges had received this report on its AM radio. At 10:00 p.m. on the same day, the Arlington bureau predicted "increasing east and southeast winds, becoming fresh to strong Friday night and increasing cloudiness followed by rain on Friday." On the basis of the morning report, one tug owner towing cargo in the vicinity had anchored at the Delaware Breakwater. Even the captain of the defendant tug conceded at trial that, had he heard the evening report, he would have done the same.

Place yourself in the position of a judge resolving this case. In your first step, aided by the arguments of the lawyers, you try to discover how much, if any, of this problem the law already makes clear. You soon find that the law of admiralty—a branch of common law for our purposes—imposes an absolute liability on ship owners for the loss of cargoes in their ships if unseaworthiness of the ship caused the loss. Note that this unseaworthiness doctrine does not simply extend the law of negligence to the sea. The ship owner may have no knowledge of the faulty condition. It may have been impossible even for a reasonable and prudent man to prevent the unseaworthy condition—hidden rot in some of a hull's wooden planking, for example. The rule creates a guarantee of seaworthiness.

But is a ship—in 1928, you must remember—that does not

carry a radio therefore unseaworthy because it won't receive weather reports? On this point the law gives no help. You find that Congress has passed a statute requiring steamers carrying more than 50 passengers to carry two-way radios so that they can call for help and receive information, but the statute does not include tugs and barges. You find no precedents whatsoever linking seaworthiness with possession of radios or any other new invention.

At this point you have several choices. Think carefully about each. Choice one:

> Congress in its wisdom chose not to require two-way shortwave radios of tugs and barges. Furthermore, Congress has made no law requiring AM radios. Therefore, Congress has intended that tugs without AM radios are seaworthy and the tug owners are not liable for the loss.

Choice two:

> I find no law requiring receiving sets. Since legislatures, not the courts, are the lawmakers in our democratic nation, I have no legal authority to find the tug owners liable. Therefore they are not liable.

You can, I trust, reject both these choices immediately. Choice one possesses many of the evils described in Chapter IV. We have no evidence whatsoever that Congress thought about AM receivers, much less intended or decided to pass a statute calling tugs without them nevertheless seaworthy. We could just as easily conclude that the statute recognizes the general importance of radios in improving navigation safety. Therefore, the statute gives ship owners a positive signal that they should seriously examine whether radios can help them navigate better. If you have any further doubts about the weakness of the first choice, consider the fact that no congressional statute required tugs to carry compasses.

The second choice conflicts with the common law tradition. Courts do continue to make law as conditions change; courts have specifically fashioned the principles of admiralty and of seaworthiness within admiralty law over the years.

Choice three:

I admit that judges retain their general lawmaking power in admiralty. In this case, however, only a legislature can decide whether ships must carry radios. Only through legislative hearings could we learn, for example, how common it was in 1928 for people to own radios. It would hardly be fair to hold the tug owners liable if, in 1928, radios were only novel. Similarly, only legislative hearings can learn whether shipowners themselves carry radios and think it wise or necessary to do so. If they do, then the fact dictates a new policy of seaworthiness, but we can't tell. As in ancient common law, custom may hold the key to justice, but only a legislature today is equipped to find the key.

The third choice may sound like an improvement, but it's not. Its major premise, that courts can't obtain the facts, is, as I argued in Chapter III, totally false. The actual case, from which this example is derived, shows that the courts were able to make the necessary factual determinations.[17] The brief for the cargo owners documented the phenomenal growth in the sales of radios, over 1,000 percent between 1922 and 1928. It quoted Frederick Lewis Allen's *Only Yesterday*. "At the age of three and a half years, radio broadcasting had attained its majority. Behind those figures of radio sales lies a whole chapter of the life of the Post-war Decade: radio penetrating every third home in the country; giant broadcasting stations with nation-wide hookups...."[18] The cargo owners also elicited testimony on the witness stand from one tug captain to the effect that, although only one tug line required radios, at least 90 percent of the tugs had them, if only for entertainment.

The lesson here is critically important. As a rule, courts can find background facts as effectively as can legislatures. We

---

[17] *The T.J. Hooper*, 60 F.2d 737 (2nd Cir. 1932). As is customary in admiralty law, the name of the ship whose seaworthiness is questioned provides the name of the case.

[18] Quoted in Henry M. Hart and Albert M. Sacks, *The Legal Process* (Cambridge: Harvard Law School, 1958), pp. 432–433. My selection of illustrative cases in this section draws heavily upon the much larger variety of cases that Hart and Sacks provide. Although I use these cases for somewhat different purposes, I cannot improve upon their choice of working materials; here, as elsewhere, I am much indebted to them.

applaud the adversary system in courts precisely because we believe it gives lawyers the incentive to present the fullest possible range of facts to support their position. Legislatures may prove superior lawmakers where complex problems require a simultaneous set of solutions and the means to coordinate them, but well-established judicial practices allow courts in cases like this one to determine the background facts that determine whether a given legal choice is wise and fair.

Choices four and five:

> Custom is a time-honored source of common law. In this case it has been convincingly shown that tugs customarily carry radios. Radio has become a part of our everyday lives. The absence of the radios in this case caused the loss.

> Custom is a time-honored source of common law. In this case it has been convincingly shown that a majority of tug owners do not customarily require radios. Since we cannot say that the customs of the sea require radios, we cannot conclude that the absence of a radio in this case caused the loss.

Choices four and five are improvements over earlier choices. They are better judicial choices because they do not shrink from judicial responsibility for lawmaking. They succeed where the other choices failed in that they create a clear rule to guide future conduct. But, of course, you should still feel unsatisfied, for custom appears to produce two contradictory results. How should you choose between them?

Choice six:

> Is it then a final answer that the business had not yet generally adopted receiving sets? There are, no doubt, cases where courts seem to make the general practice of the calling the standard of proper diligence.... Indeed, in most cases reasonable prudence is in fact common prudence; but strictly it is never its measure; a whole calling may have unduly lagged in the adoption of new and available devices. It may never set its own tests, however persuasive be its usages. Courts must in the end say what is required; there are precautions so imperative that even their universal disregard will not excuse their omission.... We hold the tugs...had they been properly equipped...would have got the Arlington reports. The injury was a direct consequence of this unseaworthiness.

The language of choice six speaks with a power and persuasiveness that the other choices lack, but not simply because I have created here what I believe to be the wisest solution. The language here compels primarily because it is not mine at all but Judge Learned Hand's, taken from his opinion finally disposing of the case.[19] Hand's choice sets a clear standard, one that, anticipating the certain further growth of the radio industry, would occur sooner or later. Note, however, that with the exception of choice four, any other choice could well have created a precedent that would delay considerably any judicial decision requiring tugs to carry radios. These choices say tugs don't need to carry radios. Judicial change would require overruling any of these alternative decisions. In short, the timid and deferential judge potentially creates a common law precedent with just as much policy impact as does the active judge. This was our main criticism of the highest *Hoffman* case.

Above all, Hand's choice avoids the problem of lawmaking by default. Judges can never know whether or when or how Congress will act on any but dramatic national issues. Courts that wait for better legislative solutions may wait for a solution that never comes. Do you disagree with Hand's choice? Is it not the courts' proven capacity to establish the facts about the use of radios, coupled with Hand's sound ethical judgment that tugs ought to carry radios, that makes his opinion persuasive?

Keeping the Tradition Alive:
Stare Decisis in Common Law

We have now covered two of the three basic types of common law problems. The first we can call the "normal" case of reasoning from factually related but not identical cases. It is a process in which precedents do not command results, they merely suggest to judges various ways of classifying legal conflicts and resolving them. Sometimes the precedents are simply the framework on which the judge can rationalize his secret "real reasons" for decision. This reasoning is a process that, over time, occasion-

---

[19] *The T.J. Hooper*, p. 740.

ally produces Levi's cycle in which concepts move in and out of law. Generally, however, common law grows erratically and unsteadily, influenced continually by the fortuitous judicial choices of precedents and outcomes.

The second case, obviously, involves the "no precedent" instance that the tug boat case has illustrated.

There remains the final common law problem category of stare decisis. How should judges respond to precedents that seem completely to cover and control the outcomes of cases before them? Lawyers label these precedents "precisely in point" or "on all fours with the case at bar." Their existence does not, however, contradict the concept that law remains ambiguous. Judges always choose the results. Some judges, faced with a precedent that produces an unwanted conclusion, will choose to ignore it, much to the anger of the losing lawyer. A judge always retains the choice to overrule or to refuse deliberately to follow a precedent, even when he doesn't choose to ignore it. Choices remain. However, they no longer resemble choices reasoned by example. Instead, ideally, they rest on choices of purpose much like those discussed in Chapter IV. The purposes of stare decisis, as we have seen, seek to promote legal stability, to protect honest reliance, to preserve efficient judicial administration, to maintain similar treatment of persons similarly situated, and to promote public confidence in courts. The judge must always decide whether adherence to a precedent will accomplish any of these values.

Chapters II and IV detailed the theory of stare decisis. We may here proceed directed to illustrations of the same theory in the common law context.

First Illustration:
Rightly Adhering to Precedent Because
the Need for Stability and Reliance Are Present

The law of tort, especially the law of negligence, creates enticing moral questions because, almost by definition in the case of negligence, courts apply the law only when it has in fact failed to control how people behave. The negligent driver simply does not plan to have or avoid an accident based on his knowledge of negligence law, even if he has some understanding of it. As a result, negligence law does not, unless the expectations expressed in an insurance contract are thwarted, confront a judge with the problem of upsetting someone's expectations if he changes the law. Negligence law defines when someone owes someone else a remedy for a past wrong, and this focus leads inevitably to the moral question of how man ought to relate to his fellow man.

The need for stability in law more often exists with respect to laws that deal with people's business and contractual relations and with their related planning of the use and disposition of their property. Here we may not reach ultimate moral questions so quickly. When plans depend on law, the law's philosophical shortcomings may not justify changing it. We therefore temporarily abandon tort law and turn to one very small problem in a very complicated subject, the law of business contracts.

Contracts, among many other items, are agreements among businessmen that allow them to formalize their buying and selling of each other's goods and services. Plans involving millions or even billions of dollars can rest on such agreements. For example, a construction company specializing in high-rise office buildings may conditionally contract with a supplier of steel to buy steel at a given price in order to know what to bid on a construction project. If the company receives the award, its entire profit margin could disappear if its steel supplier at the last minute insisted on a higher price for the steel.

But what legal rules convert an ordinary agreement—He: "Can you come to dinner at my place at 8:00?" She: "I'd love to! See you then."—into a legally binding contract? In early common law, if a written agreement contained the impression of a promise-making person's seal in wax, then the beneficiary of the promise could hold him to his promise. Men wore signet rings etched with their sign, their seal, with which to impress the wax. The only exception for a time was the king. He sealed the wax on his agreements with the impression of his front teeth. Gradually the use of wax, seals, and front teeth declined, to the point where printing the word "seal" or the letters "L.S." (for the Latin *locus sigilli*) created the contractual tie.

Today, seals do not make agreements legally binding: half

the American states have passed statutes abolishing the seal. But, in many jurisdictions in the past and in some today, when people have sealed their contract (perhaps simply by adding at the end "Seal" or "L.S."), the law has made it very difficult for the contracting parties to dispute it. The law has rendered it difficult if not impossible to argue that the contract has been made fraudulently or to prove that the promisor has already performed the act he promised.

Long after agreements became enforceable in law without a seal, the law preserved some of the special rigidities for those contracts with seals. In one specific example, unlike an unsealed contract, only the person named in a sealed contract could be held to it. When, for example, a buyer seeks to disguise his interest by having another contract for him, using the agent's name but remaining the interested party, he along with the agent may find himself bound, but only if the contract of sale bears no seal. The sealed purchase contract, on the other hand, would only bind the agent named in it, not the interested party.

Businessmen regularly transact business through agents. Sometimes, and this is particularly true in commercial real estate transactions, a businessman will fund another to buy or sell property for him. He will fund the agent but insist that the agent assume all the responsibilities of the contract. The legal name for such a backer is "undisclosed principal." This technique of preserving anonymity is not necessarily unfair to the other side. If someone buys up various lots in an area in order to build a factory in his own name, the owners approached last may insist on a highly inflated price, knowing that if the buyer fails to get the last lot in order to proceed, all his other purchases will become meaningless.

Beginning in the nineteenth century, by both statute and judicial decision, the legal gap between the protections of sealed and unsealed contracts began to narrow. However, in the 1920s, this New York case arose. In a contract under seal, an agent agreed to buy land without naming an undisclosed principal. The seller agreed, but the agent shortly thereafter withdrew from the agreement. The seller, having learned the name of the principal, sued the principal. He asked the judge to order the principal to pay for the land and accept the deed.

The court ruled for the defendant. It noted many New York

precedents limiting the significance of a seal on a contract. Nevertheless it concluded:

> We find no authority for the proposition that a contract under seal may be turned into the simple contract of a person not in any way appearing on its face to be a party to or interested in it,...and we do not feel at liberty to extend the doctrine applied to simple contracts executed by an agent for an unnamed principal so as to embrace this case....
>
> Neither do we find any authority since 1876 in this court for the proposition. *Briggs v. Partridge*[20] has been cited by us many times with no hint of disapproval.... We repeat that we do not feel at liberty to change a rule so well understood and so often enforced. If such a change is to be made it must be by legislative fiat....
>
> ....Thousands of sealed instruments must have been executed in reliance upon the authority of *Briggs v. Partridge*. Many times the seal must have been used for the express purpose of relieving the undisclosed principal from personal liability. It may not be unwise to preserve the distinction for this especial purpose. But whether wise or unwise the distinction now exists.[21]

Any doctrine, stare decisis included, has impact only when it leads to action not likely otherwise. Stare decisis affects judicial choices when, because of judges' commitment to it, they reach decisions they might in general terms think to be poorly constructed law.

In many respects it is inequitable to allow the undisclosed principal to avoid contractual responsibility because of a seal. New York's Justice Crane, who did not participate in the *Crowley* decision, wrote:

> However much the courts in some instances have relaxed the rules of the common law upon this subject, they have adhered very strictly to the principles enunciated in *Briggs* v. *Partridge*, that none but the parties can be held to a sealed instrument.... The state of the law today upon this point is as follows: A principal may be charged upon a written parol executory

---

[20]*Briggs v. Partridge,* 64 N.Y. 357 (1876).
[21]*Crowley v. Lewis,* 239 N.Y. 264 (1925), pp. 265–267.

contract entered into by an agent in his own name within his authority, although the name of the principal does not appear in the instrument and was not disclosed, and the party dealing with the agent supposed that he was acting for himself; and this doctrine obtains a well in respect to contracts which are required to be in writing, as to those where a writing is not essential to their validity. If, however, a seal be put to the instrument, agency cannot be proved nor the real principal held. Thus, if an unsealed contract to sell real estate is signed by the agent in his own name, and the fact that he is acting for another and not for himself appears nowhere upon the face of it, the real principal can always sue and be sued upon the instrument. But if it should happen that the printed letters "L.S." appear after the agent's name, all would be different. The principal could neither sue nor be sued. The absurdity of this is apparent upon the face of the statement, and the danger and pitfall of such a doctrine in business transactions is realized when we pause to consider how many printed forms of agreements have the letters "L.S." stamped upon them, or how easy it is to make the scroll. The numerous instances where the courts have been appealed to for the modification of this rule evidence not only its deep intrenchment in the law but also the restiveness of the Bar in submitting without protest to its application to the facts in hand.[22]

But another justice who joined the *Crowley* opinion, Benjamin Cardozo, later praised the result:

The rule was settled at common law that an undisclosed principal might not be held to liability upon a contract which had been executed under seal. Much of the law as to seals has small relation in society as now organized to present-day realities. The question came up whether we would adhere to the rule that I have mentioned, or hold it to have faded away with the fading significance of seals. The decision was that the old rule would be enforced. Precedents of recent date made departure difficult if *stare decisis* was not to be abandoned altogether, but there were other and deeper grounds of policy. Contracts had been made and transactions closed on the faith

[22]Frederick E. Crane, "The Magic of the Private Seal," 15 *Columbia Law Review* 24 (1915), pp. 34–35.

of the law as it had been theretofore declared. Men had taken title in the names of "dummies," and through them executed deeds and mortgages with the understanding, shared by the covenantees, that liability on the covenant would be confined to the apparent principal. They had done this honestly and without concealment. Something might be said, too, in favor of the social utility of a device by which the liability of the apparent principal could be substituted without elaborate forms for the liability of another back of him who was to reap the profits of the transaction. The law has like devices for limiting liability in other situations, as *e.g.,* in joint stock associations, corporations, and limited partnerships. In any event retrospective change would be unjust. The evil, if it was one, was to be eradicated by statute.[23]

Both Crane and Cardozo are in a sense correct. The rule may work to an unfair advantage, and it is the place of courts, not just legislatures, to minimize unfair advantages in law. However, the court rightly left legal change to the legislature because it understood that many businessmen, without acting unfairly, regularly employed that legal technique in planning their affairs. Judicial action would upset existing plans made by fair men, but the legislature would make law for the future. This difference, not a difference in lawmaking authority, gives the *Crowley* decision its wisdom.

Second Illustration:
Rightly Overruling Because No Need
for Stability or Reliance Exists

Here we return to and further explore the borderland between tort and property. We have seen that the common law distinguished between trespassers and guests, invitees in legal language. Had Carter invited Beck onto Carter's land, Carter would without question have become liable to Beck for injuries he suffered by tripping and falling into the hole Carter negligently left uncovered. The New York Central, had it sponsored a swim-a-thon on the banks of the Harlem, would have been liable for Harvey's death.

---

[23] Benjamin N. Cardozo, *The Paradoxes of Legal Science* (New York: Columbia University Press, 1928), pp. 70–71.

Common law also created a third category, that of licensee, a person who receives permission to use land or whose entry upon property the owner expressly or by implication tolerates. The common law rules of negligence applied equally to trespassers and licensees: The landowner owed no duty to protect the safety of either one.

In the early 1800s, a policeman, Officer Parker, entered a building at night to check suspicious activities. In the gloom he did not see an open and unprotected elevator shaft. He fell, suffered serious injuries, and sued the building's owner, Mr. Barnard, for damages.

In preparing the lawsuit, Parker's attorney obviously confronted the common law rule, stated in many decisions of the courts in Massachusetts, where the accident occurred. His client was a prototypical licensee. Barnard had not invited him onto the premises, but surely Barnard willingly allowed policemen to enter the building to protect his property. Fortunately, the lawyer discovered that Massachusetts had a statute, a criminal statute, imposing a fine and/or jail for any owner of a building whose elevator well was not "protected by a good and substantial railing." Although the statute said nothing about civil liability in tort to those who were injured, Parker's lawyer used the statute to argue that the courts should abandon licensee precedents in such cases.

He argued first that the common law rule denying recovery to licensees was unfair and outdated and that modern notions of one person's obligation to another ought to encompass keeping your property safe for people you want or allow to use it. He urged that, in tort, the main legal question for the court is a moral one: Either Mr. Parker or Mr. Barnard must pay the medical bills for Parker's injuries. Generalizing from this situation, should not the person at fault, the person who could have prevented the injuries in the first place, bear the burden?

Barnard's attorney, of course, had an answer to that question: No. This is simultaneously a problem in property rights, one in which the utility of stare decisis is traditionally recognized. Many property owners decide how to maintain their property and to avoid the expense of eliminating dangers precisely because they do not expect guests to expose themselves to the dangers. It is unfair to Barnard to change the rules. Had he known this rule in advance, he might have arranged for the railing or taken out insurance to cover losses to licensees.

Parker's attorney responded as anticipated: Regardless of the general need for reliance in common law, including such a need regarding the use of property, in this case what Barnard did was a crime. Obviously it cannot be said that the legislature intended Parker to recover, but it can be said that the criminal statute told Barnard to install the railing. Barnard cannot claim he had no duty to erect the railing. He had! Although the criminal statute does not control this civil case, its purpose includes protecting those who enter an unfamiliar building in the dark, a category that certainly includes Officer Parker.

The court agreed with Parker. It said simply:

> The fact that there was a penalty imposed by the statute for neglect of duty in regard to the railing and protection of the elevator well does not exonerate those responsible therefor from such liability....
>
> As a general rule, where an act is enjoined or forbidden under a statutory penalty, and the failure to do the act enjoined or the doing of the act forbidden has contributed to an injury, the party thus in default is liable therefor to the party injured, notwithstanding he may also be subject to a penalty....[24]

The court thus created a new rule. It did so rightly because, given the criminal statute, the excuse for reliance on the older rule diminished.

Third Illustration:
Wrongly Overruling When Stability Is Preferable

Should a court in the future follow the *Parker* decision? Note this subtle but important point. If we assume that the basic rule of *Parker* is correct, then it would not matter even if the *Parker* decision did wrongly upset reliance interests. If we believe that owners should pay for injuries to licensees as a general matter, then we may want to follow precedents that boldly state such a rule, even if, for reliance reasons, the court's boldness was unwise. The new decision becomes law. It undercuts the sup-

---

[24]*Parker v. Barnard*, 135 Mass. 116 (1883), p. 120.

port that honest men have for relying on an outdated rule. Similarly, if the *Crowley* court had boldly done away with the ability of businessmen to hide their interests in sealed contracts, we would want courts to follow the decision in the future if we believed that seals should be thus abandoned.

Unfortunately, the Massachusetts courts chose not to follow *Parker*. Instead, they took the approach, condemned in Chapter IV, of hiding behind legislative skirts. Since criminal statutes do not expressly create civil liability, they do not alter common law duties. Thus, in 1936, a police officer injured much in the same manner as Parker failed to recover. The court said:

> Moreover, in this Commonwealth, contrary to the rule prevailing in many jurisdictions, violation of a criminal statute of this general class does not ordinarily in and of itself, independently of common law duties, give rise to a civil cause of action. Such a statute has that effect only when by its express terms or by clear implication that appears to have been the legislative intent. That there was no such intent as to one of the very statutes here involved was decided in *Palmigiani v. D'Argenio*, 234 Mass. 434, and again with full discussion in *Garland v. Stetson*, 292 Mass. 95, 100, a case very similar to this. See also *Richardson v. Whittier*, 265 Mass. 478. In view of these cases, so far as there is in *Parker v. Barnard*, 135 Mass. 116, anything inconsistent with what is now decided, we are unable to follow it.[25]

Perhaps by 1936 this result was justified. After all, one justification for stare decisis is its prompting of courts to treat similarly situated people similarly. If all other licensees (or, for that matter, any person claiming to recover for injuries sustained from another's violation of a criminal law) failed to recover with the one exception of policemen who fell down elevator shafts, the law would not treat similarly situated people similarly. Hence the *Wynn* decision, though weak in its deference to nonexistent legislative intent, is not the main problem. Its predecessors that refused to adhere to the sensible development of *Parker* did the damage.

But perhaps the *Wynn* decision itself was not justified. At

[25] *Wynn v. Sullivan*, 294 Mass. 562 (1936), p. 566.

least the officer in that case must have felt he didn't receive the treatment that the similarly situated Officer Parker had received. The *Wynn* argument may, however, fail for more substantial reasons. If common law changes and grows, admittedly erratically over time, might not a court, mindful that the old law was inadequate, at least add an incremental move in the right direction? It could do so simply by saying, "We believe *Parker* rightly decided. Without attempting to change the entire relationship of owners and licensees in tort, and without adopting negligence *per se* in all situations, we believe the case for adherence in this instance is compelling." Might not such a result encourage other related changes in law over time? To do so would hardly violate the spirit of the common law tradition.

Fourth Illustration:
Wrongly Adhering to Precedent When
Stability Is Unnecessary

I hope I have not left the impression that courts should always follow precedents in business, contract, and property matters but never in the case of negligence. It is not that simple. Tort law can, for example, influence a person's decision to insure against loss. In this final illustration, however, let us look at a property problem in which a court, in a thoughtless opinion, followed precedent when the reasons for stare decisis did not support adherence.

The case involved a section of the will of a New Jersey resident. In it the deceased, Rosa E. Green, stated: "I give and bequeath unto my husband, William L. Green all the money which I have on deposit at the Paterson Savings and Trust Company, Paterson, New Jersey, however, any money which is in the said account at the time of my said husband's death, the said sum shall be held by my niece, Catherine King Fox, absolutely and forever." William died without removing the money.

Naturally Ms. Fox attempted to withdraw the money from the bank. However, heirs of William claimed that the conditional gift to Ms. Fox was invalid. Lawyers for the heirs cited many New Jersey precedents stating that an unconditional

bequest in a will, like the one to William, gave him unconditional ownership. Any conditional gift of the same property
would have to be invalid; otherwise, the first gift would not be
absolute. William's heirs won. The court said:

> Appellants ask this Court to explicitly and expressly overrule
> the long established law of this state. This we decline to do.
> Such action would be fraught with great danger in this type of
> case where titles to property, held by bequests and devises, are
> involved. A change of the established law by judicial decision
> is retrospective. It makes the law at the time of prior decisions
> as it is declared in the last decision, as to all transactions that
> can be reached by it. On the other hand a change in the settled
> law by statute is prospective only.[26]

Think briefly about this result in terms of the reasons for
stare decisis. For whom should this law remain stable? Who
could plan on the basis of this rule? Certainly not Rosa. She
intended to make a conditional gift to Catherine but failed.
William, if he wanted the money, had only to withdraw it. For
William to plan, we must suppose some reasoning like this: "I
am going to die. I don't want the money, but I don't want
Catherine to obtain the money, either. I could prevent her from
receiving it by depositing it in another bank, but, since the
clause is invalid, I'll leave it there." Such planning is possible,
but is it probable? Is it the sort of planning that the law needs to
preserve at the expense of carrying out the wishes of the deceased? Many people do not know rules of law of this kind. Is it
not more probable that William also intended the money to go to
Catherine? Is it plausible that, once William died leaving the
money in the bank, Catherine made plans on the assumption
that she did have the money?

Consider the other purposes of stare decisis: Is the image of
justice improved by defeating Rosa's wishes? How important is
equality of treatment in this kind of situation? How important
is it to say that because courts have refused to carry out the wishes
of past testators (the creators of wills) they must treat current
testators in the same way for equality's sake?

Finally, efficiency in the judicial process does matter.

[26]*Fox v. Snow*, 6 N.J. 12 (1950), p. 14.

Judges should not have to question the wisdom of every point of law that arises, but that hardly means they can never do so.

One judge disagreed with the majority in *Fox*. Chief Justice Vanderbilt's dissent is one of the finest essays from the bench on the subject of stare decisis. It provides a fitting summary of this section:

VANDERBILT, C.J. (dissenting):
I am constrained to dissent from the views of the majority of the court, first, because they apply to the case a technical rule of law to defeat the plain intent of the testatrix without serving any public policy whatever in so doing and, secondly—and this seems to me to be even more important—because their opinion involves a view of the judicial process, which, if it had been followed consistently in the past, would have checked irrevocably centuries ago the growth of the common law to meet changing conditions and which, if pursued now, will spell the ultimate ossification and death of the common law by depriving it of one of its most essential attributes—its inherent capacity constantly to renew its vitality and usefulness by adapting itself gradually and piecemeal to meeting the demonstrated needs of the times.…

By the words in the third paragraph, "any money which is in said account at the time of my said husband's death, the said sum shall be held by my niece, Catherine King Fox, absolutely and forever," the testatrix beyond any doubt intended that her husband could use up the bank account but that if he did not, the plaintiff should take what was left of it on his death. To hold otherwise is to proceed on the untenable assumption that the quoted words are meaningless and to ignore the elementary principle that the provisions of a will are not to be construed as meaningless except on the failure of every attempt to render them effective.… This principle is an integral part of the most fundamental rule of testamentary construction, *i.e.,* the duty of the court is to ascertain what the intent of the testator was and, then, having ascertained it, to give it effect.…

The opinion of the majority of the court, like every other decision in this State on the subject, makes no attempt to justify the rule it perpetuates either in reason or on grounds of public policy. Despite the deleterious effects of the rule and the lack of any sound principle to support it, the majority maintains that it should not be overthrown, because it has been the long established law of this State and because overruling it"would be fraught with great danger in this type of case where titles to property, held by bequests and devises, are involved" by reason of the retroactive effect of all judicial decisions. This view, if it had been consistently applied in the past, would have prevented any change whatever in property law by judicial decisions. There would have been *e.g.*, no rule against perpetuities, no restraints on the alienation of property, no right to redeem mortgaged premises, no foreclosure of the equity of redemption, and so on endlessly. Every change in the law by judicial decision necessarily creates rights in one party to the litigation and imposes corresponding duties on the other party. This is the process by which the law grows and adjusts itself to the changing needs of the times.

The process is necessarily used not only to create new rights and corresponding duties but, where necessary, to strike down old ones. *Cessante ratione legis, cessat et ipsa lex* (the reason for a law ceasing, the law itself ceases) is one of the most ancient maxims known to our law and it is constantly followed by our courts. Of this maxim it was said in *Beardsley v. City of Hartford*, 50 Conn. 529, 47 *Am. Rep.* 677, 682 (1883), "This means that no law can survive the reason on which it is founded. It needs no statute to change it; it abrogates itself." The same thought was enunciated by Lord Coke in *Milborn's Case*, 7 *Coke* 7a (K.B. 1609): "*Ratio legis est anima legis, et mutata legis ratione, mutatur ex lex*" (the reason for a law is the soul of the law, and if the reason for a law has changed, the law is changed). "It is revolting," says Mr. Justice Holmes, "to have no better reason for a rule of law than that so it was laid down in the time of Henry IV. It is still more revolting if the grounds upon which it was laid down have vanished long since, and the rule simply persists from blind imitation of the past," and "To rest upon a formula is a slumber that, prolonged, means death." *Collected Legal Papers* (1920) 187, 306. Holdsworth, in commenting on this quotation from Mr. Justice Holmes, has described how the Anglo-American system of case law has enabled "the judges, within fairly wide limits, to apply to old precedents a process of selection and rejection which brings the law into conformity with modern conditions." "This process of selection and rejection," he says, "has been applied to the law laid down in the Year Books; and generally the rules there laid down, which are still part of our modern law, have survived because they suit modern needs."

Essays in Law and History (1946) 161, 162. It is as important to the growth of the law that it should have the inherent power to cast off outmoded or erroneous rules of law as that it have the capacity for developing new doctrines suited to the needs of the times. The only difference between these two phases of the same process is that the one proceeds almost automatically out of sheer necessity and often without any open admission that new law is being created, while the other involves an open recognition of past mistakes or an express repudiation of a rule once sound but now outmoded. Unfortunately, it is not considered in good judicial taste to overrule erroneous or outworn doctrines *sub silentio*.

To hold, as the majority opinion implies, that the only way to overcome the unfortunate rule of law that plagues us here is by legislation, is to put the common law in a self-imposed straitjacket. Such a theory, if followed consistently, would inevitably lead to the ultimate codification of all of our law for sheer lack of capacity in the courts to adapt the law to the needs of the living present. The doctrine of *stare decisis* neither renders the courts impotent to correct their past errors nor requires them to adhere blindly to rules that have lost their reason for being. The common law would be sapped of its life blood if *stare decisis* were to become a god instead of a guide. The doctrine when properly applied operates only to control change, not to prevent it. As Mr. Justice Cardozo has put it, "Few rules in our time are so well established that they may not be called upon any day to justify their existence as means adapted to an end. If they do not function they are diseased,... they must not propagate their kind. Sometimes they are cut out and extirpated altogether. Sometimes they are left with the shadow of continued life, but sterilized, truncated, impotent for harm." *Nature of the Judicial Process* (1921) 98. All lawyers as well as laymen have a perfectly natural longing to think of the law as being as steadfast and immutable as the everlasting hills, but when we face the realities, we must agree with Dean Pound when he says, "Law must be stable, and yet it cannot stand still," *Interpretations of Legal History* (1923) I, and with Professor Williston when he tells us, "Uniform decisions of 300 years on a particular question may, and sometimes have been overthrown in a day, and the single decision at the end of the series may establish a rule of law at variance with all that has gone before." *Some Modern Tendencies in the Law* (1929) 125....

Particularly in the realm of testamentary construction should the courts feel free to depart from precedent when the dictates of justice and reason demand it. Even Chancellor Kent was of this opinion: "Though we are not to disregard the authority of decisions, even as to the interpretation of wills, yet it is certain that the construction of them is so much governed by the language, arrangement, and circumstances of each particular instrument, which is usually very unskillfully and very incoherently drawn, that adjudged cases become of less authority, and are of more hazardous application, than decisions upon any other branch of the law." 4 *Commentaries on American Law* 535. "Blind adherence to precedent as respects the meaning of a particular phrase is fraught with peril to the testamentary design, for, as said, intention is to be gathered from the instrument as a whole, and it rarely happens that the wills are substantially alike." *National State Bank of Newark v. Stewart*, 135 N.J. Eq. 603, 605 (1944).... Even in England where the doctrine of the judicial infallibility of the House of Lords has prevailed for a century, we find Lord Chancellor Simon declaring in the case of *Perrin v. Morgan* (1943) 1 All E.R. 187, 194, when an ancient and well established rule of testamentary construction was urged upon the court: "The present question is not, in my opinion, one in which this House is required on the ground of public interest to maintain a rule which has been constantly applied but which it is convinced is erroneous. It is far more important to promote the correct construction of future wills in this respect than to preserve consistency in misinterpretation."

The dangers that the majority fear, it is submitted, are more apparent than real. The doctrine of *stare decisis* tends to produce certainty in our law, but it is important to realize that certainty *per se* is but a means to an end, and not an end in itself. Certainty is desirable only insofar as it operates to produce the maximum good and the minimum harm and thereby to advance justice. The courts have been reluctant to overthrow established rules when property rights are involved for the simple reason that persons in arranging their affairs have relied upon the rules as established, though outmoded or erroneous, and so to abandon them would result sometimes in greater harm than to observe them. The question whether the doctrine of *stare decisis* should be adhered to in such cases is always a choice between relative evils. When it appears that the evil resulting from a continuation of the accepted rule must be productive of greater mischief to the community than can possibly ensue from disregarding the previous adjudications on the subject, courts have frequently and wisely departed from precedent, 14 Am. Jur., Courts, Section 126.

What then, are the relative evils in the instant case? First, we should consider the evils that will result from a perpetuation of the rule here involved. It has already been demonstrated that the rule, in each and every instance in which it is applied, results in a complete frustration of the legitimate intention of the testator. It can only operate to take property from one to whom the testator intended to give it and to bestow it upon another....

Having considered the evils flowing from continuing to follow the rule, let us now inquire into the evils, if any, which might result from its rejection. It is pertinent at this point to recall the words of Mr. Justice Cardozo minimizing the effect of overruling a decision: "The picture of the bewildered litigant lured into a course of action by the false light of a decision, only to meet ruin when the light is extinguished and the decision is overruled, is for the most part a figment of excited brains." *The Nature of the Judicial Process* (1921) 122 [sic.] The rule in question by its very nature is never relied upon by those who are seeking to make a testamentary disposition of their property, for if the rule were known to a person at the time of the drawing of his will, its operation would and could be guarded against by the choice of words appropriate to accomplish the result desired. This rule is truly subversive of the testator's intent. It is relied upon only after the testator's decease by those who seek, solely on the basis of its technical and arbitrary requirements, to profit from the testator's ignorance and to take his property contrary to his expressed desires. Certainly it is not unjust or inequitable to deny such persons resort to this rule....[27]

THE COMMON LAW TRADITION TODAY

Chief Justice Vanderbilt's dissent in *Fox* does more than state a sound theory of stare decisis. It also describes the essence of the common law tradition. Judicial choices continue to change

[27] *Fox v. Snow*, pp. 14–15, 21–27.

common law today. Indeed, only within the past 100 years have judges recognized the inevitability and desirability of choice and change. Thus the full political consequences of choice and change have just come sharply into focus.

By this I mean that understanding the nature of judicial choice has more than academic consequences in law. Common law has in the past changed even when judges *believed* they merely chose the one applicable statute or line of precedents that "correctly" resolved the conflict before them. When judges *think* they solve problems by mechanically finding the one right solution from the past, the slow and erratic developments in law do not occur deliberately. Judges do not grapple with moral and economic aspects of policy choices when judges do not believe they choose policies.

But, when the point of view shifts, when judges begin believing they *do* make policy choices, this consciousness changes the kind and quality of law that judges make in several ways.

The first of these changes we have already studied and condemned. It occurs when judges throw up their hands and say, "In a democracy only the legislature can make new law, not the courts. We must, therefore, deliberately avoid making changes." These decisions, in spite of themselves, do make changes, of course, just as the *Fox* decision, by rejecting Vanderbilt's powerful arguments, more deeply imbedded a mechanical view of stare decisis as well as the rule against conditional gifts, in New Jersey's law.

A second modern view of the consequences of acknowledged judicial discretion can avoid this evil. Judges, acknowledging that they can and do make law, pay closer attention, as we are about to see, to the facts and values that help them (and us) decide that some policy choices are wiser than others. Modern decisions do tend to be less mechanistic and more concerned with the consequences for the future of various alternative choices of policy. This quality, after all, gave the *Lyman* case its modern flavor.

There is, however, a third consequence of this shift in viewpoint, one that raises today's most challenging unsolved problem in legal reasoning. Judges may dramatically increase the speed of change and deliberately broaden the lengths of the legal jumps they take from old law to new. When judges realize they rightly possess authority to remake common law, they may overreact and enact what *they* believe are ideal legal solutions without properly honoring competing needs for stability. Similarly, they may ignore the possibility that, while both courts and legislatures share authority to make law, they do not necessarily possess identical institutional characteristics for making wise law.

The problem is so central to reasoning in constitutional law that a thorough canvass of the "judicial limits" territory must be postponed until the following chapter, which deals with reasoning in constitutional interpretation. This problem does, however, arise in common law (and statutory) interpretation.

In this perspective, consider the next case. It illustrates deliberate lawmaking. It exemplifies a dramatic expansion of common law, and it faces squarely the double problem of determining whether a given policy is wise and whether the courts were the wise place to make it. The case, *Tarasoff v. Regents of the University of California,* takes the law of negligence on a substantial jump outward.[28]

Tatiana Tarsoff spent the summer of 1969 in Brazil. She had, with her parents' consent and assistance, left the United States, in part, to escape the almost fanatical affections of one Prosenjit Poddar. During her absence Poddar kept his contact alive. He persuaded Tatiana's brother to share an apartment with him near Tatiana's home in Berkeley, California.

Tatiana returned from Brazil in October. On October 27, 1969, Poddar killed her.

In due course, Tatiana's parents learned that Poddar had, during the summer, received psychological therapy on an out-patient basis from Cowell Memorial Hospital at the University of California, Berkeley. Their further investigation uncovered these facts:

- On August 20, 1969, Poddar told his therapist, Dr. Moore, that he planned to kill his girlfriend when she returned from Brazil.

---

[28] *Tarasoff v. Regents of the University of California,* 551 P.2d 334 (1976).

- When Poddar left, Dr. Moore felt Poddar should be committed for psychiatric examination in a mental hospital. He urgently consulted two of his colleagues at Cowell. They concurred.
- Moore then told two campus police officers that he would request commitment of Poddar. He followed up with a letter of request to the campus police chief.
- Three officers, in fact, took Poddar into custody. Poddar promised them he would leave Tatiana alone in the future. The officers believed Poddar was rational and released him.
- After, and presumably in part because the officers released Poddar, Dr. Moore's supervisor, Dr. Powelson, asked the police to return Moore's letter. Dr. Powelson also ordered destroyed all written evidence of the affair and prohibited any further action to commit Poddar for examination or observation.
- At no point did any members of the hospital staff or the campus police attempt to notify Tatiana, her brother, or her parents of Poddar's threat.
- The staff could easily have determined Tatiana's identity as well as her location and that of her family.

The Tarasoffs sued the doctors, the officers, and the university's board of regents, claiming damages for the loss of their daughter. Among other charges, they alleged that "defendants negligently permitted Poddar to be released from police custody without 'notifying the parents of Tatiana Tarasoff that their daughter was in grave danger from Prosenjit Poddar.'"[29] They claimed, in other words, that the defendants had a duty to use reasonable care to protect Tatiana.

The California Supreme Court upheld the legality of this claim, but only against the regents and the doctors. Reasoning by example played a major part in its result. The court cited precedents from California and elsewhere holding a doctor liable for the damage caused by illness contracted by people in contact with his patient *if* the doctor negligently failed to diagnose the disease as contagious and to isolate the patient. It

[29] Ibid., p. 341.

also cited a case holding a doctor liable for damages where, following his negligent refusal to admit a mental patient to a hospital, the mental patient assaulted the plaintiff.

The directly relevant case law in California, however, imposed a duty only where the defendant already assumed some responsibility for the victim. If, for example, a mental hospital failed negligently to protect one patient from another's violence, the hospital became liable. In California, no law extended the duty further.

Using fact freedom, however, the court ignored the distinction. It said, "[W]e do not think that the duty should logically be constricted to such situations."[30] Let us review the majority's reasons for the conclusion.

The majority first stated a general framework for determining the existence or absence of a duty, a statement amply supported by recent California precedents. Note above all how different this statement is from earlier mechanical statements like "duty to invitees but no duty to trespassers or licensees." The court, quoting precedents, said the existence of a duty depends:

> only upon the "balancing of a number of considerations"; major ones "are the foreseeability of harm to the plaintiff, the degree of certainty that the plaintiff suffered injury, the closeness of the connection between the defendant's conduct and the injury suffered, the moral blame attached to the defendant's conduct, the policy of preventing future harm, the extent of the burden to the defendant and consequences to the community of imposing a duty to exercise care with resulting liability for breach, and the availability, cost and prevalence of insurance for the risk involved."
>
> The most important of these considerations in establishing duty is foreseeability. As a general principle, a "defendant owes a duty of care to all persons who are foreseeably endangered by his conduct, with respect to all risks which make the conduct unreasonably dangerous."[31]

Having said this much the majority then noted that at common law a duty to warn of foreseeable harm done by a

---

[30] Ibid., p. 344.
[31] Ibid., p. 342.

dangerous person existed only when the defendant had a "special relationship" with either the source of danger or the potential victim. The court admitted that the doctors had no special relationship to Tatiana, but it asserted that because they did have such a relationship to Poddar, they therefore owed Tatiana a duty of care.

The court cited no convincing precedent or other authority for this expansion of law, but that did not seem to bother it. The court did pay attention to the arguments sustaining and attacking the practical wisdom and effect of the new policy.

The court had to deal first with the possibility that the harm was not foreseeable in the first place. The issue was made even more difficult because only a few years earlier the court had based an important mental health ruling on the fact that psychological and psychiatric predictions of future behavior are notoriously inaccurate.[32] To this the court responded:

> The role of the psychiatrist, who is indeed a practitioner of medicine, and that of the psychologist who performs an allied function, are like that of the physician who must conform to the standards of the profession and who must often make diagnoses and predictions based upon such evaluations. Thus the judgment of the therapist in diagnosing emotional disorders and in predicting whether a patient presents a serious danger of violence is comparable to the judgment which doctors and professionals must regularly render under accepted rules of responsibility.
>
> We recognize the difficulty that a therapist encounters in attempting to forecast whether a patient presents a serious danger of violence. Obviously we do not require that the therapist, in making that determination, render a perfect performance; the therapist need only exercise "that reasonable degree of skill, knowledge, and care ordinarily possessed and exercised by members of [that professional specialty] under similar circumstances." (*Bardessono v. Michels* (1970) 3 Cal.3d 780, 788...) Within the broad range of reasonable practice and treatment in which professional opinion and judgment may

---

[32] In this particular case, *People v. Burnick,* 14 Cal. 3rd 306 (1975), the court held that a person could be committed to an institution for mentally disturbed sex offenders only after proof at trial beyond reasonable doubt that the defendant was, in fact, likely to repeat the offense.

differ, the therapist is free to exercise his or her own best judgment without liability; proof, aided by hindsight, that he or she judged wrongly is insufficient to establish negligence.

In the instant case, however, the pleadings do not raise any question as to failure of defendant therapists to predict that Poddar presented a serious danger of violence. On the contrary, the present complaints allege that defendant therapists did in fact predict that Poddar would kill, but were negligent in failing to warn.[33]

The court then turned to the most complex policy issue of all: Will imposition of the duty to warn discourage patients from seeking the psychiatric help they need, thus preventing not only their own improvement but perhaps increasing the actual incidence of violent harm to others because people don't get help? The court insisted that such a prediction is entirely speculative. It noted that both the California code of evidence and the Principles of Medical Ethics of the American Medical Association permit a doctor to reveal information about a dangerous person if doing so could protect the patient, other individuals, or the community. The court concluded that

the public policy favoring protection of the confidential character of patient-psychotherapist communications must yield to the extent to which disclosure is essential to avert danger to others. The protective privilege ends where the public peril begins.

Our current crowded and computerized society compels the interdependence of its members. In this risk-infested society we can hardly tolerate the further exposure to danger that would result from a concealed knowledge of the therapist that his patient was lethal. If the exercise of reasonable care to protect the threatened victim requires the therapist to warn the endangered party or those who can reasonably be expected to notify him, we see no sufficient societal interest that would protect and justify concealment. The containment of such risks lies in the public interest.[34]

Backed by powerful opposition communicated to the court in an amicus ("friend of the court") brief from the American

[33] *Tarasoff v. Regents,* p. 345.
[34] Ibid., pp. 347–348.

Psychiatric Association, Justice William Clark heatedly disputed the court's policy conclusion.[35] He began by noting that a California statute *prohibits* the release of "all" information about a patient once a person authorized to begin commitment proceedings does so. The majority had avoided that issue by insisting that the pleadings in the case did not state that Dr. Moore was so authorized. Clark insisted he was and further argued that the purpose of the statute applied clearly in the *Tarasoff* case. "The Legislature," he wrote, "obviously is more capable than is this court to investigate, debate, and weigh potential harm through disclosure against the risk of public harm by nondisclosure. We should defer to its judgment."[36]

Clark then turned to common law analysis itself:

Generally, a person owes no duty to control the conduct of another.... Exceptions are recognized only in limited situations where (1) a special relationship exists between the defendant and injured party, or (2) a special relationship exists between defendant and the active wrongdoer, imposing a duty on defendant to control the wrongdoer's conduct. The majority does not contend the first exception is appropriate to this case.

Policy generally determines duty.... Principal policy considerations include foreseeability of harm, certainty of the plaintiff's injury, proximity of the defendant's conduct to the plaintiff's injury, moral blame attributable to defendant's conduct, prevention of future harm, burden on the defendant, and consequences to the community....

Overwhelming policy considerations weigh against imposing a duty on psychotherapists to warn a potential victim against harm. While offering virtually no benefit to society, such a duty will frustrate psychiatric treatment, invade fundamental patient rights and increase violence.

The importance of psychiatric treatment and its need for confidentiality have been recognized by this court. (*In re Lifschutz* (1970) 2 Cal.3d 415, 421–422, 85 *Cal. Rptr.* 829, 467 P.2d 557.) "It is clearly recognized that the very practice of

---

[35] As of this writing in 1984, William Clark is U.S. Secretary of the Interior, replacing James Watt. He formerly served as National Security Advisor to President Ronald Reagan.

[36] Ibid., p. 358.

psychiatry vitally depends upon the reputation in the
community that the psychiatrist will not tell." (Slovenko,
Psychiatry and a Second Look at the Medical Privilege (1960) 6
Wayne L.Rev. 175, 188.)

Assurance of confidentiality is important for three
reasons....

First, without substantial assurance of confidentiality,
those requiring treatment will be deterred from seeking
assistance. (See Sen. Judiciary Com. comment accompanying
Sec. 1014 of Evid.Code; Slovenko, *supra*, 6 Wayne L.Rev. 175,
187–188; Goldstein & Katz, *Psychiatrist-Patient Privilege: The
GAP Proposal and the Connecticut Statute* (1962) 36 Conn.Bar
J. 175, 178.) It remains an unfortunate fact in our society that
people seeking psychiatric guidance tend to become
stigmatized. Apprehension of such stigma—apparently
increased by the propensity of people considering treatment to
see themselves in the worst possible light—creates a well-
recognized reluctance to seek aid. (Fisher, *The
Psychotherapeutic Professions and the Law of Privileged
Communications* (1964) 10 Wayne L.Rev. 609, 617; Slovenko,
supra, 6 Wayne L.Rev. 175, 188; see also Rappeport,
Psychiatrist-Patient Privilege (1963) 23 Md.L.J. 39, 46–47.)
This reluctance is alleviated by the psychiatrist's assurance of
confidentiality....

Second, the guarantee of confidentiality is essential in
eliciting the full disclosure necessary for effective treatment.
(*In re Lifschutz, supra*, 2 Cal.3d 415, 431, 85 Cal.Rptr. 829, 467
P.2d 557; *Taylor v. United States* (1955), 95 U.S. App.D.C. 373,
222 F.2d 398, 401; Goldstein & Katz, *supra*, 36 Conn.Bar J. 175,
178; Heller, *Some Comments to Lawyers on the Practice of
Psychiatry* (1957) 30 Temp.L.Q. 401; Guttmacher & Weihofen,
Privileged Communications between Psychiatrist and Patient
(1952) 28 Ind.L.J. 32, 34.* The psychiatric patient approaches
treatment with conscious and unconscious inhibitions against
revealing his innermost thoughts. "Every person, however
well-motivated, has to overcome resistances to therapeutic
exploration. These resistances seek support from every possible

---

*One survey indicated that five of every seven people interviewed said they
would be less likely to make full disclosure to a psychiatrist in the absence of
assurance of confidentiality. (See Comment, *Functional Overlap Between the
Lawyer and Other Professionals: Its Implications for the Doctrine of Privileged
Communications* (1962) 71 Yale L.J. 1226, 1255). [Asterisk note in original.]

source and the possibility of disclosure would easily be employed in the service of resistance." (Goldstein & Katz, *supra*, 36 Conn. Bar J. 175, 179; see also, 118 Am.J.Psych 734, 735.) Until a patient can trust his psychiatrist not to violate their confidential relationship, "the unconscious psychological control mechanism of repression will prevent the recall of past experiences." (Butler, *Psychotherapy and Griswold: Is Confidentiality a Privilege or a Right?* (1971) 3 Conn. L.Rev. 599, 604)....

Third, even if the patient fully discloses his thoughts, assurance that the confidential relationship will not be breached is necessary to maintain his trust in his psychiatrist— the very means by which treatment is effected. "[T]he essence of much psychotherapy is the contribution of trust in the external world and ultimately in the self, modelled upon the trusting relationship established during therapy" (Dawidoff, *The Malpractice of Psychiatrists*, 1966 Duke L.J. 696, 704). Patients will be helped only if they can form a trusting relationship with the psychiatrist. (*Id.* at 704, fn. 34; Burham, *Separation Anxiety* (1965) 13 Arch.Gen. Psychiatry 346, 356; Heller, *supra*, 30 Temp. L.Q. 401, 406.) All authorities appear to agree that if the trust relationship cannot be developed because of collusive communication between the psychiatrist and others, treatment will be frustrated. (See, e.g., Slovenko (1973) *Psychiatry and Law*, p. 61; Cross, *Privileged Communications between Participants in Group Psychotherapy* (1970) Law and the Social Order, 191, 199....

Given the importance of confidentiality to the practice of psychiatry, it becomes clear the duty to warn imposed by the majority will cripple the use and effectiveness of psychiatry. Many people, potentially violent—yet susceptible to treatment—will be deterred from seeking it; those seeking it will be inhibited from making revelations necessary to effective treatment; and, forcing the psychiatrist to violate the patient's trust will destroy the interpersonal relationship by which treatment is effected.[37]

Is Justice Clark correct? Should the court defer here to the legislature's fact-finding abilities? Or is he only using the time-worn argument that legislatures, not courts, should make pol-

---

[37] Ibid., pp. 358–360.

icy? A complete framework for an answer must wait until the next chapter. Consider here only two possibilities. First, the court did in fact hear a wide variety of points of view on the policy questions. The American Psychiatric Association did file an amicus brief. Interest groups lobby courts much as they do legislatures. Is there any reason to believe that a legislature facing this issue would hear substantially more or different or better policy arguments? Does not Justice Clark's dissent tend to undercut his position, in the sense that he appears to have digested and incorporated into his thinking a wide range of literature bearing on the subject? Second, if Clark's analysis is so compellingly correct, nothing in the common law prevents the California legislature from amending the statute Clark cites to include within its scope the type of situation that occurred in *Tarasoff*.

Any final analysis of this case must not lose sight of an important technical element in *Tarasoff*. The Supreme Court of California did not hold that the doctors and the board of regents were liable to the Tarasoffs. It held only that they might be if a full trial on the facts showed that the doctors had not used reasonable care in assessing the likelihood that Poddar would carry out his threat. In this case the trial judge did not allow a trial at all. The trial judge had ruled that the law did not permit the Tarasoffs to recover even if all their allegations were true. It is this interpretation of law that the California Supreme court here reversed. Thus the case comes down to this: If a doctor has reason to believe the threat is a serious and real one, then he must warn the victim. It does not mean he must tell all.

How frequently do you think people who need psychiatric help will reason this way: "I need psychiatric help. I think I might kill someone. However, I've read about *Tarasoff* and I know that if I tell the psychiatrist the name of the person I might kill, the psychiatrist, if he or she thinks I really mean it, will warn the person whose killing I'm trying to avoid by seeking help. Therefore I won't seek help." Do you believe the psychiatric profession will suffer a setback because people will reason that way?

There are two more interesting points in the *Tarasoff* case. One is the reliance of courts on law review articles for assistance in legal reasoning. I have not included the California court's footnotes in my quotations. A complete reading of this fascinating case will, however, reveal that the court relied very heavily on the analysis of this problem published in 1974 in the *California Law Review*.[38] The authors wrote the article precisely because they knew of the Tarasoff killing and recognized that it raised important legal questions. In doing so, they effectively wrote the majority's opinion.

Second, among the many amicus parties noted at the beginning of the *Tarasoff* opinion you will see the name Melanie Bellah. In October 1977, the Associated Press wire carried the following story:[39]

SUICIDE WARNING NOT REQUIRED

The state Court of Appeal has ruled that a psychiatrist cannot be sued for failing to warn parents of their 18-year-old daughter's potential for suicide.

The court also ruled that the physician was not bound legally to restrain the young woman from killing herself.

Melanie and Robert Bellah sought unspecified damages from Berkeley psychiatrist Dr. Daniel Greenson in the suicide death of their daughter, Tammy, on April 12, 1973.

Tammy, a freshman at the University of California at Berkeley, had been under the care of the doctor, and the court said it appeared Greenson knew she was disposed to suicide.

When Tammy died, her parents were temporarily living in New Jersey and claimed they had no personal contact with her and were unaware of her suicidal tendencies.

The suit, filed two years later, alleged the doctor had failed to take measures to prevent Tammy's suicide and failed to warn others of her true condition.

The appeal court noted the California Supreme Court's 1976 *Tarasoff* ruling that in certain circumstances a therapist

---

[38] John G. Fleming and Bruce Maximov, "The Patient or His Victim: The Therapist's Dilemma," 62 *California Law Review* 1025 (1974). One measure of freedom in the United States is surely that the law review of a state-run school can, without state interference, publish an article concluding that the very school ought to be found legally liable.

[39] *The Atlanta Constitution*, 7 October, 1977, p. 14-B.

had a duty to warn others when a patient was likely to harm another.

"The [state Supreme] court did not hold that such disclosure was required where the danger presented was that of self-inflicted harm or suicide or where the danger consisted of a likelihood of property damage," said the appeal court.

Note that in the *Bellah* case the physician's own patient died, but the court held that no law imposed potential liability on the doctor. On the other hand, in *Tarasoff*, a third party died and yet the court did impose a legal obligation on the physician. Why this apparent anomaly? Could it be that Tammy Bellah's condition might have worsened if her parents, when notified of her problem, had then intruded into the therapeutic efforts of the doctor? Common law fact freedom marches on.

SUMMARY

- What is the historical origin of common law?
- Who was Henri de Bracton? How did his work over 700 years ago help produce the modern emphasis on reasoning by example in common law?
- Describe the recent transition from natural law to reasoning by example, and hence acknowledged and accepted judicial law-making today.
- Why don't general principles such as the rules of negligence and battery described in this chapter clearly resolve all legal problems of that type?
- How and why do the beliefs and values of individual judges influence the growth of law?
- What is the fatal flaw in Professor Goodhart's famous method for finding the *ratio decidendi* (the principle) of a case?
- How do legal principles move into common law and then out again? In analyzing reasoning in common law, why is it not sufficient to trace the rise and fall of such principles?
- How do the five justifications for stare decisis articulated in Chapter II apply to the cases described in this chapter?
- If judicial lawmaking is part of the common law tradition, are there any reasons why, in modern American political culture, judges should now discard that tradition and refuse to make new common law when the legislature has created no law of its own? Why not?

ILLUSTRATIVE CASE

Like *Tarasoff,* this case went to the court of appeals on a question of law before any trial occurred to test the actual facts. Thus the court's holding here does not mean that defendant O'Daniels is liable to the plaintiff for damages. In a telephone conversation with Judge Andreen in July of 1983, I learned that the defendants had chosen not to appeal this ruling to the California Supreme Court.

Soldano v. O'Daniels
California Court of Appeals, Fifth District
190 *California Reporter* 310 (1983)

ANDREEN, Associate Justice.

Does a business establishment incur liability for wrongful death if it denies use of its telephone to a good samaritan who explains an emergency situation occurring without and wishes to call the police?....

Both briefs on appeal adopt the defense averments:

"This action arises out of a shooting death occurring on August 9, 1977. Plaintiff's father [Darrell Soldano] was shot and killed by one Rudolph Villanueva on that date at defendant's Happy Jack's Saloon. This defendant owns and operates the Circle Inn which is an eating establishment located across the street from Happy Jack's. Plaintiff's second cause of action against this defendant is one for negligence.

"Plaintiff alleges that on the date of the shooting, a patron of Happy Jack's Saloon came into the Circle Inn and informed a Circle Inn [bartender] that a man had been threatened at Happy Jack's. He requested the [bartender] either call the police or allow him to use the Circle Inn phone to call the police. That [bartender] allegedly refused to call the police and allegedly refused to allow the patron to use the phone to make his own call. Plaintiff alleges that the actions of the Circle Inn [bartender] were a breach of the legal duty that the Circle Inn owed to the decedent."....

There is a distinction, well rooted in the common law, between action and nonaction. (*Weirum v. RKO General, Inc.* (1975) 15 Cal.3d 40, 49). It has found its way into the prestigious Restatement Second of Torts (hereafter cited as "Restatement"), which provides in Section 314:

> The fact that the actor realizes or should realize that action on his part is necessary for another's aid or protection does not of itself impose upon him a duty to take such action.

The distinction between malfeasance and nonfeasance, between active misconduct working positive injury and failure to act to prevent mischief not brought on by the defendant, is founded on "that attitude of extreme individualism so typical of anglo-saxon legal thought." (Bohlen, *The Moral Duty to Aid Others as a Basis of Tort Liability*, part I, (1908) 56 U.Pa.L.Rev. 217, 219–220.)....

The refusal of the law to recognize the moral obligation of one to aid another when he is in peril and when such aid may be given without danger and at little cost in effort has been roundly criticized. Prosser describes the case law sanctioning such inaction as a "refus[al] to recognize the moral obligation of common decency and common humanity" and characterizes some of these decisions as "shocking in the extreme.... Such decisions are revolting to any moral sense. They have been denounced with vigor by legal writers." (Prosser, *Law of Torts* (4th ed. 1971) §56, pp. 340–341, fn. omitted.) A similar rule has been termed "morally questionable" by our Supreme Court. (*Tarasoff v. Regents of University of California* 551 P.2d 334 (1976).)

Francis H. Bohlen, in his article "The Moral Duty to Aid Others as a Basis of Tort Liability," commented:

> Nor does it follow that because the law has not as yet recognized the duty to repair harm innocently wrought, that it will continue indefinitely to refuse it recognition. While it is true that the common law does not attempt to enforce all moral, ethical, or humanitarian duties, it is, it is submitted, equally true that all ethical and moral conceptions, which are not the mere temporary manifestations of a passing wave of sentimentalism or puritanism, but on the contrary, find a real and permanent place in the settled convictions of a race and become part of the normal habit of thought thereof, of necessity do in time color the judicial conception of legal obligation....

As noted in *Tarasoff v. Regents of University of California, supra*, the courts have increased the instances in which affirmative duties are imposed not by direct rejection of the common law rule, but by expanding the list of special relationships which will justify departure from that rule....

Here there was no special relationship between the defendant and the deceased. It would be stretching the concept beyond recognition to assert there was a relationship between the defendant and the patron from Happy Jack's Saloon who wished to summon aid. But this does not end the matter.

It is time to re-examine the common law rule of nonliability for nonfeasance in the special circumstances of the instant case.

The Legislature has recognized the importance of the telephone system in reporting crime and in summoning emergency aid. Penal Code section 384 makes it a misdemeanor to refuse to relinquish a party line when informed that it is needed to call a police department or obtain other specified emergency services. This requirement, which the Legislature has mandated to be printed in virtually every telephone book in this state, may have wider printed distribution in this state than even the Ten Commandments. It creates an affirmative duty to do something—to clear the line for another user of the party line—in certain circumstances.

In 1972 the Legislature enacted the Warren-911-Emergency Assistance Act. This act expressly recognizes the importance of the telephone system in procuring emergency aid....

The above statutes are cited without the suggestion that the defendant violated a statute which would result in a presumption of a failure to use due care under Evidence Code section 669. Instead, they, and the quotations from the prestigious national commissions, demonstrate that "that attitude of extreme individualism so typical of anglo-saxon legal thought" may need limited re-examination in the light of current societal conditions and the facts of this case to determine whether the defendant owed a duty to the deceased to permit the use of the telephone.

We turn now to the concept of duty in a tort case. The Supreme Court has identified certain factors to be considered in determining whether a duty is owed to third persons. These factors include:

> The foreseeability of harm to the plaintiff, the degree of certainty that the plaintiff suffered injury, the closeness of the connection between the defendant's conduct and the injury suffered, the moral blame attached to the defendant's conduct, the policy of preventing future harm, the extent of the burden to the defendant and consequences to the community of

imposing a duty to exercise care with resulting liability for breach, and the availability, cost, and prevalence of insurance for the risk involved. (*Rowland v. Christian* (1968) 443 P.2d 561.)

We examine those factors in reference to this case. (1) The harm to the decedent was abundantly foreseeable; it was imminent. The employee was expressly told that a man had been threatened. The employee was a bartender. As such he knew it is foreseeable that some people who drink alcohol in the milieu of a bar setting are prone to violence. (2) The certainty of decedent's injury is undisputed. (3) There is arguably a close connection between the employee's conduct and the injury: the patron wanted to use the phone to summon the police to intervene. The employee's refusal to allow the use of the phone prevented this anticipated intervention. If permitted to go to trial, the plaintiff may be able to show that the probable response time of the police would have been shorter than the time between the prohibited telephone call and the fatal shot. (4) The employee's conduct displayed a disregard for human life that can be characterized as morally wrong: he was callously indifferent to the possibility that Darrell Soldano would die as the result of his refusal to allow a person to use the telephone. Under the circumstances before us the bartender's burden was minimal and exposed him to no risk: all he had to do was allow the use of the telephone. It would have cost him or his employer nothing. It could have saved a life. (5) Finding a duty in these circumstances would promote a policy of preventing future harm. A citizen would not be required to summon the police but would be required, in circumstances such as those before us, not to impede another who has chosen to summon aid. (6) We have no information on the question of the availability, cost, and prevalence of insurance for the risk, but note that the liability which is sought to be imposed here is that of employee negligence, which is covered by many insurance policies. (7) The extent of the burden on the defendant was minimal, as noted.

The consequences to the community of imposing a duty, the remaining factor mentioned in *Rowland v. Christian, supra,* is termed "the administrative factor" by Professor Green in his analysis of determining whether a duty exists in a given case. (Green, *The Duty Problem in Negligence Cases,* I (1929) 28 Colum.L.Rev. 1014, 1035–1045.... The administrative factor is simply the pragmatic concern of fashioning a workable rule and the impact of such a rule on the judicial machinery. It is the policy of major concern in this case.

As the Supreme Court has noted, the reluctance of the law to impose liability for nonfeasance, as distinguished from misfeasance, is in part due to the difficulties in setting standards and of making rules workable. (*Tarasoff v. Regents of University of California, supra....*)

Many citizens simply "don't want to get involved." No rule should be adopted which would require a citizen to open up his or her house to a stranger so that the latter may use the telephone to call for emergency assistance. As Mrs. Alexander in Anthony Burgess' *A Clockwork Orange* learned to her horror, such an action may be fraught with danger. It does not follow, however, that use of a telephone in a public portion of a business should be refused for a legitimate emergency call. Imposing liability for such a refusal would not subject innocent citizens to possible attack by the "good samaritan," for it would be limited to an establishment open to the public during times when it is open to business, and to places within the establishment ordinarily accessible to the public....

We conclude that the bartender owed a duty to the plaintiff's decedent to permit the patron from Happy Jack's to place a call to the police or to place the call himself....

The creative and regenerative power of the law has been strong enough to break chains imposed by outmoded former decisions. What the courts have power to create, they also have power to modify, reject and re-create in response to the needs of a dynamic society. The exercise of this power is an imperative function of the courts and is the strength of the common law. It cannot be surrendered to legislative inaction.

Prosser puts it this way:

New and nameless torts are being recognized constantly, and the progress of the common law is marked by many cases of first impression, in which the court has struck out boldly to create a new cause of action, where none had been recognized before.... The law of torts is anything but static, and the limits of its development are never set. When it becomes clear that the plaintiff's interests are entitled to legal protection against the conduct of the defendant, the mere fact that the claim is novel will not of itself operate as a bar to the remedy."
(Prosser, *op. cit. supra*, at pp. 3–4, fns. omitted.)

The possible imposition of liability on the defendant in this case is not a global change in the law. It is but a slight departure from the "morally questionable" rule of nonliability for inaction absent a special relationship. . . . It is a logical extension of Restatement section 327 which imposes liability for negligent interference with a third person who the defendant knows is attempting to render necessary aid. However small it may be, it is a step which should be taken.

We conclude there are sufficient justiciable issues to permit the case to go to trial and therefore reverse.

FRANSON, Acting P.J., and STANTON, J., concur.

QUESTIONS

1. This case overrules a long-standing common law rule. Do you agree that the old rule was "bad law?" (Remember that for the doctrine of stare decisis to come into play, you must believe that the old rule is unwise in the abstract.) If you so agree, do the principles of stare decisis permit overruling in this instance? Why or why not?
2. Note Judge Andreen's citation of *Tarasoff*. Is *Tarasoff* really a precedent for the *Soldano* holding? In what sense? In what sense is it no precedent at all?
3. Recall the cyclical model of common law principles. Of course it is too early to be sure, but might not *Tarasoff* mark the rise and *Soldano* the fall of the "special relationship" principle on such a cycle?
4. I edited out of the case many references to acts of the California legislature the purpose of which is to attempt to reduce the crime rate by increasing community responsibility. Be sure you see how Judge Andreen uses these references. How helpful and convincing do you find his use of legislative support here?
5. Do you believe this case is only a "slight departure" from prior law? Why or why not?
6. Judge Andreen sent me copies of the parties' briefs in this case. The large majority of Judge Andreen's reasoning appears nowhere in either brief. That is, despite our adversary system, this judge felt no hesitation to go beyond the parties' arguments to decide on the basis that he and a unanimous court felt best. Are you comfortable with this practice?
7. Most modern common law opinions do not explicitly rest on a philosophy of innovation in common law as does the opinion in *Soldano*. What reasons might explain why such opinions are

relatively rare? Is it necessarily helpful in every case for judges to follow the *Soldano* pattern? Why or why not?

8. At the beginning of August, 1983, a Minnesota statute went into effect which required witnesses of crimes go to the aid of a victim in grave physical danger or face misdemeanor charges and a fine of $200. The statute does not require intervention where doing so would endanger the witness. Does this evidence of legislative action on the Good Samaritan problem issue in common law indicate that it was wrong of the *Soldano* court to address the issue itself?

SOME EXPLORATORY PROBLEMS

1. *The T.J. Hooper* appeared in this chapter to illustrate an instance in which judges make new common law. You should not, however, let yourself be misled into the belief that the case is entirely new. Review the description of that case, pulling out all the previously settled legal points on which Learned Hand's opinion drew. Is it not fair to say that the novelty of a case is always a matter of degree?

2. Problem 1 suggested we can find settled legal principles at work in even a novel case. At the other extreme, students of law can take a case and project its consequences into the future. Indeed, a careful, innovative opinion, like Judge Andreen's, will attempt to anticipate obvious applications of the doctrine and to reassure the legal community that the new principle will not explode in destructive ways. Use the principle of a case like *Hynes*, *Hooper*, or *Soldano* to resolve the following two hypothetical cases:

   (a) A mother of two small children dies after ingesting a cyanide-filled Extra-Strength Tylenol capsule in Chicago during the "tampering" scare of 1982. Her husband and her two surviving children sue the makers of Tylenol—Johnson and Johnson, Inc.—for damages for their negligence in not anticipating the tampering and not selling the product in a tamper-proof package.

   (b) A wife contracts a venereal disease—herpes simplex—after engaging in normal marital sexual relations with her spouse. She sues him for failure to tell her of his condition. The husband contends that to do so would have amounted to a confession of his infidelity and that his concern for his wife and marriage prompted him not to confess.

3. A couple with several children decides to avoid further children through vasectomy of the husband. The urologist performs the operation negligently, and the couple conceives another child. Should a court modify the common law to allow the couple to recover from the doctor the costs of raising the unwanted child? See *Cochran v. Baumgartner,* 425 N.E.2d 968 (1981). A couple with a known risk that its offspring will be born with the invariably debilitating Tay-Sachs Disease has tests done that will predict the health of their offspring. The lab performs the tests negligently and informs the couple they face no risk. The mother gives birth to a Tay-Sachs child 15 months later. Should the child recover damages from the laboratory for its "wrongful life?" See *Curlender v. Biological Science Laboratories,* 165 *California Reporter* 447 (1980). The courts, incidentally, permitted recovery in both these cases. See also *Turpin v. Sartini,* 643 P.2d 953 (California, 1982).

4. I imply in my introduction to the *Tarasoff* case that the California Supreme Court may have leaped too much into new law. I am actually inclined to believe that the leap here was not too large, but strong arguments on both sides of this question exist. What are they? Do they not have to do with the relative competence of courts and legislatures to make policies of this sort? What does *relative competence* mean in the context of *Tarasoff*? Can you imagine a problem, a human conflict, in which the courts would clearly be less competent to find the facts and articulate the values on which acceptable policy depends than a legislature or a president or a regulatory agency? Do we not believe that some problems require no government policy at all, that private agreements (private laws), suited to the interests of the immediately affected parties provide the wisest solutions?

5. Write an opinion in the *Bellah* case that reaches the outcome depicted in the Associated Press news item that concluded this chapter.

6. The immediate policy issues raised in *Tarasoff* remain very much in the forefront of law a decade later. Thus, in the 1970s, a man who murdered a total stranger, thinking him to be a food poisoner, was found not guilty by reason of insanity and confined to a mental hospital. He was released four years later because the psychiatrists involved felt he was no longer a threat. Fifty-eight days later he decided another total stranger, Felix

Richardson, whom he saw walking down the street, was about to poison his food. He killed him, too. Should Richardson's heirs recover from the psychiatrists? See "When Can a Shrink Be Sued?" *Newsweek,* March 7, 1983, p. 77. See, generally, Sisella Bok, *Secrets: On the Ethics of Concealment and Revelation* (New York: Pantheon Books, 1982).

7. *Soldano* shows the common law alive and kicking. In fact, any reasonably diligent review of the popular news media will reveal interesting innovations in common law almost weekly. Here are a few more examples to ice this chapter's cake:

(a) A wife works hard to put her husband through medical school. Shortly after he begins to make money in his practice, the marriage crumbles. After the divorce his ex-wife sues for part of the proceeds of the professional education she helped, through her work, to make possible for her husband. Should she recover part of his income for the rest of her life? See "California Court to Decide in Divorce Case if Professional Education Is Like Property," The *Wall Street Journal,* March 14, 1983, p. 33.

(b) A mugger snatches the purse of a woman in a poorly lighted shopping center parking lot as she loads her groceries into her car at night. Does the owner of the shopping center owe a duty to shoppers to keep the lots well-lit in order to reduce crime? See "Let the Seller Beware," *Newsweek,* August 16, 1982, p. 63.

(c) Do you agree with a Michigan court that recently awarded Dennis Polonich $850,000 in damages for injuries received from Wilfrid Paiement, a hockey player who hit Polonich with a swing of his hockey stick during a hockey brawl in a game between the Detroit Red Wings and the Colorado Rockies on October 25, 1978? Polonich received a broken nose, multiple cuts of the face, and a concussion. See, "Should Courts be Refereeing Sports Fights?", The *Wall Street Journal,* September 1, 1982, p. 17.

(d) A California statute requires law enforcement officials to obtain dental records of any person missing more than 30 days. Plaintiffs' son, a victim of the 1979 Los Angeles "Freeway Killer," was reported missing, but the police of the city of Westminster never obtained his dental records as required by law. As a result his body was found in August of 1979 but not identified until April 1, 1980. The parents sued for the expenses of their pain and suffering, both medical and physical, caused by the unnecessary prolonging of their uncertainty about their son's condition. Should the Court find the city liable? Should the answer depend on whether the police have a *Tarasoff*-like "special relationship" with the parents once they report a missing child and 30 days have elapsed? Why or why not? Is the *Parker* case relevant to this issue? See *Shelton v. City of Westminster*, 188 *California Reporter* 205 (1982). Would the 1983 *Soldano* case bear on this problem if *Soldano* had instead predated *Shelton?*

Chapter VI

REASON AND THE CONSTITUTION

*[Be it] regarded hereafter as the law of this
Court, that its opinion upon the construction
of the Constitution is always open to
discussion when it is supposed to have been
founded in error, and that its judicial
authority should hereafter depend altogether
on the force of the reasoning by which it is
supported.*
   *—Chief Justice Roger B. Taney,
      dissenting in* The Passenger Cases

*We are under a Constitution—but the
Constitution is what the Judges say it is.*
   —Charles Evans Hughes

As I begin this chapter, I keep thinking about an incident from
my college days. A friend and I were driving home late one
Sunday afternoon from a weekend skiing trip in Vermont. As I
drove, the friend punched the buttons on the car radio hunting
for something to divert us from the depressing thoughts of the
exams and term papers ahead. But religious exhortations of
various sorts, at least in that place and time, dominated Sunday
afternoon radio. We were not consoled or diverted until my
companion's random punching produced this sequence of

excerpts: [punch] "Jesus Christ came to earth to save mankind from sin!" [punch] "a fool's errand!" [punch] "Let us pray."

Any attempt to capture the essence of constitutional reasoning in a single chapter has multiple parallels to that incident. The problem is not so much the quantity of constitutional law; the majority of judges most of the time do not tackle major constitutional issues when they resolve conflicts. The problem is, rather, that constitutional law raises so many fundamentally different issues and questions, all of them potentially important. Courts strike down laws prohibiting abortions in the first trimester of pregnancy. Courts tell states what property they can and cannot tax. Courts order busing to integrate schools. Courts order legislatures to reapportion. Courts reverse the convictions of killers because of what some critics call "technicalities." The field inevitably seems disjointed, like punching from one program to another. Scholars and laymen alike take the issues so seriously that discussion often resembles theological exhortations, at least their intensity if not their logic. There is so much to say that any attempt to create a comprehensive chapter on constitutional reasoning may amount to a fool's errand. In this field, prayer may offer the only prudent recourse.

More than the preceding chapters, these materials on constitutional reasoning present a point of view that requires a lifetime of pondering and refinement. I have no doubt that this chapter asks the right questions. However, in the course of your deliberations you may reject some or all of the answers my point of view prescribes.

My point of view, in a nutshell, holds that in constitutional law courts must be prepared to abandon many of the principles of sound reasoning that earlier chapters described. In some circumstances, these sound principles suffice in constitutional law. The "mischief rule" of statutory interpretation, defined in Chapter IV, is often helpful here, too. But, in other circumstances, courts must reason in unique ways in constitutional law because the structure of the American political system makes it necessary and because it is ethically proper to do so.

The view that the constitutional work of courts properly differs from common law and statutory interpretation rests heavily on the assumption that constitutions create rules that differ in important ways from the other kinds of law. Hence, the next section describes the special legal qualities of constitutions. Next we examine, with the help of another role play, the unique nature of the constitutional role of courts. This unique role helps explain why constitutional reasoning is itself unique. The final sections describe some limits on this awesome judicial power.

Before plunging in, let me remind you that in both this chapter and the final chapter, we deliberately expand the territory. Here, in Chapter VI, our thinking about law must expand to include some understanding about how the American political system ought to operate. In Chapter VII our thinking will expand even further to struggle with the nature of reason itself and the nature of reason in public life.

THE CONSTITUTION AS LAW[1]

The United States possesses the world's oldest written constitution. Its age should not surprise us. The framers, with the philosophical guidance of Locke, Montesquieu, and others, all but invented the idea.

The invention amounts to this: Law should govern both the citizens and the government. Just as the government makes laws creating and controlling private institutions, like corporations, so constitutions should create and control the lawmaking and law enforcing institutions of government. Moreover, since governments necessarily contain many institutions, legal rules should seek to prevent a disorderly and chaotic scramble for power among them, just as the law of contract injects some orderliness into the private scramble for money. Most impor-

---

[1]To simplify this discussion, if only slightly, this chapter focuses almost exclusively on the United States Constitution and the United States Supreme Court's reasoning about it. This simplification also distorts the subject matter of this chapter to the extent that state supreme courts do not deal with constitutional issues of the same political magnitude and with the finality of the U.S. Supreme Court.

tant, the inventors recognized that, just as the criminal law proscribes some conduct altogether, constitutions should state, at least generally, the kinds of actions institutions of government should not do at all.

Our Constitution, like all our law, has grown out of the political beliefs and conflicts of specific times. Initially, the framers felt government must effectively function—as the confederation of "united states" had not functioned—and at the same time avoid the tendency of effective government to function too well, to become oppressively efficient and effective. The framers felt strongly that an order—law—superior to government should separate public from private prerogatives and make the separation endure. Unquestionably the framers worried about protecting property (including their property!) from the suspected tyranny of the less affluent majority. But it discredits them to insist that they worried only about property. The framers worried, more profoundly, about the task of reconciling personal freedom and the power of the state.

The framers believed that the familiar result—a government partially of separated but coequal powers; partially of overlapping, checking, and balancing powers; *and* a government forbidden from exercising some powers altogether— would realize their goal of an effective but limited state. The important fact is that history, which rapidly makes the work of most politicians obsolete, has continued to prove these colonial politicians mostly correct and hence to validate the wisdom of their work.

Unfortunately, creating written documents and calling them constitutions do not automatically define and limit the power of rulers in reality. Many countries now possess elaborate written constitutions that rulers and ruled alike ignore. For reasons that we can only partly understand, the belief that constitutional limits matter—perhaps that law itself matters— varies from culture to culture. How, then, did the work of men who resemble medieval princes more than computer programmers create law that actually limits government today?

Perhaps the belief in the legal authority of the Constitution developed because the United States Constitution in Article VI calls itself and the laws of the United States "made in pursuance thereof...the supreme law of the land." By itself, however, such a verbal bootstrapping operation should no more convince us that the Constitution is law than if I concluded this book with the declaration that "These lessons in legal reasoning are the supreme law of the land."

Unlike this book, however, the Constitution looks and reads like a legal document. See how often the legally potent word "shall" (and to a lesser extent "may") appears in these typical constitutional clauses:

- "All legislative powers herein granted shall be vested in a Congress of the United States, which shall consist of a Senate and House of Representatives." [Article I, Section 1]*
- "No person shall be a Representative who shall not have attained to the age of twenty-five years, and been seven years a citizen of the United States, and who shall not, when elected, be an inhabitant of that State in which he shall be chosen." [Article I, Section 2(2)]
- "The President shall at stated times, receive for his services, a compensation, which shall neither be increased nor diminished during the period for which he shall have been elected, and he shall not receive within that period any other emolument from the United States, or any of them." [Article II, Section 1(7)]
- "Each House may determine the rules of its proceedings, punish its members for disorderly behavior, and with the concurrence of two-thirds, expel a member." [Article I, Section 5(2)]
- "The judicial power of the United States shall be vested in one supreme court, and in such inferior courts as the Congress may from time to time ordain and establish." [Article III, Section 1]

I trust you noted how these excerpts define institutions, separate powers, and functions, and limit government action. The main point here is that these excerpts use the same legal

*This chapter's quotations from the Constitution use modernized forms of spelling and capitalization.

language as do the statutes cited in earlier chapters. But again, I could list at the end of this book a set of lawlike judicial commands—"Judges shall interpret statutes in terms of an intelligible statutory purpose; they shall never resolve a dispute in terms of isolated and misleading evidence of legislative intent," for example—and this book would still not create law.

Chapter I defined law as the process in which lawyers and judges try to prevent or resolve conflicts using rules made by the state as their starting point. Just as a statute or a common law principle is not part of law unless lawyers and judges use it in resolving conflicts, so the Constitution has become law that actually binds government because judges have made a leap of faith and actually resolved conflicts in constitutional terms. More precisely, judges make two leaps. First, they assert that the constitution is a legally binding document rather than a philosophical expression of public values. Second, they assert, as Chief Justice John Marshall (1801–1835) did so powerfully throughout his judicial career, that the Constitution binds judges. The Constitution is law only as long as judges say that, in a controversy involving governmental power, the government's power triumphs only if the Constitution permits. Judges must say that the government actually loses from time to time because the Constitution requires it. Otherwise, the rules will not limit government behavior in practice. Thus one of the main assumptions in my argument is that constitutions will actually govern the government only as long as judges, in the name of constitutions, willingly assume the task of governing the government. The conventional name of this task is "judicial review."

Later we must deal with the difficulties arising from the fact that judges are part of the government and perhaps its least democratic part. For now, consider what our political world would have to be like in order to relieve judges of their constitutional tasks. We would have to believe that government consists entirely of people who are intelligent enough to decide in every case what the Constitution means and conscientious enough to act upon it—all the way from presidents and legislators to policemen. We would have to reject the possibility that human self-interest and the buzzing confusion of political life combine to produce governmental decisions that do not always conform to legal norms.

The political history of the human race, to say nothing of the more modern discovery that tentative incrementalism pervades all organizational life, commands us to accept this possibility. History shows how difficult it is to preserve the legal authority of the Constitution without entrusting to some organization the specific responsibility for deciding what the Constitution means and ordering people to obey it.

For the moment, however, suppose a different world in which human behavior did make the first belief defensible. Suppose we *could* assume that every governmental representative, the legislator before voting for a statute or the policeman before deciding to arrest, stopped and made a conscientious determination of the constitutionality of the decision. Under our Constitution, we would still need a constitution-interpreting organization like the courts. The Constitution is so vague, general, and ambiguous that people with the best of intentions do not necessarily reach the same interpretation. What does it mean to give Congress "the legislative power" or the president the "executive power"? What are these powers and how do they differ? "Congress shall make no law respecting an establishment of religion." But what is an establishment? What is religion?

Federalism compounds the problem. We have one national constitution but many states. If we take its legal status seriously, then the Constitution should mean the same everywhere, just as the Mann Act should not have one meaning in Utah and another in the District of Columbia. If we lived under a unitary government, then maybe (but only maybe) we could count on a conscientious Congress to determine uniform constitutional applications. Under our Constitution, however, Congress is neither structured nor empowered to review the constitutionality of the actions of state and local governments.

Thus, under even the idealistic and unrealistic conditions and assumptions, we would need a body like the Supreme Court to apply the meaning of constitutional language uniformly. Under realistic assumptions, courts must *enforce* that language as well.

ANOTHER ROLE PLAY

At this point, you may protest that I have hardly explained why, in constitutional law, judges sometimes must abandon what I have so far described as wise principles of legal reasoning. Your protest is quite in order. Showing the legal character of the Constitution is simply the first step toward understanding the unique elements of constitutional reasoning. We may best take the next step by entering another role play.

Suppose that you are 38 and work in a middle management position for any large corporation—Polaroid or RCA or the Chase Manhatten Bank, for example. Stop for a moment and think about the kinds of decisions you will and will not probably have to make, and how you will expect, by and large, to make them.

In this role, are you not primarily a "facilitator"? You must link the basic policy decisions of the ranking executives and directors to the daily operation of the organization. I hope you sense that it is perfectly proper for you to apply policy decisions in terms of their purpose as best you can determine it. I trust you sense that you have considerable discretion in the way you resolve daily problems and that you may also have the "common law" responsibility to make intermediate policies about sales strategies or sick-leave benefits for employees in order to help keep the company functioning. I trust that you feel some obligation, in making and applying these intermediate policies, to state them so that your employees can understand them and so that they feel you apply them fairly and equitably. But I also trust that you sense powerful limits on your authority. Your job is to act for the general welfare of the company, not as you would prefer to define it, but as you believe top management has chosen to define it.

Now make yourself an active member of the board of directors. How do the decisions you must make differ from those facing the middle manager? How do the ways, the bases, of making these decisions differ?

I trust you feel that your basic role shifts substantially. You no longer think of your job primarily as facilitative. Unlike the specific policy decisions that top management makes for middle managers to implement, no governing body above the directors regularly reviews and changes the charter and bylaws to give you instructions. Of course you are constrained by a corporate charter and bylaws. The charter and bylaws impose some specific obligations on you. Part of your job as director is to facilitate, to mediate among the various not-entirely-compatible bodies—the unions, the stockholders, the banks, and the government—that make demands on the corporation. But at a deeper level the charter and bylaws obligate you to work to insure the survival of the corporation and of the purposes for its being that the charter and bylaws create. These documents, the corporate "constitution," won't tell you how to make decisions. They do little more than instruct you to care about the corporate mission. They merely imply that you should search diligently for the ideas and conditions—new technologies, improved accounting and financial systems, better balances between internal reinvestment and dividend payouts to stockholders and more sophisticated approaches to the demands of labor—that will insure the survival of the organization. *Your job requires you to remain always open to the possibility of change. More important, it requires you to initiate the changes that will insure the corporation's continued health.*

As a director, you would *not* decide a current corporate question based primarily upon: (1) a 50-year-old bylaw created to cope with a problem that has long since evaporated; (2) what old J.B., the corporation's Victorian founder, would have done 100 years ago; or (3) a policy the directors adopted five years ago that has in the interim proved itself a failure.

Your orientation must be to the future. Therefore, would you not feel that looking only to the intent of the founders or to the words of an old bylaw or to a failed policy of a few years back would lead to ruin?

When appellate judges interpret statutes, their main task is to resolve conflicts in a way that reflects statutory purpose. Judges in this role facilitate. They work out the detailed linkages between the general decision of legislators and the specific problem that caught the legislators' attention. Like the middle manager, they do not perform their job effectively if they do not apply policies in terms of their purposes. Similarly, in common law, the courts seek above all to facilitate the ability of people to live as safely and trustingly with one another as possible in those areas where no superior legislative policy imposes its own commands. Each judge's decision, just like that of the middle manager, is only a small contribution to the process. But individual judges, and managers must nevertheless keep the need for facilitation foremost in their heads or, collectively, they will fail to meet their goals.

Our previous emphasis on the necessity for judges to decide in order to enable people to rely on law and plan their affairs, is imply the jurisprudential equivalent of saying that judges should facilitate. In the interpretation of statutes and in common law, judges are in many ways like middle managers.

Let us now expand the assertions made in this chapter about the Constitution. If you believe in the trust and propriety of each of these assertions, then you will find that the courts must behave like directors, not middle managers, when they make constitutional decisions:

- The Constitution enunciates certain fundamental values of good government.
- The Constitution is the supreme law of the land. Therefore, unless it changes, the fundamental values it expresses bind government legally.
- The Constitution expresses values about government that vary a great deal in specificity. Some provisions— the president must be at least 35 years old—pose only minor interpretive problems. Many other provisions— the allocation of "legislative," "executive," and "judicial" powers, or the mandate for freedom of "religion" or for "equal protection of the law"—are so imprecise that someone somewhere must perpetually be prepared to translate these values into concrete meanings. Some provisions contain values that clash directly, like the clash between "free press" and "fair trial."[2]
- Because the Constitution is law, courts are the natural place to which to look for interpretation. If, however, we

[2] For a more complex example of clashing principles see *Yarborough v. Yarborough*, 290 U.S. 202 (1933), counterposing the due process clause and the "full faith and credit" clause.

could trust government officials at all levels to make—
and make consistently—decisions that perpetuated constitutional values, then courts might not need to exercise
this responsibility often. But both human history and
the actual distribution of powers and responsibilities in
a federal system suggest that, if the courts do not interpret and apply the Constitution, no one else will.

- Finally, we cannot depend on the process of formal
Constitution-changing, the amending process, to respond to each and every new question about governmental power and every new social background fact that
concrete lawsuits bring to courts. The amendment process allows either minorities in Congress or minorities
of states to block constitutional change. Of the roughly
10,000 amendments introduced in Congress in our national lifetime, dealing most recently with equal rights
for women and balanced budgets, only 26 have been
ratified. Indeed, only 33 have ever left Congress for state
ratification at all, presumably because most proposed
amendments do not really seek to govern the government but to impose a private policy preference directly
on society. This is precisely what our one great amendment failure, the Prohibition Amendment, attempted.
This intractability is part of the constitutional scheme.
The major difficulty is that, in the pressure of daily
political business, the proposal to amend in order to
address the concrete issue of a lawsuit may not come up
for serious discussion at all.

Hence our charter and bylaws, the Constitution, leave in
the hands of the courts, primarily the Supreme Court, the same
responsibilities and discretion that a board of directors possesses. The Constitution's vaguely worded provisions do little
more than command the courts to *care* about basic political and
governmental values without specifying with any precision the
values or the problems to which the provisions apply.

- "Care," says the First Amendment to the courts, "that
government not take sides on religious matters. Care
that it not constrain religious freedom, or speech, or the
press, unduly. But it's up to you to define religion,

speech, and press and to decide when government action and those values simply cannot stand together.

- "Care," say the Fourth, Fifth, Sixth, and Eighth Amendments, "that government not become too zealous in fighting crime. Respect people's homes and property. Give them a fair chance to prove their innocence in court and do not punish the guilty too harshly. In short, be fair. But it's up to you to decide what's fair."
- "Men must be able to trade effectively," say the commerce clause and the contract clause. "Work it out so they can."

And that, for better or worse, is about all the Constitution says. Like the charter and bylaws, which in effect urge directors to preserve the economic value of profitability, hence survival, the Constitution is little more than a command to the courts to be conscientious political and social philosophers.

Not all legal scholars agree that the courts can or must assume this role. Indeed, the conventional judge habitually insists that, in declaring a statute unconstitutional, he does not concern himself with its "wisdom." I hope by the end of this chapter that you will see why the conventional position, although politically attractive, is intellectually fraudulent. The short of the matter is simply that, since the words don't yield clear answers to many constitutional questions, the solutions will come from somewhere else. In selecting the "somewhere else," judges who eschew wisdom will by definition decide foolishly.[3]

---

[3] One currently popular way to frame this controversy counterposes "interpretivism" and "noninterpretivism." The literature in this field has mushroomed and improved in the last decade. I do not find this distinction convincing because, whether one reasons from the text and history of the constitution itself or from the political realities in which it is embedded, one is interpreting something. The real issue is not whether we interpret but what counts as properly "constitutional" material to interpret. If forced to choose, I would go along with those presently defined as "noninterpretivists." After all, there is no more flagrant illustration of this position than *Marbury v. Madison* itself! In any event, in addition to other recent works noted in this chapter, see Michael J. Perry, *The Constitution, the Courts, and Human Rights* (New Haven: Yale University Press, 1982); "Symposium," 90 *Yale Law Journal,* Part 2 (1981); "Symposium," 42 *Ohio State Law Journal* 3 (1981); Walter Murphy, "The Art of

CONSTITUTIONAL REASONING AS POLITICAL AND SOCIAL PHILOSOPHY

By now I hope you begin to sense how the role play uncovers some unique problems in constitutional reasoning. The words of a statute often prevent judges from interpreting it in ways that, words aside, would seem sensible. The words of "White Slave" act, after all, unambiguously cover voluntary prostitution. But the words of the Constitution, as we shall see in a moment, should not constrain judges any more than the words of an obsolete bylaw constrain directors. Judges should always probe for defensible definitions of statutory purpose when they interpret statutes, but in constitutional law the purpose of a provision to the framers may sometimes, though not always, mean no more than did old J.B.'s purpose in founding the corporation. Stare decision plays an occasional role in the judicial facilitation of conflict resolution. But, despite reliance and other reasons for stability, neither directors nor judges resolving constitutional issues can afford to follow even recently adopted policies if evidence of their inadequacy calls for a more promising approach. In short, words, purposes, and stare decisis take on a different significance in constitutional law. Here are some illustrations.

Words as Channels of Meaning

Article I, Section 10 of the Constitution prohibits the states from engaging in certain activities altogether. It prohibits them from making treaties, coining money, or keeping a state militia during times of peace without Congressional permission. The section also includes these words: "No state shall...pass any... law impairing the obligation of contracts...."

Debts provide the best example of the kind of contract the state may not impair under the contract clause. In the typical

---

Constitutional Interpretation," in M. Judd Harmon, *Essays on the Constitution* (Port Washington, N.Y.: Kennikat Press, 1978). Chapter 8; Mark Tushnet, "Following the Rules Laid Down: A Critique of Interpretivism & Neutral Principles," 96 *Harvard Law Review* 781 (1983).

case of such a contract—"executory" contracts in legal language —Pauline borrows money, say from the bank, and promises to pay the money back some time in the future. Until she pays the money back (and at the stated time), she has a contractual obligation to do so. The contract clause prevents the state from impairing Pauline's "obligation" to repay. At minimum, these words seem clearly to mean the state can't pass a law saying people don't have to pay back what they owe, even if a popularly elected legislature voted to do so. Note also that the word "impairing" also presumably means something. An impairment is something different from a destruction. Someone with impaired vision is not necessarily totally blind. Thus the words would also seem to prevent the state from allowing Pauline to forget about paying the interest or to pay back years later than she promised.

During the Great Depression, a number of states passed laws allowing owners of homes and land to postpone paying their mortgage payments as the mortgage contracts required. These statutes forbade banks and other mortgage holders from foreclosing. The Depression, of course, destroyed the financial ability of hundreds of thousands of Paulines to repay mortgages on time, but these mortgage moratorium laws spared the Paulines from this peril. These laws spared the Paulines precisely and only because they impaired the bank's ability to recover the debt, yet the Supreme Court ruled, in *Home Building and Loan Association v. Blaisdell,* that these laws did not violate the contract clause.[4]

How can we defend such a result? Just as in nature, survival of economic and political values depends on adaptation, on changefulness, and on the ability to re-evaluate policies in light of new information. The Supreme Court rightly rejected the contract clause's words and upheld the Depression's mortgage moratorium laws because these laws were based on economic knowledge not fully available to the framers. In the forced panic sale of land following massive numbers of foreclosures of mortgages what would happen to the price of land?

[4]*Home Building and Loan Association v. Blaisdell,* 290 U.S. 398 (1934). See also *East New York Savings Bank v. Hahn,* 326 U.S. 230 (1945) and *El Paso v. Simmons,* 379 U.S. 497 (1965).

Supply and demand analysis predicted that the price would drastically decline, quite possibly to the point where creditors as well as debtors would lose because the land could be sold for only a fraction of what the banks had originally loaned on it. The Court upheld the law as a defensible method for attempting to prevent the further collapse of the economy.

A decision in the monumental school desegregation cases provides another example of prudent judicial flight from constitutional words. In its celebrated decision, *Brown v. Board of Education*, the Court held that the equal protection clause of the Fourteenth Amendment prohibited laws and policies designed to maintain segregation in public schools of the then 48 states.[5] The case concerned the problem of segregation of schools in the nation's capital. The Fourteenth Amendment's sentence containing the equal protection clause begins with the words "no state shall." It does not govern the District of Columbia. The original Bill of Rights does govern the national government and hence the district, but it contains no equal protection clause. The Court forbade segregation in the District's public schools by invoking the due process clause of the Fifth Amendment.[6] Unfortunately, the due process clause does not address the problem of equality. Its words—"No person shall... be deprived of life, liberty, or property, without due process of law..."— seem to address the problem of the fairness of procedures, the "due process," in the courts. The Fourteenth Amendment contains *both* due process and equal protection clauses, which further suggests that they convey different messages.

Nevertheless, the Court rightly prohibited segregation in the district. If the Constitution denies government the power to segregate schools by race, it is proper to avoid the absurdity of permitting segregation only in the national capital. It is proper to say in this instance that the due process clause of the Fifth Amendment *does* address this problem of equality despite its words.[7]

[5] *Brown v. Board of Education*, 347 U.S. 483 (1954).
[6] *Bolling v. Sharpe*, 347 U.S. 497 (1954). See also *Hirabayashi v. United States*, 320 U.S. 81 (1943).
[7] Some of the Court's creative manipulations of words in constitutional law come disguised as statutory interpretations. For example Section 6 (j) of the old

The Intent of the Framers and the Purpose of Constitutional Provisions

Searching for the actual intent of the framers of the original Constitution (or of its later amendments) proves just as frustrating as the search for legislative intent. The processes of constitution and statute making are equally political. People make arguments they don't fully intend in order to win support. Others do not express what they do intend in order to avoid offending. The painful process of negotiation and accommodation that produced the Constitution in 1787 left many questions unresolved. Most confounding of all, the authors could have had no intent in relation to the new facts that have surfaced since their work concluded. Here, for example, is Justice Brennan concurring in the Court's 1963 decision forbidding devotional reading from the Bible (including reading the Lord's Prayer) in public schools:

> (A)n awareness of history and an appreciation of the aims of the Founding Fathers do not always resolve concrete problems. The specific question before us has, for example, aroused vigorous dispute whether the architects of the First Amendment—James Madison and Thomas Jefferson

---

draft law stated, "Nothing contained in this title shall be construed to require any person to be subject to combatant training and service...who, by reason of religious training and belief, is conscientiously opposed to participation in war in any form. Religious training and belief, in this connection means an individual's belief in a relation to a Supreme Being involving duties superior to those arising from any human relation, but does not include essentially political, sociological, or philosophical views or a merely personal moral code." In 1966, one Elliott A. Welsh, II, was convicted for refusing to submit to induction. He had applied for an exemption as a conscientious objector under Section 6 (j), but he insisted that his feelings were not religious but moral, based upon "reading in the fields of history and sociology," he said. He believed that taking any life was "morally wrong" and "totally repugnant." The Court reversed Welsh's conviction. Hugo Black, speaking for himself and three other Justices (Blackmun did not sit; Harlan concurred on other grounds), said that Section 6 (j) exempted all those who held moral and philosophical beliefs "with the strength of more traditional religious convictions." To avoid invalidating Section 6 (j), Black made it say precisely what the words in Section 6 (j) take pains to avoid. *Welsh v. United States*, 398 U.S. 333 (1970).

particularly—understood the prohibition against any "law respecting an establishment of religion" to reach devotional exercises in the public schools. It may be that Jefferson and Madison would have held such exercises to be permissible.... But I doubt that their view, even if perfectly clear one way or the other, would supply a dispositive answer to the question presented by these cases. A more fruitful inquiry, it seems to me, is whether the practices here challenged threaten those consequences which the Framers deeply feared; whether, in short, they tend to promote that type of interdependence between religion and state which the First Amendment was designed to prevent....

A too literal quest for the advice of the Founding Fathers upon the issues of these cases seems to me futile and misdirected for several reasons: First, on our precise problem the historical record is at best ambiguous, and statements can readily be found to support either side of the proposition....

Second, the structure of American education has greatly changed since the First Amendment was adopted.... Education, as the Framers knew it, was in the main confined to private schools more often than not under strictly sectarian supervision....

Third, our religious composition makes us a vastly more diverse people than were our forefathers. They knew differences chiefly among Protestant sects. Today the Nation is far more heterogeneous religiously, including as it does substantial minorities not only of Catholics and Jews but as well of those who worship according to no version of the Bible and those who worship no God at all.... In the face of such profound changes, practices which may have been objectionable to no one in the time of Jefferson and Madison may today be highly offensive to many persons, the deeply devout and the nonbelievers alike.[8]

Notice how, like the director in the role play, Brennan senses how changing conditions may require new constitutional policy despite the initial purposes of constitutional provisions. If, in other words, the "establishment clause" appeared only in a

---

[8]*Abington Township v. Schempp*, 374 U.S. 203 (1963), pp. 234–241. If you agree with Justice Brennan you will reject, as I do, the conclusions by Raoul Berger and Learned Hand that the Court must always confine itself to the original intent underlying constitutional provisions. See Raoul Berger, *Gov-*

statute passed, say, in 1792, the Court should have reached the opposite result.

Similarly the Court ignored the original purpose of the Sixth Amendment's command when it expanded the right to counsel. This amendment states in part that "In all criminal prosecutions, the accused shall enjoy the right...to have the assistance of counsel for his defense." The framers who drafted it sought to alter the common law rule that prohibited accused felons from having any lawyer at all. They wanted to stop the government from preventing the accused from bringing his lawyer to court with him. It makes no reference to the problem that a man's *poverty* may stop him from hiring a lawyer. Yet in 1938 the Court held that these words required the federal government to provide lawyers for the poor, and the Court has since expanded the right to protect those accused of felonies and misdemeanors in state and local courts.[9]

Finally, consider again the mortgage moratorium laws of the Depression. If we examine the purpose of the contract clause from the framers' viewpoint, we discover that they feared excessive democracy, feared that popularly elected legislators would enact the "selfish" interests of the masses. The masses contain more debtors than creditors, and it was precisely in economically difficult times that the framers most feared that debtors would put irresistible pressure on legislators to ease their debts.

---

ernment by Judiciary: The Transformation of the Fourteenth Amendment (Cambridge: Harvard University Press, 1977), and Learned Hand, *The Bill of Rights* (Cambridge: Harvard University Press, 1958). See also Justice Rehnquist, dissenting, in *Roe v. Wade*, 410 U.S. 113 (1973). For a most convincing brief explanation of why the intent of the original framers is unknowable, see Harold Spaeth, *Supreme Court Policy Making* (San Francisco: Freeman, 1979) pp. 65–66. See also Perry, *supra*, Chapter 1. Thomas C. Grey has argued that the framers themselves contemplated that the Constitution embodied an unwritten higher law of natural rights in addition to its written commands. See "Do We Have an Unwritten Constitution?" 27 *Stanford Law Review* 703 (1975). See also Grey's "Origins of the Unwritten Constitution: Fundamental Law in American Revolutionary Thought," 30 *Stanford Law Review* 843 (1978).

[9] *Johnson v. Zerbst*, 304 U.S. 458 (1938), *Gideon v. Wainwright*, 372 U.S. 335 (1963), *Argersinger v. Hamlin*, 407 U.S. 25 (1972). For a persuasive defense of this trend see Anthony Lewis's classic, *Gideon's Trumpet* (New York: Random House, 1964).

Hence the court in *Home Building and Loan* rejected more than constitutional words; it rejected the purpose of the provision. But it did so correctly because it understood, as presumably the framers did not, how postponing mortgage foreclosures could benefit creditors and debtors alike. The moratorium laws, to use Brennan's phrase, did not "threaten those consequences which the Framers deeply feared," even though they did violate the framers' specific purpose.

Stare Decisis

In 1940 the Supreme Court held that a public school could require all children, including Jehovah's Witnesses whose religious convictions forbade it, to salute the flag each day. In 1943 the Court overruled itself and held the opposite.[10] In 1942, four years after it required the federal government to provide counsel for the poor, the Court held that the states did not have to do so.[11] In the famous *Gideon* case cited above, the Court changed its mind. In 1946 the Court refused to require state legislatures to make electoral districts roughly equal, but in 1962 the Court began to do just that.[12]

The Justices themselves have from time to time recognized the limited utility of stare decisis in constitutional law. After all, no legislature sits mainly to update constitutional policy in light of new conditions. It is not simply that the Court should correct its own mistakes—that, as indicated in Chapter IV, is always wise policy. It is rather that wise policy at one time is not necessarily wise policy at another. If we take seriously the idea that the Constitution is law—ought to have teeth—then the courts must do the updating. As Justice William O. Douglas once said:

> The place of *stare decisis* in constitutional law is...tenuous. A judge looking at a constitutional decision may have compulsions to revere past history and accept what was once written. But he remembers above all else that it is the

[10]*Minersville School District v. Gobitis,* 310 U.S. 586 (1940), and *West Virginia State Board of Education v. Barnette,* 319 U.S. 624 (1943).

[11]*Betts v. Brady,* 316 U.S. 455 (1942).

[12]*Colegrove v. Green,* 328 U.S. 549 (1946), and *Baker v. Carr,* 369 U.S. 186 (1962).

Constitution which he swore to support and defend, not the gloss which his predecessors may have put on it. So he comes to formulate his own views, rejecting some earlier ones as false and embracing others. He cannot do otherwise unless he lets men long dead and unaware of the problems of the age in which he lives do his thinking for him.[13]

Of course people rely on constitutional decisions. Teachers in 1943 believed they could require even Jehovah's Witnesses in the classroom to salute the flag. State judges in 1963 did not believe they had to appoint counsel in all felonies. Candidates for political office and their parties in the early 1960s may have created their election strategies assuming malapportionment in voting districts. The point is that constitutional values may be important enough to override reliance on past policy.

SUMMARY

This section has explained my choice of Chief Justice Taney's words to begin this chapter. If we believe that the Constitution should be enforced so as to limit government in fact, then courts must do that job. If we believe that the Constitution's vague, ambiguous, and general words often fail to resolve concrete cases, then courts must say what the words mean. If we believe that no other agency of government is structured to give close, careful, and continuous attention to the meaning of the supreme law of the land, then what Taney called "the force of reasoning" behind the decisions of courts becomes the center of our scheme of constitutional law. When the force of reasoning fails, constitutional law must adjust.

Before we proceed further, however, let me remind you what I am *not* asserting. First, I am *not* asserting simply that in constitutional law judges *should* attempt to reason as political, social, and economic philosophers. I am asserting that they have no choice. The judge who invokes a prior constitutional rule and resolves a conflict by invoking stare decisis simply applies, wisely or unwisely, the philosophy of an earlier time to the case

[13] William O. Douglas, "Stare Decisis," 4 *Record of the Association of the Bar of the City of New York* 152 (1949), pp. 153–154.

before him. Second, I do not mean to imply that philosophizing—deciding in terms of assessments about basic social relationships and values—necessarily and inevitably forces judges to reject words, purposes, or stare decisis. It is rather that these decisional aids cannot come first and preclude reasoning at a deeper level. Finally, I do not mean to imply that reasoning by example has no place in constitutional law. Fact freedom pervades all law, and constitutional opinions cite precedents in many creative ways.

LIMITING THE CONSTITUTIONAL POWER OF COURTS

A large dark paradox now looms on our horizon: We take the concept that *law* should limit government so seriously that we assign one branch of government, the courts, the task of making that law and enforcing it, practically without limits! The constitutional command to "care" hardly limits judges at all.

I am not, in a few deft pages, about to resolve that paradox. The problem of policing the police is, after all, as durable as any in government. I do hope, however, to show that we can live with it. Perhaps continuously worrying about the problem of policing the police is the most effective means of policing police that societies will ever achieve. In any event, the remaining material in this chapter reviews how philosophizing about the role of the U.S. Supreme Court can justify some—but not all—active constitutional law making. We shall see first that some constitutional problems only indirectly raise the problem of limits. Here, in order to *facilitate* the working of government, courts must create rules that tell the various branches and levels of government which powers are and are not theirs. Second, we shall see how some conditions and values in American politics can yield at least rough conclusions about where limits on constitutional powers of judges ought to lie.

Where Limits on Judges Don't Matter: Facilitation of Intergovernmental Relations

Just as corporate leaders must at times facilitate, the Constitution also calls on the Court to facilitate. By facilitation I mean umpiring the inevitable disputes that arise among the divisions of government about who has power to do something. These squabbles will always exist in any complex organization, and, when they exist, the squabblers will inevitably go to the legal system for refereeing help. In 1983, for example, we saw the House of Representatives threatening to arrest the head of the Environmental Protection Agency, and the President in turn suing the House of Representatives on the matter. Like many intergovernmental squabbles, this squabble over the legislature's power to investigate wrongdoing in the EPA ended up in court.

Facilitation is part of constitutional law because, as we saw near the beginning of the chapter, the Constitution accomplishes more than one goal. It sets absolute limits on governmental power, but it also coordinates the powers of different parts of the government. To illustrate, the clause stating "Congress shall have power to regulate commerce among the several states" begins the laborious task of working out just who can tax, who can regulate, and who can forbid what without infringing upon the other jurisdictions trying to perform the same function.

Laying aside the question of what the commerce clause actually empowers the Congress to do, let us examine the problem from the state's side. Does the commerce clause mean that no state can ever regulate any commercial activity that in some way involves other states? Does it mean that the state cannot impose safety regulations on a business (or tax that business's profits) if that business buys some of its supplies from out of state or sells some of its product to customers in other states? On the other hand, the commerce clause does not necessarily prohibit the states from competing with, perhaps even nullifying the effects of, federal regulation of commerce. Maybe the states can do that, too.

The Court has not, over the course of history, always reached precisely the right division of state and federal responsibilities over commerce, but it has, in large part, reached workable results. More important, it has done so by approaching the problem as facilitator.

The Court began in 1824 to define the regulatory power of states over interstate commerce when Justice Marshall, for the

Court, ruled that, once federal law regulates a commercial enterprise specifically, then state law must not interfere. Beveridge, in his classic biography of Marshall, describes the problem that the framers designed the commerce clause to meet in this way:

> Finance, commerce, and business assembled the historic Philadelphia Convention; although it must be said that statesmanship guided its turbulent councils. The senseless and selfish nagging at trade in which the States indulged, after peace was declared, produced a brood of civil abuses as noisome as the military dangers which State control of troops had brought forth during the Revolution. Madison truly said that "most of our political evils may be traced up to our commercial ones." The States passed tariff laws against one another as well as against foreign nations; and, indeed, as far as commerce was concerned, each State treated the others as foreign nations. There were retaliations, discriminations, and every manner of trade restrictions and impediments which local ingenuity and selfishness could devise.
>
> The idea of each State was to keep money from going outside its borders into other States and to build up its own business and prosperity at the expense of its neighbors. States having no seaports were in a particularly hard case. Madison picturesquely describes their unhappy plight: "New Jersey placed between Phil^a & N. York, was likened to a cask tapped at both ends; And N. Carolina, between Virg^a & S. Carolina to a patient bleeding at both Arms." Merchants and commercial bodies were at their wits' end to carry on business and petitioned for a general power over commerce.[14]

Marshall's decision in 1824 was consistent with constitutional purpose as Beveridge describes it.[15]

In 1851, however, the Court upheld local regulations of interstate commerce. In this case of harbor and river pilots, the Court refined the earlier decision:

> Whatever subjects of this power are in their nature national, or admit only of one uniform system, or plan of regulation, may

---

[14]Albert J. Beveridge, *The Life of John Marshall*, Vol. 1 (New York: Houghton Mifflin, 1916), pp. 310–312.

[15]*Gibbons v. Ogden*, 22 U.S. 1 (1824).

justly be said to be of such a nature as to require exclusive legislation by Congress.[16]

Translated, this meant that the states, as well as the cities and counties within them, may impose separate and nonuniform regulations on interstate commerce as long as businessmen can adjust to these regulations without suffering great costs or being placed at a competitive disadvantage with local businesses.

The essence of the doctrine in *Cooley* remains law today. When Arizona by statute limited the length of passenger trains to 14 cars and freight trains to 70 cars, the Court found the law unconstitutional. The Arizona statute was a safety measure designed to alleviate a danger inherent in the railroad business: The more the couplings, the greater the jolt to the tail cars when they start up. (Because each coupling has some slack in it, the locomotive can actually build up significant speed before its pull reaches the tail cars at all. When it does, the tail cars jerk forward immediately to the locomotive's speed.) The Court held, however, that the expense of breaking up and recombining trains at Arizona's borders was costly and would become much more costly if every state had a different train limit law of its own. The Court said:

> For a hundred years it has been accepted constitutional doctrine that the commerce clause, without the aid of Congressional legislation, thus affords some protection from state legislation inimical to the national commerce, and that in such cases, where Congress has not acted, this Court, and not the state legislature, is under the commerce clause the final arbiter of the competing demands of state and national interests....
>
> Congress has undoubted power to redefine the distribution of power over interstate commerce. It may either permit the states to regulate the commerce in a manner which would otherwise not be permissible,...or exclude state regulation even of matters of peculiarly local concern which nevertheless affect interstate commerce....
>
> But in general Congress has left it to the courts to formulate the rules thus interpreting the commerce clause in its application, doubtless because it has appreciated the

[16]*Cooley v. Board of Wardens of Part of Philadelphia,* 53 U.S. 299 (1851), p. 319

destructive consequences to the commerce of the nation if their protection were withdrawn, . . . and has been aware that in their application state laws will not be invalidated without the support of relevant factual material which will "afford a sure basis" for an informed judgment. . . . Meanwhile, Congress has accommodated its legislation, as have the states, to these rules as an established feature of our constitutional system. There has thus been left to the states wide scope for the regulation of matters of local state concern, even though it in some measure affects the commerce, provided it does not materially restrict the free flow of commerce across state lines, or interfere with it in matters with respect to which uniformity of regulation is of predominant national concern.[17]

Note the Court's emphasis here on the need to develop clear accommodations between state and federal power and then to hold to them. In a later case, the Court held that Illinois could not require all trucks and trailers operating in the state to use a certain rear fender mudguard that differed from those 45 other states allowed and that was flatly illegal in yet another state.[18]

The Court has reached similar results in cases where state or local policy seems to work for the benefit of local businesses at the expense of out-of-state competitors. In 1949 it invalidated a New York decision that limited the sales of New York milk to out-of-state buyers at lower cost, even though New York was simply attempting to maintain adequate milk prices for New York dairymen and supplies for New York consumers.[19] And in 1951 the Court struck down a Madison, Wisconsin, ordinance that forbade the sale of milk in Madison that was not pasteurized and bottled within five miles of town. The Court said no such barrier to commerce should stand under the commerce clause as long as the city had less discriminatory means of equally insuring the safety of its milk. The Court concluded that the city could ask any producer to pay the extra cost of time and travel of inspectors to its plant and reach the same result. No doubt the Court suspected that the measure was designed to protect the business of local processors.[20]

---

[17]*Southern Pacific v. Arizona*, 325 U.S. 761 (1945), pp. 769–770.
[18]*Bibb v. Navajo Freight Lines, Inc.*, 359 U.S. 520 (1959).
[19]*Hood & Son v. Du Mond*, 336 U.S. 525 (1949).
[20]*Dean Milk Co. v. City of Madison*, 340 U.S. 349 (1951).

You will not find absolute consistency among the Court's many decisions attempting to separate state from federal power over commerce. In 1938 the Court upheld a South Carolina statute that prohibited trucks over 20,000 pounds or more than 90 inches wide from using South Carolina's highways. No one denied that these limits substantially increased the costs of trucking in interstate commerce through that state. The Court emphasized that South Carolina owned the roads and that the law did not discriminate against interstate commerce, since local trucks had to meet the same requirements. The Court did not, however, show convincingly why these factors justified the substantial burden on interstate commerce.[21]

Yet how crucial is a high level of consistency? The central problem is that, in a federal system, different units of government from time to time inevitably step on each other's toes. As long as judges, on a case-by-case basis, delineate state and federal power over highways, railroads, taxes, and a thousand other commercial problems, facilitation occurs. The results need not all conform to the same overall standard of federal relations. A series of narrow solutions to practical problems serves the purpose. Of course we need a rule telling states whether they can or cannot limit the weights of trucks. The Supreme Court is the most plausible place to articulate such a rule and apply it uniformly. But the same rule need not govern the constitutional capacity of states to limit trains.

In the world of facilitation, which draws lines that, despite

---

[21] *South Carolina State Highway Department v. Barnwell Bros.*, 303 U.S. 177 (1938). See also *Brotherhood of Locomotive Firemen and Enginemen v. Chicago, R.I. and P. Railroad*, 393 U.S. 129 (1968). Commentators often note considerable legal and policy inconsistencies between *Barnwell* and *Southern Pacific*. A careful reading of the two opinions reveals the explanation. In the earlier case *(Barnwell),* the Court refused to examine or deem relevant the social background facts in the case. But seven years later, the Court's personnel had changed significantly, and the *Southern Pacific* Court looked into the costs and other facts about the railroad freight business quite extensively. For a view that the courts should not even bother facilitating at all, based in part on the fact that the members of Congress, being elected state-by-state, have much pressure on them to represent state interests effectively, see Jesse H. Choper, *Judicial Review and the National Political Process: A Functional Reconsideration of the Role of the Supreme Court* (Chicago: University of Chicago Press, 1980).

occasional arbitrariness, tell governmental units what they can and can't do, how serious is the problem of limits on judicial power? Virtually any decision, or even the refusal to decide altogether, will encourage some policies and discourage others. We hope that the Court acts wisely and that it retains its capacity to correct its own mistakes, but we do not want to limit it from acting at all. Judicial inaction here only makes the task of facilitation more difficult.

Where Limits on Judges Matter: Defining Individual Rights

The most celebrated constitutional cases in this century have not facilitated; they have defined prohibitions on governmental power that limit *all* levels of government. No level of government may segregate schools by race. No level of government may impose a scheme of prior censorship on the press. No level of government may win a conviction of an accused criminal through the use of a coerced confession. No level of government may require prayers in public schools. No level of government may, as a rule, impose criminal penalties upon those performing or undergoing an abortion in the first trimester of pregnancy.

I do not mean to belittle or oversimplify the practical and philosophical hazards of defining human rights and liberties convincingly. In many cultures other than our own—Islam, for example—the oft-spoken claim that the regime advances and protects "human rights" means something very different from our own culture's protection of the individual's autonomy and dignity.[22]

In our culture, at least, the absolute prohibitions I have just listed do create individual rights. These judicial rulings do not overturn the work of elected governmental bodies because other elected governmental bodies should do the work instead, as the train length decision did. Decisions creating rights often prevent

---

[22] Jack Donnelly, "Human Rights and Human Dignity: An Analytical Critique of Non-Western Conceptions of Human Rights," 76 *American Political Science Review* 303 (1982).

any elected group from adopting certain policies. If we take the concept of limited government seriously, this awesome power itself must also have its limits.

Let us begin to examine these limits by reviewing one of the most notorious examples of unlimited judicial power: *Lochner v. New York.* At the turn of the century, the New York legislature passed a law regulating the hours of bakers. The statute said no employee should be "required or permitted to work in a biscuit, bread, or cake bakery or confectionery establishment more than ten hours in any one day unless for the purpose of making a shorter day on the last day of the week."

The health problem in bakeries appeared to be serious. Professor Hirt, in his treatise, *Diseases of the Workers,* had observed:

> The labor of the bakers is among the hardest and most laborious imaginable, because it has to be performed under conditions injurious to the health of those engaged in it.... [T]he erratic demands of the public [compel] the baker to perform the greater part of his work at night, thus depriving him of an opportunity to enjoy the necessary rest and sleep, a fact which is highly injurious to his health.

Another source stated:

> The constant inhaling of flour dust causes inflammation of the lungs and of the bronchial tubes. The eyes also suffer through this dust, which is responsible for the many cases of running eyes among the bakers. The long hours of toil to which all bakers are subjected produce rheumatism, cramps and swollen legs. The intense heat in the workshops induces the workers to resort to cooling drinks, which together with their habit of exposing the greater part of their bodies to the change in the atmosphere, is another source of a number of diseases of various organs. Nearly all bakers are pale-faced and of more delicate health than the workers of other crafts, which is chiefly due to their hard work and their irregular and unnatural mode of living, whereby the power of resistance against disease is greatly diminished. The average age of a baker is below that of other workmen; they seldom live over their fiftieth year, most of them dying between the ages of forty and fifty. During periods of epidemic diseases the bakers are generally the first to succumb to the disease, and the number

swept away during such periods far exceeds the number of other crafts in comparison to the men employed in the respective industries. When, in 1720, the plague visited the city of Marseilles, France, every baker in the city succumbed to the epidemic, which caused considerable excitement in the neighboring cities and resulted in measures for the sanitary protection of the bakers.[23]

Mr. Lochner was indicted and convicted of requiring and permitting a bakery employee to work more than 60 hours a week, but the Supreme Court ruled that the statute deprived Mr. Lochner and his baker of their freedom to contract with one another. The Court invoked the Fourteenth Amendment's words, "No state shall...deprive any person of life, liberty, or property, without due process of law."[24] The court admitted that the state could prohibit making contracts to the extent necessary to preserve public health and morality. But the majority said, "We think that there can be no fair doubt that the trade of a baker, in and of itself, is not an unhealthy one...." In effect the Court said the Constitution does not allow the government to tell individuals what kinds of contracts they can make unless public health and morals are involved. Ailing bakers do not necessarily make unhealthy bread for public consumption.

The Court wrongly decided *Lochner*, but why? Notice that the earlier explanations of this chapter seem to corner me. I *cannot* say that *Lochner* was wrong because the Fourteenth Amendment says nothing about freedom of contract. If the Justices only protect those civil rights that the Constitution clearly and concretely defines, most of the freedoms the Constitution only generally describes would have no legal force. Similarly, we cannot resort to the purpose of the framers of the Fourteenth Amendment or to earlier precedents. Except for its disregard for the social background facts about the health of

---

[23] Quoted in the dissenting opinion of Justice Harlan in *Lochner*, 198 U.S. 45 (1905), pp. 70–71.

[24] *Lochner*, p. 53. Of Justice Peckham, the author of the majority opinion, Justice Holmes once wrote that "his major premise was 'God damn it,' meaning thereby that emotional predilections somewhat governed him on social themes." See Alpheus Mason and William Beaney, *American Constitutional Law* (Englewood Cliffs, N.J.: Prentice-Hall, 1978), p. 361.

bakery workers, the majority engaged in precisely the political and social philosophy I have applauded. Freedom of contract, the majority thought, greatly enhanced individual and social well-being.

Hence the central question comes down to this: When should the Supreme Court actively protect personal freedom by proscribing governmental power?

The rest of this chapter concerns three possible answers that judges may give. Each answer presents a distinct way of thinking about limits on judicial power. Each of my three formulations concludes that the Court decided *Lochner* wrongly, but you should feel comfortable only with the third.

1. Rarely, if ever. We are not elected. We do not speak for the people. The more the courts decide such issues, the more we overrule the results of the democratic process. The more we do so, the more we both injure our own authority as a court and the more we enfeeble the democratic process. *Lochner* wrongly overruled a democratic decision.

2. We the Justices can, through reason and the careful study of the human condition, determine what really are fundamental freedoms. When we do discover and articulate the nature of a freedom, then it is up to us as a court to make the government toe this legal line. That's part of the function of any court. "Freedom of contract" simply isn't a fundamental freedom; hence *Lochner* was wrong. But the right to an integrated education is fundamental. So is the right to have one's vote counted equally. So are freedom of speech, religion, and privacy.

3. The Constitution obligates the government, indeed the entire polity, to respect the fact that limits on public power do exist. We the Justices can never be entirely sure what those limits are. Indeed, their definition will shift over time. But in order to preserve the *belief* that limits exist, we must make rough guesses about what these limits, these freedoms, are. We can also make rough guesses about whether the political processes — in Congress, in state legislatures, in bureaucracies, and all other agencies of government down to the police

station—is likely to persuade other people besides judges to think about, to wrestle with, the fundamental problem of defining freedom in ways that keep the basic freedoms intact. When we believe that a party in a lawsuit raises a question of fundamental freedom *and* when we worry that the political process outside courts may not take that value into account, then it is our duty to articulate the value and make it stick as far as we can. In some cases we shall guess wrongly. If so, either through amendment, or widespread noncompliance, or a change in the views of the Justices wrought by the presidential appointment process, or criticism in the law reviews, we shall be forced to back off. But when our hunches are valid, our decisions will help the polity remember to care, as we do, about the often bothersome task of preserving freedom.

   Lochner was wrong because, if we know anything about the political process, we know that money influences. We have every reason to believe that legislators hear lobbyists for well-funded interests. We have every reason to believe that people with money finance candidates of their choice to attempt to win votes for their positions. If legislatures pass laws seemingly at odds with our hunches about the freedoms of the well-funded, we still have every reason to believe that the proponents of the losing position had their chance to persuade. There is nothing about wearing our robes that makes us any better qualified than a legislator or a policeman to decide in the abstract what really are fundamental freedoms. But there is something about our position that allows us to judge whether others have made or are likely to make the effort. Our decisions are not perfect, but they are better than silence. We cannot keep alive through silence the idea that government has limits.

   By this point you should, without my help, sense why the first answer fails, but do you see the important differences between the second and third answers? The second assumes that the members of the Supreme Court somehow possess the capacity to decide what are and are not fundamental public and private values. The second choice almost makes a claim of judicial infallibility, or at least clear ethical superiority.

But the third answer presents for the Court a more modest claim. Here judges need not sit as Platonic guardians. They must study the actual operation of the political process, the daily ways of national life, and act when available evidence indicates that the political process may not consider a liberties problem seriously. Briefly, I prefer the third choice because I think judges can philosophize in this manner. They can, in a crude way, comprehend the knowledge on which defensible constitutional judgments of this sort rest.

The Court itself has never officially adopted this view of its constitutional function, though I suspect that many civil rights decisions are consistent with it. However, in a famous footnote to an otherwise ordinary constitutional case, Justice Stone did provide essentially this justification for greater judicial protection of political and personal freedoms than of economic freedoms:

> There may be narrower scope for operation of the presumption of constitutionality when legislation appears on its face to be within a specific prohibition of the Constitution, such as those of the first ten amendments, which are deemed equally specific when held to be embraced within the Fourteenth....
>
> It is unnecessary to consider now whether legislation which restricts those political processes which can ordinarily be expected to bring about a repeal of undesirable legislation, is to be subjected to more exacting judicial scrutiny under the general prohibitions of the Fourteenth Amendment than are most other types of legislation....
>
> Nor need we inquire whether similar consideration enter into the review of statutes directed at particular religious...or national...or racial minorities...: whether prejudice against discrete and insular minorities may be a special condition, which tends seriously to curtail the operation of those political processes ordinarily to be relied upon to protect minorities, and which may call for a correspondingly more searching judicial inquiry....[25]

[25] *United States v. Carolene Products Company*, 304 U.S. 144 (1938), pp. 152–153, note 4. See also Jesse Choper, supra, and John Hart Ely, *Democracy*

This is certainly a backhanded way of explaining the point, but the footnote has had substantial impact on the way in which both judges and scholars conceive of the judicial role.

The next section develops a more complete defense of this third way of limiting the Court's power to protect individual liberties. First, however, consider several additional cases illustrating the third answer. We begin by returning to the flag salute cases. The Court first allowed public schools to require every student to salute the flag, but quickly changed its view.

The Supreme Court's initial approach to the flag salute issue reflected the philosophy of Mr. Justice Frankfurter. Frankfurter believed that most attempts by the courts to set civil liberties standards for state and local governments did, at least in the long run, more harm than good. He believed that the more the courts resolved these issues, the more state and local politicians would assume the habit of passing on constitutional questions to the courts. He preferred always the course of action that encouraged the electoral process to face such issues directly. He felt that both politicians and the population would, by deliberating the issue themselves, become more sophisticated about and sensitive to the importance of constitutional values.

At the threshold, notice that Frankfurter reasoned precisely in the way the third choice applauds. Frankfurter philosophized not about ethical absolutes but about the operation of the political process itself. One of the many reasons for Frankfurter's deserved respect as a jurist is that he did not pretend that he could escape philosophizing or that he could divine ethically perfect answers.

By and large, however, the background facts about the political world simply do not support the premises in Frankfurter's argument. Our electoral system builds on the foundation of self-interest. Men in office want to keep their jobs. They

---

and *Distrust* (Cambridge: Harvard University Press, 1980). The *Carolene Products* approach is more an analytical starting point than a conclusion. For a provocative analysis of its limitations, see Owen Fiss, "Foreword: The Forms of Justice," 98 *Harvard Law Review* 1 (1979) and Lawrence Tribe, "The Puzzling Persistence of Process-Based Constitutional Theories," 89 *Yale Law Journal* 1063 (1980).

do so by helping as many interests (as many sources of votes) as possible as long as they can reconcile their positions. In those relatively rare cases in which a politician senses strong and stable majority support for a policy, he or she will certainly not take the initiative to change it. The "flag, motherhood, and apple pie" do not regularly receive careful legislative scrutiny, yet this is what Frankfurter assumed. By upholding the flag salute, Frankfurter thought the Court would encourage candidates competing for office to take sides against the flag to win the votes of a tiny number of voters, the Jehovah's Witnesses. But successful politicians are not suicidal, and Frankfurter was incorrect. The process of setting legislative agendas in a democracy will exclude some interests altogether, and this is precisely the kind of political fact that the court should and can—and in this example did—consider.

Frankfurter also opposed judicial intervention in legislative electoral districting, yet legislative reapportionment is perhaps this century's most persuasive case for judicial intervention. This is one of those rare issues in which not even majorities can affect the politician's self-interested choice. Reapportionment to a politician in a badly apportioned state may carry only one meaning: redrawing the lines and changing the kinds of voters he has successfully appealed to in the past and must appeal to in the future. If cities receive seats at the expense of rural areas, some rural legislators will almost surely lose their jobs altogether. Badly apportioned districts by their very nature return to office each election day men who have every reason to avoid reapportionment. Our third answer thus justifies some direct judicial interference in the political process, such as the Court's decision in 1944 invalidating "white only" primary elections.[26]

The list continues. The Court, ever since it held unconstitutional the laws promoting segregated housing, has moved aggressively to protect that group of citizens most systematically excluded from political participation, black Americans.[27] Another dramatic change, wrought primarily by the Warren Court, advanced the interest of the accused. Imagine how atten-

[26]*Smith v. Allwright*, 321 U.S. 649 (1944).
[27]*Buchanan v. Warley*, 245 U.S. 60 (1917).

tively legislators would listen to a hypothetical interest group (of course, under the fanciful assumption that such a group could possibly fund any kind of lobbying campaign) titled "The League for the Protection of the Rights of Accused Rapists, Muggers, and Killers."

Again the point is not that the civil rights decisions, primarily of the Warren Court, were right in any final, absolute sense. Rather, their overall thrust was to add to the political processes of the nation an institutional "ear" for those whose voices the political process tended not to hear.

The Scholarly Critique of Judicial Activism and a Response

Let me summarize my position. I think it essential to preserve the idea that law limits government. I think this far more essential than any notion that the courts should only decide in those rare instances in which no reasonable argument stands against judicial activism. Sometimes the courts will decide erroneously. Sometimes the social price will be high, but the price is worth paying. I believe the Constitution requires judges to be nothing more or less than political philosophers. As a political scientist, I believe the modern Supreme Court Justice generally asks the right question when he or she asks, "Do the normal political processes reflect the claims for a given governmental limit, or freedom, so as to shape it coherently? Does the normal political process, perhaps only by imperfect compromise, nevertheless preserve the basic integrity of these liberties?" However, the issue is certainly an open one, particularly because the limits on the courts themselves seem so tentative. This chapter concludes with my own solutions to these open puzzles of judicial activism. My purpose here is to stimulate you to begin to formulate your own solutions, not to force you into accepting mine.

The Problem of Democracy and the Courts

Question: The entire argument for judicial activism hinges upon the need to maintain limits on government. But the courts are one of the three branches of government. The most important limit upon government, placed there by the Constitution itself, is the electoral process. If people do not like a decision, they ought to be able to change it. But the Justices of the Supreme Court have lifetime appointments. The political process does not reach them. Mustn't they have an overwhelmingly persuasive case before they consider destroying the work of a democratic body like a legislature?

Response: At the outset, do not lose sight of the meaning of limited government.[28] Assuming for the moment that a given law represents the majority will, the Constitution still means that there are some decisions majorities cannot impose on individuals. The existence of the Constitution itself prevents us from having an absolute democracy. Remember also that many constitutional decisions do not invalidate a statutory provision at all. The bulk of decisions protecting the accused do not correct "democratic" legislative decisions. They correct the decisions of policemen, trial judges, and other bureaucrats whose actions receive even less scrutiny by voters than do actions of the Supreme Court.

The more we study the electoral process, however, the more we realize that most acts of the bulk of elected officials generally do not really correspond to the majority will, for the very simple reason that the majority has no will on the issue whatsoever. Elections do not matter primarily because they insure that all laws will correspond to majority wishes. We benefit from elections primarily because they make politicians listen, not to "the majority" but to people and group interests of all kinds that come to politicians with problems. The election campaign the

---

[28] Professor Lawrence Tribe has nicely refined the fallacies in any view that automatically prefers the interest group–dominated world of daily politics to any form of judicial activism. Three such fallacies are:

1. The assumption that issues affecting large numbers, perhaps majorities, of citizens will automatically find their way onto the priority lists of specific and politically active interest groups.
2. The assumption that individual cases can receive fair treatment in noncourt settings.
3. The belief that infrequent judicial pronouncements of normative constitutional principles will suffice to keep these principles alive. See "Seven Pluralist Fallacies: In Defense of the Adversary Process." 33 *University of Miami Law Review* 43 (1978).

politician hopes to win requires votes from as many sources as possible. It is in his self-interest to help as many as he can. It is also in his interest—this is particularly true of governors, presidents, and the leaders of parties in power—that the affairs of state not deteriorate. The elected politician's desire to prevent economic and social decay because he or she can lose office if this occurs, keeps politicians searching for policies that contribute to the general welfare and encourages them to be open to the possibility of change. Elections tend to overcome the natural inertia of all organized human effort.

It is a partial solution to our problem to note that some state judges are actually elected and that the president fills a vacancy on the Supreme Court, on the average, about once in two years. These political facts of life do have an impact on judicial decisions. For a complete response, we must realize that, if elections mainly accomplish the positive value of persuading officials to listen and change, then the judicial process accomplishes the *same* result by other means. At least at the levels below the Supreme Court, unlike other governmental officials, judges must listen. Anyone can file a lawsuit as the innovative cases reported at the end of Chapter V show. A judge, unlike a senator or representative, cannot politely file away a request from a powerless minority because time does not permit consideration or because there is no political gain in listening. For every lawsuit filed, a judge must listen long enough to determine whether the plaintiff alleges an injury for which the law may give relief. The judicial process therefore has its own built-in parallel to elections that requires judges, like other politicians, to listen to the complaints of citizens.

The Supreme Court has discretion over its docket, true enough, but this brings us to another feature of the judicial process that corresponds to the electoral process. Elections force officials to be prepared to justify their decisions and their behavior. The press asks questions. An opponent in the campaign will press the politician to explain a vote. The tradition that appellate judges write opinions explaining their decisions also imposes a requirement of justification.[29] A questionable

[29] Legal reasoning itself is a form of justification. Chapter VII develops the point further.

justification in an opinion provokes not only dissents, it provokes, as did the first flag salute case, the criticism of the community of legal scholars, expressed both in bar association speeches and in law reviews.

The legal system thus contains its own dynamics for listening and correcting mistakes. If, however, none of this persuades you, do consider the following facts. In less than one-half of one percent of all statutes passed by Congress since World War II has the Court found a point to invalidate. In nearly all of these instances, the Court has invalidated not an entire statutory scheme or policy but only an offending clause or provision.[30] The most activist of courts touches only a tiny fraction of the democratic work of Congress. Nor, conversely, does the Court's constitutional approval of law or administrative practice necessarily seal that practice forever. A judicial decision upholding the constitutionality of a governmental action does not impair the ability of political interests to lobby that the policy is wasteful and erroneous on other grounds.

In summary, some of the political forces that affect other politicians also affect judges. Where they don't, the judicial process contains other mechanisms that accomplish many of the same results. The political similarities outweigh the differences and do not dictate judicial abstinence from constitutional decision making.

The Problem of Judicial Information Processing

Question: Judges are lawyers, and probably lawyers who knew politicians. They are certainly not trained to evalute all the complexities of modern policy questions. For that matter, they are not trained as political scientists, either. What assurance have we that judges will not reject socially beneficial policies, as *Lochner* did, or will sense correctly when the political process succeeds or fails to make acceptable judgments about civil liberties on its own?

---

[30] Through the year 1978, the Supreme Court had invalidated portions of about 100 Acts of Congress, 900 State Statutes, and 124 local ordinances. My thanks to Professor Sam Krislov for calling these tabulations to my attention.

Response: We have no absolute assurance. Worse, the long history of *Lochner*-like judicial nullification of social and economic legislation illustrates the danger that courts can ignore social background facts most people believe to be true. Of course the Court ultimately retreated, but that is not itself a satisfying response.

A more complete response must return to our discussion of *The T.J. Hooper* and the barges that sank in Chapter V. We saw there that courts process information very much as other decision makers do. Various sides present positions. Lawyers file briefs containing abundant factual as well as legal assertions. They criticize the positions their opponents take. The problem lies not so much in the judges' ability to get facts but in their capacity to understand them.

On this score, we cannot escape the wisely ambiguous answer that the capacity of judges to understand information "all depends." It depends on two things. First, does the issue really depend on the intelligent digestion and interpretation of a complex body of facts at all? Many of the most dramatic civil rights questions are so fundamentally normative and depend so extensively on moral rather than factual reasoning, that the technical competence of judges really does not seem relevant. The decision to forbid mandatory flag salutes does not depend on scientific analysis of data revealing the beneficial and harmful consequences of such practices.

Notice this is a different question than that raised by *Lochner*, for there, as we saw, the wisdom of the law did depend on whether it promoted health, a medical question. Second, therefore, when the issue does depend on an understanding of facts, then we should really expect judges to have the capacity to understand the facts before they proceed.

By understanding the facts, I mean this. First, judges must understand the language through which the problem expresses itself. Most judges are well equipped to understand the dimensions of a right-to-counsel issue. Most judges are not equipped to understand the econometric analysis on which the Federal Reserve Board determines its national monetary policy. Second, the problem must not be of the sort in which part of the information is necessarily hidden from judges, as it is in many foreign policy matters because the information is secret or because the only people who possess it do not live or work within the reach of the court's jurisdiction. Finally, if a given decision generates feedback information that will produce improved policy, the courts should have access to that information in the course of further litigation.

The inability of trial courts to find some kinds of facts and to make acceptable decisions at the implementation stage is a serious problem, perhaps the most serious in all of constitutional law. Judges are insulated from many pragmatic sources of political knowledge. When the sensitive and hard-working Judge Arthur Garrity was forced personally to oversee the integration of the Boston public school system, he was not and could not realistically have been in a position to make all the practical adjustments the situation called for. Specifically, he used police department geographical lines for organizing some phases of integration, not realizing that, to ease tensions within zones, the police lines were deliberately drawn to maximize homogeneity, not integration, in the population. Boston's schools are not in 1983 substantially more integrated than in 1972 when the Boston litigation began.[31]

My own contentment with the Warren Court's expansion of the rights of the accused rests largely on the fact that these decisions arose out of the legal system itself. I do not doubt the capacity of an Earl Warren, himself a former district attorney and attorney general of California, to understand the strengths and shortcomings of the criminal justice system. I do, on the other hand, doubt the capacity of judges to assess adequately the facts surrounding questions of foreign and military policy. The Court wisely refrained from interfering in the conduct of the Vietnam War, despite the fact that the war was disastrously bad policy.[32]

On the whole, I believe the judicial history of the last

---

[31] George V. Higgins, "Boston's Busing Disaster," *The New Republic,* February 28, 1983, p. 16.

[32] *Holtzman v. Schlesinger,* 414 U.S. 1304 (1973). See more generally, Lief H. Carter, "When Courts Should Make Policy: An Institutional Approach," in *Public Law and Public Policy,* John A. Gardiner, ed. (New York: Praeger, 1977), pp. 141–157; Donald L. Horowitz, *The Courts and Social Policy* (Washington, D.C.: The Brookings Institution, 1977); J. Woodford Howard, "Adjudication

quarter century reveals a Court that has moved most forcefully in fields which it possesses this capacity to comprehend. Where judicial understanding has proved itself naive, as it did in some of the more extreme versions of its "one man, one vote" requirement, the Court has retreated, just as the constitutional-reasoning model suggests it should.

But the most important justification of an active judicial defense of liberties is simply this: Constitutional decisions possess all the characteristics of the common law tradition. No one decision permanently sets the course of law. The process is a thoroughly incremental one in which, case by case, new facts and new arguments pro and con repeatedly come before the courts. The law can change and adjust to new facts and conditions. A judicial commitment to protecting liberties does not require the courts to articulate a complete theory of equal protection or due process.[33]

Of course courts will often fail, and it is critically important that scholars criticize judges for their failures, as Donald Horowitz has recently done. But to conclude from these failures, as Horowitz does, that judicial defense of liberties must attend more to the case and less to social policy misses a central point.[34] *All* organized problem solving is incremental, disjointed, and prone to error. Judges need only recognize this fact. Hiding from it prevents judges from processing information to improve the quality of constitutional law.

The Problem of Legitimacy

Question: Conceding that courts could carve out a politically sensible approach to the defense of rights, we still have not faced

---

Considered as a Process of Conflict Resolution: A Variation on Separation of Powers," 18 *Journal of Public Law* 39 (1969); Stephen Wasby, "Horowitz: The Courts and Social Policy," 31 *Vanderbilt Law Review* 727 (1978).

[33] Felix Cohen, "Transcendental Nonsense and the Functional Approach," 35 *Columbia Law Review* 809 (1935). See also Martin Shapiro, "Stability and Change in Judicial Decision Making: Incrementalism or Stare Decisis?" 2 *Law in Transition Quarterly* 134 (1964).

[34] *Horowitz*, Chapter 7.

the most important problem of all. The fact remains that some people do not believe the Supreme Court ought to make policy. The Court, like any other court, is a legal institution designed to resolve lawsuits. Since courts do not have the legitimacy-giving power of elections to fall back on, they can rely only on the quality of their reasoning. If the Court behaves flexibly, if the Court willingly changes unwise policies and thus makes the definition of rights seem to change at whim, does it not in the long run destroy itself? Isn't it, in other words, a contradiction in terms for the Court to say that rights are so important that a nondemocratic body should preserve them and then turn around and say that the process of defending these rights must be flexible and variable because the courts can never tell precisely what the rights really are?

Response: This final question raising the problem of legitimacy is, I think, the most persuasive argument against an active judicial defense of civil rights. This is so despite judicial lawmaking's roots in the common law tradition. In his last book, Alexander Bickel addressed the problem most elegantly. In any modern complex society, one in which the strongest of interests, both symbolic and economic, can always clash and explode, government's primary task is to generate workable tradeoffs and compromises. Policy in this political environment almost inevitably fails when it becomes captured and controlled by absolute principles. The disaster of the Vietnam War occurred because our policy became the prisoner of ideology.[35] The Supreme Court has many techniques for avoiding the obligation to make constitutional decisions.[36] But when it speaks, it cannot avoid speaking in principled fashion. Whenever it speaks, it injects into the political process absolutes that only make it more difficult to achieve the absolutely essential compromises and unprincipled decisions that allow complex societies to survive. What elections really accomplish more than any other objective is to make acceptable in the public eye a process of compromise that produces decisions that no one can fully justify in the abstract.

---

[35] Alexander Bickel, *The Morality of Consent* (New Haven: Yale University Press, 1975).

[36] Bickel, *The Least Dangerous Branch,* Chapter 4, pp. 111–198.

Why does this approach, with its impeccable scholarly pedigree, fail to persuade me? To begin, reread the judicial position I prefer (the third answer on page 252). That position makes paramount not the protection of any given right but the protection of the idea of rights, the preservation of the idea that government has limits. The precise definition of limits may change as times and political conditions change as long as the *idea* of limits remains in tact.

The key question is whether people can accept that approach. Here I think the political reality of public opinion and judicial legitimacy is in conflict with the antiactivist position. The general public does not read judicial decisions or analyze lines of precedent for consistency. If judicial legitimacy depends on public reaction, then it depends almost exclusively on the way the public perceives the basic results of judicial action.[37] If the public believes the Warren Court coddled criminals, no amount of principled reasoning in the opinion will change that perception.

But, if judicial legitimacy depends on the reaction of the legal profession to a decision, we may have little to fear, for lawyers already know and accept the inevitable failures, the inevitable errors that judges, being human, will make. The lawyer is trained to accept as inevitable the basic common law teaching that in a common law system, law constantly changes.

My own feeling is that the Court will preserve its authority to impose constitutional limits on government as long as the majority of its decisions meets three requirements. I see no reason that those fallible human beings who become judges cannot meet these requirements.

In this century, the court has, by and large, successfully met the first requirement: Taken as a whole the work of the Court must not appear consistently to favor one faction or party within the electorate. The Court cannot protect the political speech of liberals while refusing to protect the political speech of conservatives, or the reverse. Similarly, the Court's authority would suffer if people believed other political forces and institutions controlled it. If the citizenry came to believe that the Court

---

[37] See David Adamany, "Legitimacy, Realigning Elections, and the Supreme Court," 1973 *Wisconsin Law Review* 790 (1973).

had actively worked to protect or to remove President Nixon during the Watergate crisis, its authority would have seriously weakened.

The first requirement is *not* a constitutional requirement. The Constitution does not tell judges how to preserve their authority. This is a political requirement, and judges can satisfy it only by paying attention to the political realities around them.

This very political requirement to stay, paradoxically, above politics, is what makes so fascinating the Court's "decision" concerning racial quotas in university admissions.[38] Since no clear majority opinion addresses the totality of the *Bakke* case, it is difficult to speak of a decision in this case. I do sense, however, that Justice Powell's "compromise" position, one that permits universities to consider race as one factor for admission but not as the determining factor, represents a wise sensitivity to our political requirement.

Notice carefully that this requirement qualifies the position I have taken in defense of the third answer. In the *Bakke* case, the Court could easily have said that white and relatively affluent engineers like Allan Bakke simply do not typify those who lack the power to be heard in the political process. The Court could have equated a university racial quota with New York's bakers' law and assumed that, because whites, like businesses, have substantial political clout, decisions that fail to reflect their interests meet constitutional standards. It could have said the University of California's admissions policy was a legitimate attempt to cope with a serious social problem we widely believe needs a solution, namely the problem of racial discrimination and inequality. In arguing as he did, however, Justice Powell acknowledges another belief we also widely share: Race alone does not automatically determine disadvantage. Whites from Appalachian mining families may suffer the same disadvantages as do Mexican-American migrant workers. The children of successful black professional families may not suffer those disadvantages. I do not mean that either approach to *Bakke* is necessarily the one correct legal solution for that problem. I mean that among many possible approaches, the one

---

[38]*Regents v. Bakke*, 98 *Supreme Court Reporter* 2733 (1978).

that maximizes the appearance that decisions rise above the simple endorsement of one interest group rather than another may prove politically the wisest approach.

My second requirement, the second precondition for preserving the constitutional authority of courts, I call "consistency in method." I do not ask for total consistency among all cases. I mean that judges must set some internal limits, internal criteria, that govern not what they decide but how they decide constitutional questions, and they must take their own self-made limits seriously.[39]

Internal limits on the process of deciding play a critically important symbolic or public role. When a judge has the final word, when there is no hope of appeal (as when the umpire calls a pitch the ball that walks in the winning run), his power seems enormous. People often react to the threat of such power misused with frightening intensity. The booing of an enraged sports crowd has more than once made me taste bits of true terror. Such judges need to shield themselves with an impartiality of their procedures so unshakable as to assure the angry losers that the decision, if wrong, was no more than an honest mistake.

The Supreme Court, being supremely final, would be particularly wise to do so, and the final chapter of this book focuses directly on the impartiality problem. Unfortunately, the Court has met this requirement erratically at best. Indeed, the great failing of the modern Supreme Court is not so much its activism or its restraint or its doctrinal inconsistencies from case to case. Its greatest shortcoming is the failure of the Justices to confront collectively what it means to have constitutional responsibility in the first place and to translate that shared sense of responsibility into decisions.

Justice Brandeis, referring often to previous judicial decisions, codified one such set of internal limits:

1. The Court will not pass upon the constitutionality of legislation in a friendly, non-adversary, proceeding, declining because to decide such questions "is legitimate

---

[39] See Charles Fried, "Two Concepts of Interests: Some Reflections on the Supreme Court's Balancing Test," 76 *Harvard Law Review* 755 (1963).

only in the last resort, and as a necessity in the determination of real, earnest and vital controversy between individuals...."

2. The Court will not "anticipate a question of constitutional law in advance of the necessity of deciding it...."

3. The Court will not "formulate a rule of constitutional law broader than is required by the precise facts to which it is to be applied...."

4. The Court will not pass upon a constitutional question although properly presented by the record, if there is also present some other ground upon which the case may be disposed of....

5. The Court will not pass upon the validity of a statute upon complaint of one who fails to show that he is injured by its operation....

6. The Court will not pass upon the constitutionality of a statute at the instance of one who has availed himself of its benefits....

7. "When the validity of an act of the Congress is drawn in question, and even if a serious doubt of constitutionality is raised, it is a cardinal principle that this Court will first ascertain whether a construction of the statute is fairly possible by which the question may be avoided...."[40]

I think these limits are sensible. They encourage the Court's exercise of its "passive virtues," as Bickel calls them, whereby the Court can avoid reaching constitutional decisions in inappropriate cases and inappropriate political circumstances.[41] Unfortunately the recent Court has not respected these limits. Perhaps these "*Ashwander* rules" are unrealistic. If so, some alternative formulation should replace them. Again, the Court has failed, not by abandoning the Brandeis formulation but by developing no coherent philosophy about its role whatsoever.

My third and final condition of judicial legitimacy in constitutional matters I call the obligation of candor. If, as I think they should, judges acknowledge a constitutional role comparable to our third answer, then part of that role obligates judges to acknowledge and act out the role publicly as well as

---

[40] *Ashwander v. Tennessee Valley Authority*, 297 U.S. 288 (1936) pp. 346–348 (citations omitted from quotation).

[41] Bickel, *The Least Dangerous Branch*, Chapter 4.

privately. If the judicial decision applying the Constitution to our affairs is really part of a continuing dialogue about the nature of personal rights in a modern society, the dialogue cannot work if judges hide their analysis behind a facade of constitutional absolutism.

I, for one, will feel more optimistic about the endurance of the idea of rights and hence of limits on governmental power when I believe that judges themselves understand both the legal and the political dimensions of the problem. The age of absolutes is gone. Relativity and change pervade modern life. Judges and the law will look increasingly foolish if they refuse to accept and work within this truth.

But perhaps you are still uncomfortable with the idea that laws can be laws without being absolutes, that laws can retain meaning even when we admit that they are imperfect, ambiguous, and capable of rapid change that courts can act like courts without always pretending to know or state what absolute law is. I am not advocating that courts should routinely decide cases without giving reasons. No case can be decided reasonably without reference to some legal standard. But must we continue to pretend that these legal standards embody absolute truths? Societies can survive without absolutes in law. Societies will not survive a loss of faith in their capacity to do justice. In the past, judges have tended to assume that only when they pretend to find absolutes do they look as if they do justice. I suspect, on the other hand, that our collective belief that courts can do justice will grow if courts face and accept the rightness of relativity and change in standards. To do so need not require a major change in how judges view their work. Judge Andreen's opinion in *Soldano* in Chapter V, accepts changeability as part of the common law tradition. The next and final chapter explains more fully how I believe people can reconcile justice and relativity in modern times.

SUMMARY

- Why is the Constitution law? In this connection, consider H.L.A. Hart's increasingly accepted view that law exists to the extent that a society develops rules and methods for deciding precisely what its "primary rules," its statements of social obligations, say and for enforcing them.[42] For what reasons does Hart's approach mandate active constitutional policy making by the courts?

- Why does the judicial responsibility for constitutional policy making alter the bases of legal reasoning in constitutional law?
- Why, in such facilitative enterprises as the interpretation of the commerce clause, is it less necessary to pay close attention to the problem of limits on judicial power? Why does the problem of limits become more important when courts, primarily the Supreme Court, define and enforce civil rights?
- Under "normal" political conditions, what characteristics of our legal and political systems make active judicial review a desirable and relatively democratic institution?
- On what factors does the "legitimacy," or public acceptability, of the constitutional work of judges depend?

ILLUSTRATIVE CASE

To understand the legal issues in the following case you need to know that the "equal protection clause" of the Fourteenth Amendment potentially invalidates any state law that classifies or differentiates people by sex. This body of law is complex and unsettled, but please assume for the moment that *Craig v. Boren* 429 U.S. 190 (1976) states accepted law. In *Craig* the Court struck down a law that limited sale of 3.2 beer to men (but not women) in their late teens. The courts conventionally permit differentiations that bear a substantial relationship to legitimate public policies, but the Court in *Craig* required some evidence that young men more frequently caused social harm from drinking 3.2 beer than did young women. It found none and invalidated the sex-based classification. Consider by contrast the Supreme Court's conclusions about what the background facts do and do not prove in the following case. Assume that both male and female in this case were about 17 years old and that at least a half hour of fully consensual foreplay occurred before the act of statutory rape itself.

---

[42] See H.L.A. Hart, *The Concept of Law* (Oxford: Clarendon Press, 1961), p. 92, and, more generally, Phillippe Nonet and Philip Selznick, *Law and Society in Transition* (New York: Harper & Row, 1978), pp. 10–14.

Michael M. v. Superior Court of Sonoma County
(California, Real Party in Interest)
460 U.S. 464 (1981)

Justice Rehnquist announced the judgment of the Court and delivered an opinion, in which The Chief Justice, Justice Stewart, and Justice Powell joined.

The question presented in this case is whether California's "statutory rape" law, Section 261.5 of the California Penal Code...violates the Equal Protection Clause of the Fourteenth Amendment. Section 261.5 defines unlawful sexual intercourse as "an act of sexual intercourse accomplished with a female not the wife of the perpetrator, where the female is under the age of 18 years." The statute thus makes men alone criminally liable for the act of sexual intercourse....

We are satisfied not only that the prevention of illegitimate pregnancy is at least one of the "purposes" of the statute, but also that the State has a strong interest in preventing such pregnancy. At the risk of stating the obvious, teenage pregnancies, which have increased dramatically over the last two decades, have significant social, medical, and economic consequences for both the mother and her child, and the State.[a] Of particular concern to the State is that approximately half of all teenage pregnancies end in abortion. And of those children who are born, their illegitimacy makes them likely candidates to become wards of the State.

We need not be medical doctors to discern that young men and young women are not similarly situated with respect to the problems and the risks of sexual intercourse. Only women may become pregnant, and they suffer disproportionately the profound physical, emotional, and psychological consequences of sexual activity. The statute at issue here protects women from sexual intercourse at an age when those consequences are particularly severe.

---

[a]The risk of maternal death is 60% higher for a teenager under the age of 15 than for a woman in her early twenties. The risk is 13% higher for 15-to-19-year-olds. The statistics further show that most teenage mothers drop out of school and face a bleak economic future. See, *e.g., 11 Million Teenagers,* supra, at 23, 25; Bennett & Bardon, "The Effects of a School Program On Teenager Mothers and Their Children," 47 *Am. J. Orthopsychiatry* 671 (1977); Phipps-Yonas, "Teenage Pregnancy and Motherhood," 50 *Am. J. Orthopsychiatry* 403, 414 (1980).

The question thus boils down to whether a State may attack the problem of sexual intercourse and teenage pregnancy directly by prohibiting a male from having sexual intercourse with a minor female. We hold that such a statute is sufficiently related to the State's objectives to pass constitutional muster.

Because virtually all of the significant harmful and inescapably identifiable consequences of teenage pregnancy fall on the young female, a legislature acts well within its authority when it elects to punish only the participant who, by nature, suffers few of the consequences of his conduct. It is hardly unreasonable for a legislature acting to protect minor females to exclude them from punishment. Moreover, the risk of pregnancy itself constitutes a substantial deterrence to young females. No similar natural sanctions deter males. A criminal sanction imposed solely on males thus serves to roughly "equalize" the deterrents on the sexes....

In any event, we cannot say that a gender-neutral statute would be as effective as the statute California has chosen to enact. The State persuasively contends that a gender-neutral statute would frustrate its interest in effective enforcement. Its view is that a female is surely less likely to report violations of the statute if she herself would be subject to criminal prosecution. In an area already fraught with prosecutorial difficulties, we decline to hold that the Equal Protection Clause requires a legislature to enact a statute so broad that it may well be incapable of enforcement....

There remains only petitioner's contention that the statute is unconstitutional as it is applied to him because he, like Sharon, was under 18 at the time of sexual intercourse. Petitioner argues that the statute is flawed because it presumes that as between two persons under 18, the male is the culpable aggressor. We find petitioner's contentions unpersuasive. Contrary to his assertions, the statute does not rest on the assumption that males are generally the aggressors. It is instead an attempt by a legislature to prevent illegitimate teenage pregnancy by providing an additional deterrent for men. The age of the man is irrelevant since young men are as capable as older men of inflicting the harm sought to be prevented....

Accordingly, the judgment of the California Supreme Court is affirmed. JUSTICE STEWART concurring....

Young women and men are not similarly situated with respect to the problems and risks associated with intercourse and pregnancy, and the statute is realistically related to the legitimate state purpose of reducing those problems and risks.

As the California Supreme Court's catalog shows, the pregnant unmarried female confronts problems more numerous and more severe than any faced by her male partner.[b] She alone endures the medical risks of pregnancy or abortion. She suffers disproportionately the social, educational, and emotional consequences of pregnancy. Recognizing this disproportion, California has attempted to protect teenage females by prohibiting males from participating in the act necessary for conception.

The fact that males and females are not similarly situated with respect to the risks of sexual intercourse applies with the same force to males under 18 as it does to older males. The risk of pregnancy is a significant deterrent for unwed young females that is not shared by unmarried males, regardless of their age. Experienced observation confirms the commonsense notion that adolescent males disregard the possibility of pregnancy far more than do adolescent females. And to the extent that Section 261.5 may punish males for intercourse with prepubescent females, that punishment is justifiable because of the substantial physical risks for prepubescent females that are not shared by their male counterparts. . . .

[Concurring opinion of Justice BLACKMUN omitted.]

Justice BRENNAN, with whom Justices WHITE and MARSHALL join, dissenting. . . .

The plurality assumes that a gender-neutral statute would be less effective than Section 261.5 in deterring sexual activity because a gender-neutral statute would create significant enforcement problems. The plurality thus accepts the State's assertion that

> a female is surely less likely to report violations of the statute if she herself would be subject to criminal prosecution. In an area already fraught with prosecutorial difficulties, we decline to hold that the Equal Protection Clause requires a legislature to enact a statute so broad that it may well be incapable of enforcement. Ante, at 473–474. . . .

However, a State's bare assertion that its gender-based statutory classification substantially furthers an important governmental interest is not enough to meet its burden of proof under *Craig* v.

[b]The court noted that from 1971 through 1976, 83.6% of the 4,860 children born to girls under 15 in California were illegitimate, as were 51% of those born to girls 15 to 17. The court also observed that while accounting for only 21% of California pregnancies in 1976, teenagers accounted for 34.7% of legal abortions.

Boren. Rather, the State must produce evidence that will persuade the court that its assertion is true. See *Craig* v. *Boren,* 429 U.S., at 200–204.

The State has not produced such evidence in this case. Moreover, there are at least two serious flaws in the State's assertion that law enforcement problems created by a gender-neutral statutory rape law would make such a statute less effective than a gender-based statute in deterring sexual activity.

First, the experience of other jurisdictions, and California itself, belies the plurality's conclusion that a gender-neutral statutory rape law "may well be incapable of enforcement." There are now at least 37 States that have enacted gender-neutral statutory rape laws. Although most of these laws protect young persons (of either sex) from the sexual exploitation of older individuals, the laws of Arizona, Florida, and Illinois permit prosecution of both minor females and minor males for engaging in mutual sexual conduct. California has introduced no evidence that those States have been handicapped by the enforcement problems the plurality finds so persuasive. Surely, if those States could provide such evidence, we might expect that California would have introduced it.

In addition, the California Legislature in recent years has revised other sections of the Penal Code to make them gender-neutral. For example, Cal. Penal Code Ann. Sections 286(b)(1) and 288a(b)(1), prohibiting sodomy and oral copulation with a "person who is under 18 years of age," could cause two minor homosexuals to be subjected to criminal sanctions for engaging in mutually consensual conduct. Again, the State has introduced no evidence to explain why a gender-neutral statutory rape law would be any more difficult to enforce than those statutes.

The second flaw in the State's assertion is that even assuming that a gender-neutral statute would be more difficult to enforce, the State has still not shown that those enforcement problems would make such a statute less effective than a gender-based statute in deterring minor females from engaging in sexual intercourse. Common sense, however, suggests that a gender-neutral statutory rape law is potentially a *greater* deterrent of sexual activity than a gender-based law, for the simple reason that a gender-neutral law subjects both men and women to criminal sanctions and thus arguably has a deterrent effect on twice as many potential violators. Even if fewer persons were prosecuted under the gender-neutral law, as the State suggests, it would still be true that twice as many persons would be *subject* to arrest. The State's failure to prove that a gender-neutral law would be a less effective deterrent than a gender-based law, like the State's failure to prove that a gender-neutral law would be difficult to enforce, should have led this Court to invalidate Section 261.5. ...

Justice STEVENS, dissenting.

Local custom and belief—rather than statutory laws of venerable but doubtful ancestry—will determine the volume of sexual activity among unmarried teenagers. The empirical evidence cited by the plurality demonstrates the futility of the notion that a statutory prohibition will significantly affect the volume of that activity or provide a meaningful solution to the problems created by it. ... [T]he plurality surely cannot believe that the risk of pregnancy confronted by the female—any more than the risk of venereal disease confronted by males as well as females—has provided an effective deterrent to voluntary female participation in the risk-creating conduct. Yet the plurality's decision seems to rest on the assumption that the California Legislature acted on the basis of that rather fanciful notion.

In my judgment, the fact that a class of persons is especially vulnerable to a risk that a statute is designed to avoid is a reason for making the statute applicable to that class. The argument that a special need for protection provides a rational explanation for an exemption is one I simply do not comprehend.[c]

In this case, the fact that a female confronts a greater risk of harm than a male is a reason for applying the prohibition to her—not a reason for granting her a license to use her own judgment on whether or not to assume the risk. Surely, if we examine the problem from the point of view of society's interest in preventing the risk-creating conduct from occurring at all, it is irrational to exempt 50% of the potential violators. ... And, if we view the government's interest as that of a *parens patriae* seeking to protect its subjects from

---

[c]A hypothetical racial classification will illustrate my point. Assume that skin pigmentation provides some measure of protection against cancer caused by exposure to certain chemicals in the atmosphere and, therefore, that white employees confront a greater risk than black employees in certain industrial settings. Would it be rational to require black employees to wear protective clothing but to exempt whites from that requirement? It seems to me that the greater risk of harm to white workers would be a reason for including them in the requirement—not for granting them an exemption.

harming themselves, the discrimination is actually perverse. Would a rational parent making rules for the conduct of twin children of opposite sex simultaneously forbid the son and authorize the daughter to engage in conduct that is especially harmful to the daughter? That is the effect of this statutory classification.

If pregnancy or some other special harm is suffered by one of the two participants in the prohibited act, that special harm no doubt would constitute a legitimate mitigating factor in deciding what, if any, punishment might be appropriate in a given case. But from the standpoint of fashioning a general preventive rule—or, indeed, in determining appropriate punishment when neither party in fact has suffered any special harm—I regard a total exemption for the members of the more endangered class as utterly irrational.

In my opinion, the only acceptable justification for a general rule requiring disparate treatment of the two participants in a joint act must be a legislative judgment that one is more guilty than the other. The risk-creating conduct that this statute is designed to prevent requires the participation of two persons—one male and one female.[d] In many situations it is probably true that one is the aggressor and the other is either an unwilling, or at least a less willing, participant in the joint act. If a statute authorized punishment of only one participant and required the prosecutor to prove that that participant had been the aggressor, I assume that the discrimination would be valid. Although the question is less clear, I also assume, for the purpose of deciding this case, that it would be permissible to punish only the male participant, if one element of the offense were proof that he had been the aggressor, or at least in some respects the more responsible participant in the joint act. The statute at issue in this case, however, requires no such proof. The question raised by this statute is whether the State, consistently with the Federal Constitution, may always punish the male and never the

---

[d]In light of this indisputable biological fact, I find somewhat puzzling the California Supreme Court's conclusion, quoted by the plurality, *ante*, at 467, that males "are the *only* persons who may physiologically cause the result which the law properly seeks to avoid." 25 Cal. 3d 608, 612, 601 P. 2d 572, 575 (1979) (emphasis in original). Presumably, the California Supreme Court was referring to the equally indisputable biological fact that only females may become pregnant. However, if pregnancy results from sexual intercourse between two willing participants—and the California statute is directed at such conduct—I would find it difficult to conclude that the pregnancy was "caused" solely by the male participant.

female when they are equally responsible or when the female is the more responsible of the two.

It would seem to me that an impartial lawmaker could give only one answer to that question. The fact that the California Legislature has decided to apply its prohibition only to the male may reflect a legislative judgment that in the typical case the male is actually the more guilty party. Any such judgment must, in turn, assume that the decision to engage in the risk-creating conduct is always—or at least typically—a male decision. If that assumption is valid, the statutory classification should also be valid. But what is the support for the assumption? It is not contained in the record of this case or in any legislative history or scholarly study that has been called to our attention. I think it is supported to some extent by traditional attitudes toward male-female relationships. But the possibility that such a habitual attitude may reflect nothing more than an irrational prejudice makes it an insufficient justification for discriminatory treatment that is otherwise blatantly unfair. For, as I read this statute, it requires that one, and only one, of two equally guilty wrongdoers be stigmatized by a criminal conviction....

Nor do I find at all persuasive the suggestion that this discrimination is adequately justified by the desire to encourage females to inform against their male partners. Even if the concept of a wholesale informant's exemption were an acceptable enforcement device, what is the justification for defining the exempt class entirely by reference to sex rather than by reference to a more neutral criterion such as relative innocence? Indeed, if the exempt class is to be composed entirely of members of one sex, what is there to support the view that the statutory purpose will be better served by granting the informing license to females rather than to males? If a discarded male partner informs on a promiscuous female, a timely threat of prosecution might well prevent the precise harm the statute is intended to minimize.

Finally, even if my logic is faulty and there actually is some speculative basis for treating equally guilty males and females differently, I still believe that any such speculative justification would be outweighed by the paramount interest in evenhanded enforcement of the law. A rule that authorizes punishment of only one of two equally guilty wrongdoers violates the essence of the constitutional requirement that the sovereign must govern impartially.

I respectfully dissent.

QUESTIONS

1. From the perspective of the average layman, does California's statute treat men and women unequally? Why or why not? By what legal route does the Court conclude that there is no unconstitutional inequality here? On what assumptions about differences between male and female psychology and sexual behavior does the decision rest? Are these assumptions *factual* in the way this book defines facts?

2. Is this a facilitation case or a case of individual rights? Why does this distinction matter in a case like this?

3. Is this decision consistent with the precedent of *Craig v. Boren*? If not, how much does the inconsistency bother you? Why should it, particularly if disregard for precedent is acceptable in constitutional law?

4. Males under the age of 18 are a group that lacks direct access to the normal electoral and legislative political processes. Why? How significant should that fact be in this case?

5. Do you think the authors of the Fourteenth Amendment intended the equal protection clause to cover sale of 3.2 beer to male versus female customers? to cover "statutory" rape statutes? to cover sex issues at all, given that women did not have the vote when the amendment was passed? How much attention do the opinions in this case pay to these questions?

6. Recall the fifth of Justice Brandeis's self-imposed limits on the Court. Has Michael M. been hurt by the operation of this statute? If his claim amounts to the assertion that the girl should be punished also, how is he hurt? Is the answer that, if Michael cannot raise the constitutional issue, no one can?

7. This case is a rich blend of case facts, background facts and values. I find the dissenters' treatment of the background factual assumptions much more realistic than those in the majority opinions. However, I have deliberately omitted one important fact in this case itself, namely that just before the intercourse occurred, the girl testified that she resisted and that Michael M. punched her two or three times on the chin, which punches eventually raised bruises. Construct a theory explaining how the presence of that fact in the case itself could subconsciously determine the Court's answer to the question of constitutional law.

SOME EXPLORATORY PROBLEMS

1. In 1956 the Supreme Court dismissed without deciding an appeal from a challenge to Virginia's statute prohibiting interracial marriages. The lower court had upheld the statute. The Court's rules allow it to dismiss without deciding cases on appeal that seem frivolous or do not "raise a substantial federal question." In light of the desegregation ruling two years earlier, the case obviously did raise a substantial federal constitutional issue. Was the Court's dismissal wise? Alexander Bickel thought so. He wrote:

> But would it have been wise, at a time when the Court had just pronounced its new integration principle, when it was subject to scurrilous attack by men who predicted that integration of the schools would lead directly to "mongrelization of the race" and that this was the result the Court had really willed, would it have been wise, just then, in the first case of its sort, on an issue that the Negro community as a whole can hardly be said to be pressing hard at the moment, to declare that the states may not prohibit racial intermarriage?[43]

How would you answer Bickel's question in view of this chapter's argument?

2. Comment on the following statement: "If courts are to keep the idea of rights alive, then it is better to err on the side of nullifying rather than upholding a governmental statute or action. In this sense the nation was better served by having to live with the *Lochner* decision for a time than to have no formal machinery for resolving the problem of freedom of contract whatsoever."

3. In several large cities under desegregation orders, black and white political interests have, for the sake of avoiding further white flight, recently agreed to support desegregation plans that leave many schools only minimally integrated. In view of the recent gains in black political power and political equality and in light of my position in this chapter that judicial activism matters most where the political process fails to hear or weigh a civil

[43]Alexander Bickel, *The Least Dangerous Branch*, p. 174. *Naim v. Naim* 350 U.S. 985 (appeal dismissed, 1956). The Court finally resolved the issue in favor of personal freedom in *Loving v. Virginia* 388 U.S. 1 (1967).

rights interest at all, should courts approve such desegregation compromises?

4. Do the Supreme Court's constitutional decisions actually become the Constitution itself, which all government officials take an oath to uphold? In the famous Little Rock desegregation case, the Court answered in the affirmative.[44] But in protecting the rights of those accused of crimes, the Court said that its decisions need not be applied retroactively to release from prison those who were convicted under the same illegality before the judicial ruling.[45] More recently the Court said that retroactivity depends on the purpose of the new ruling, the extent of law enforcement reliance on the old standard, and the effect on the administration of justice that retroactive application would have.[46] Are all these approaches consistent? Is consistency on such a point desirable? Compare the following related problem. The Court held that the equal protection clause did not prohibit literacy tests for voters. However, the Civil War amendments contain clauses allowing Congress to enforce their provisions through statutes. Congress in 1965 under this enforcement rubric outlawed literacy tests, and the Court upheld the statute in spite of its earlier ruling that the equal protection clause permitted literacy tests.[47] But then in 1975 the Court forbade the State of Oregon to create restraints on police officers that were more restrictive than those the Court's own rulings prescribed, presumably because the Court's rulings exhausted the Constitution's meaning.[48] What about Section 5 of the Fourteenth Amendment? Which approach is correct? Or are they both correct? Or are they both incorrect? Or should we substitute the words "acceptable" and "unacceptable" for "correct" and "incorrect" to make those questions meaningful?

5. Professor Bradley C. Canon has recently analysed the various forms judicial activism can take.[49] His analysis is particularly

---

[44] *Cooper v. Aaron,* 358 U.S. 1 (1958), p. 18.
[45] *Linkletter v. Walker,* 301 U.S. 618 (1965).
[46] *Stovall v. Denno,* 388 U.S. 293 (1967), p. 297.
[47] *Katzenbach v. Morgan,* 384 U.S. 641 (1966).
[48] *Oregon v. Hass,* 420 U.S. 714 (1975). See the analysis of more recent cases in Walter V. Schaefer, "Prospective Rulings: Two Perspectives," in Philip B. Kurland, Gerhard Casper, and Dennis J. Hutchinson, eds., *The Supreme Court Review* (Chicago: University of Chicago Press, 1983).
[49] "A Framework for the Analysis of Judicial Activism," in Halpern and

useful because it shows how a decision that appears highly active on one dimension may be inactive on another. His six dimensions are:

1. Majoritarianism—Does the decision nullify an act of an elected legislature?
2. Interpretive stability—Does the decision overrule prior court precedent?
3. Interpretive fidelity—Does the decision contradict the manifest intent of the framers?
4. Substance—Does the decision make new basic policy for the society, e.g., public school desegregation?
5. Specificity—Does the decision require people to follow specific, court-created rules?
6. Availability of political alternatives—Are other political institutions equally able and willing to formulate effective policy in the area the decision touches?

Try describing some of the cases discussed in this chapter using Canon's categories.

6. Evaluate the following quotation, a favorite of conservative constitutional scholar Gary McDowell of Dickenson University:

> If an honest, and I may truly affirm, a laborious zeal for the public service, has given me any weight in your esteem, let me exhort and conjure you never to suffer an invasion of your political constitution, however minute the instance may appear, to pass by, without a determined, persevering resistance. One precedent creates another—they soon accumulate and constitute law. What yesterday was fact, today is doctrine. Examples are supposed to justify the most dangerous measures; and where they do not suit exactly, the defect is supplied by analogy. Be assured that the laws which protect us in our civil rights, grow out of the constitution, and that they must fall or flourish with it.
>
> Junius
> *The Letters of Junius*, 1769

7. Bob Woodward and Scott Armstrong's *The Brethren: Inside the Supreme Court* (New York: Simon & Schuster, 1979) received

---

Lamb, eds., *Supreme Court Activism and Restraint* (Lexington, Mass.: Lexington Books, 1982), Chapter 15.

widespread and well-deserved academic criticism. The earliest criticisms were levelled at the methods used—the authors' failure to prove many assertations convincingly and publicly and the implication that they had abused their sources. The more thoughtful reactions pointed out that the book succeeded in establishing only that Supreme Court Justices are human and that they engage in the same sort of tactics and strategies that people usually employ when they must make group decisions about difficult and controversial issues. The classic work describing these truths is Walter Murphy, *Elements of Judicial Strategy* (Chicago: University of Chicago Press, 1964). Of course one consequence of the inevitably political relationships among the Justices is that their published opinions do not report anything like the actual thinking process by which they decide how to vote in a case. In Chapter VII, we will address the significance of this fact in legal reasoning.

Having warned about the seductions of rumors about the Court, however, let me report the existence of two fairly serious problems that appear to undercut the effectiveness of the modern Court. The first concerns the expanding caseload of the Court and the fears that the quantity of work reduces the quality of judicial decision making. The second analyses the apparent failure, at least of the Burger Court, to work as harmoniously together as we know many past courts have done. For recent assessments of these problems, see "Justices Seek Ways to Ease Big Caseload"[50] and "Low Roading on the High Court."[51]

8. Is it ever proper for a constitutional ruling to hinge almost exclusively on the magnitude and complexity of the task of enforcing it? The U.S. Supreme Court has refused to require states to equalize the funding of the public schools in different regions of the state. To do so would require courts to enforce fairly drastic changes in school finance and local and state taxation in nearly every state. But what if nearly all states in fact funded their schools equally and one state adopted a new policy permitting unequal funding? Archibald Cox argues that the Court might properly hold invalid on constitutional grounds such an innovation. Is he correct?[52]

---

[50]*The Wall Street Journal*, July 8, 1983, p. 23.

[51]*The Wall Street Journal*, September 13, 1982, p. 30.

[52]See *San Antonio Independent School District v. Rodriguez*, 411 U.S. 1 (1973), and Archibald Cox, *The Role of the Supreme Court in American Government* (New York: Oxford University Press, 1976), p. 94.

Chapter VII

LAW AND REASON

The ultimate goal is to break down the sense that legal argument is autonomous from moral, economic and political discourse.
    —Duncan Kennedy

When judges make law and scholars propose rules of law, they necessarily rely on their vision of society as it is and as it ought to be. If law is to be made well, those visions must be accurate and attractive.
    —Mark Tushnet

We must learn again to speak to each other with authority and not as the scribes. For the present we are all much too clever and unchildlike to be of real mutual help.
    —Karl Barth

The time has come to fit the pieces and groups of pieces of this puzzle together. To do so we must clarify the nature of law and of reason and thereby clarify the final picture of legal reasoning.

"Law" and "reason"—what feelings and beliefs, what relationships and actions do these two words symbolize? People eat, sleep, love, hate, work, and play. In this great mass of human activity, what part is "law"? People also feel, believe, and think. Feelings, beliefs, and thoughts influence choices and actions. To what extent can we separate "reason" from all the other psychological dynamics—feeling powerful; feeling reckless; feeling lustful, or empathetic, or sad—that influence choices and actions? I shall first refine our definition of law and then turn to the nature of reason and of judgment. "Moral, economic and political discourse" do affect law through the "visions" of judges. Legal reasoning is the process that makes those visions either "accurate and attractive" or erroneous and repugnant. Our ultimate goal is to see clearly how these lawmaking judges must speak "with authority" yet retain that essential quality of any legal system: *impartiality*.

WHAT IS LAW?

Law is the process by which people try to conduct their affairs in terms of rules created by government, by the "State." Rules on the books do not by themselves make law. The legal process operates only to the degree that people agree on ways of deciding what the rules mean in the context of their situation and abiding by the results of the decision process. Given this broad definition of law as process, consider the many questions that arise within it that the study of legal reasoning itself does not directly answer:

- How do elections, lobbying, and the other complexities of political and bureaucratic life affect the content of laws and regulations created and administered outside of courts?
- How do the varying political and social backgrounds of judges affect the results they reach? Some judges are elected, others appointed. Does this difference associate with different patterns of judicial decision?[1] How can personality difference affect outcomes?[2]

[1]See Joel B. Grossman, "Social Backgrounds and Judicial Decision-Making," 79 *Harvard Law Review* 1551 (1966); Martin A. Levin, *Urban Politics and the Criminal Courts* (Chicago: University of Chicago Press, 1977); Boyum and Mather, *Empirical Theories about Courts* (New York: Longman, 1983); Robert C. Carp and C.K. Rowland, *Policymaking and Politics in the Federal District Courts* (Knoxville: University of Tennessee Press, 1983).

[2]See Harold Lasswell, *Power and Personality*, 1st ed. (New York: Norton, 1948), Chapter 4.

- What impacts do legal rules and judicial and administrative decisions of all kinds actually have on the lives of citizens? When do people comply with rules; when do they ignore them, and why? When do laws and decisions produce the kinds of effects for which the people who created them had hoped? When do the unanticipated impacts of laws overwhelm the desired effects? Why? How can we tell?[3]
- The courts and the legal profession themselves are far from perfect. Chief Justice Burger has challenged the American Bar Association with the charge that many trial lawyers are incompetent. Is he correct? How sound is the Chief Justice's proposal to require specific training and certification for trial practice similar both to the British practice in law and to the common organization of medical specialities in the United States? Are court dockets overloaded? Does overload necessarily affect the quality of justice that courts deliver? (In civil cases, at least, do overload and delay serve a salutary purpose by encouraging litigants to settle out of court?) Should family relations problems of all kinds go to specialized tribunals rather than courts of general jurisdiction? Should we eliminate jury trials in most noncriminal cases?[4]
- How effectively does civil rights or environmental litigation or other efforts in "public interest" law actually influence public policy and basic human needs?[5]
- Even when the judicial process appears to conform to the textbook model, beginning with a full adversarial trial and ending, if necessary, with an appeal on the

[3]Stephen L. Wasby, *The Impact of the United States Supreme Court* (Homewood, Ill.: Dorsey, 1970); Theodore L. Becker and Malcolm Feeley, eds., *The Impact of Supreme Court Decisions*, 2nd ed. (New York: Oxford University Press, 1973); and Stewart Macaulay, "Noncontractual Relations in Business: A Preliminary Study," 28 *American Sociological Review* 55 (1963).

[4]See "Burger Steps up Attack on Unqualified Lawyers," *The Atlanta Constitution*, 13 February 1978, p. 9-A, and "Justice Delayed," *Wall Street Journal*, February 11, 1983, p. 1.

[5]Stuart A. Scheingold is pessimistic. See *The Politics of Rights* (New Haven: Yale University Press, 1974).

contested points of law, does the process find the "true" facts of the conflict and act upon them? Judge Jerome Frank wrote forcefully that the Achilles' heel in law is not the ambiguity of rules. He argued that all the lawyers' pushing and shoving over the facts—the selective calling of witnesses and the fierce baiting and misleading questioning on cross-examination, for example—tend to distort the facts so wildly that the judge conscientiously reasons legally to resolve a conflict that never happened. Judge Frank labeled his concern "fact skepticism."[6]

- In criminal cases does the widespread practice of "plea bargaining" wash out the capacity of criminal prosecution to deter crime and rehabilitate criminals? Do defense attorneys who seek delay, either to keep their clients out of jail as long as possible, to lever a fee from their clients, or both, block desirable criminal justice reform?[7]

Notice that to analyze carefully all the facets of the legal system depends upon judgments about culture, public morals, statistical data, even upon competing philosophical and emotional doctrines, and upon the nature of knowledge itself. Because these constantly change, our analysis of law never becomes complete or final.[8] Problems in the legal process constantly change; at best we can offer partial solutions. In this broad view of law we see that "law" and "politics" are no more than different labels we attach to the same process. Analysis requires mastery of all the social sciences as well as philosophy and history.

Narrowing the Terrain of Law

Benjamin Cardozo once confessed that he could find the answers to important judicial questions only in life itself. But, in this

---

[6]See Jerome Frank, *Courts on Trial* (Princeton: Princeton University Press, 1949).

[7]See Arthur I. Rosett and Donald R. Cressey, *Justice by Consent* (Philadelphia: Lippincott, 1976); James Eisenstein and Herbert Jacob, *Felony Justice* (Boston: Little, Brown, 1977); and Stuart Scheingold, *The Politics of Law and Order* (New York: Longman, 1984).

[8]See Jerome Hall, *Foundations of Jurisprudence* (Indianapolis: Bobbs-Merrill, 1973), Chapter 6.

sense, medicine is life and education is life; everything is life. In what ways can we narrow the field so as to give sensible counsel to the lawyers and judges who reason in law every day?

The legal process resolves disputes, sometimes between two individuals and sometimes among a variety of contending interests and groups. Sometimes the legal process induces social change, while at other times it lags well behind such changes. But law is not the only method—probably not even the primary one—that individuals, groups, and societies use to handle disputes. Loving, going home to mother, shaking hands on the gentleman's agreement, exercising power, unconsciously conforming to informal social rules we call customs, and many other activities in private and public life reduce conflict and cope with social change. As Malcolm Feeley writes:

> Law does not perform a unique social function, nor is it a singular form of social control.... Legal rules are only one of a number of systems of rules, often overlapping and entwined, which shape people's aspirations and actions, and by which they are judged and resolve their troubles.[9]

Thus, one way to narrow the judge's field of vision—and hence his responsibilities—is to remind him that he need not attain perfection in every case. By perfection I mean the discovery of, or the creation of, a legal rule that produces one right solution in every case. Previous chapters have explained why judges cannot attain this kind of perfection, but I am arguing here as well that they do not need to do this. Law is ultimately one of many ways of meeting needs that people feel and try to satisfy: psychological needs. Other activities and relationships can compensate if and when the legal system fails to address these interests.

But what kinds of needs do law and other social processes jointly try to satisfy? *Social processes including law seek to satisfy, above all, the psychological need for structure in people's lives, the need to believe that physical forces and moral norms can answer questions and relieve people from questioning some*

---

[9]Malcolm M. Feeley, "The Concept of Laws in Social Science," 10 *Law and Society Review* 497 (1976), p. 501. For a particularly promising alternative to traditional litigation in problem solving, see Fisher and Ury, *Getting to Yes: Negotiating Agreement without Giving In* (New York: Penguin Books, 1981).

concepts altogether. When society fails to meet its members' need for structure, law cannot achieve its immediate goal of promoting social cooperation. Note carefully that this statement emphasizes the importance of the belief in structure, not the structure itself. We do not lead our daily lives by constantly testing every decision against the rules of physics or of religion or of law, but we need to believe they are there if we need them.

Having precepts and resolving cases in terms of them help maintain that confidence in structure. For the legal system, success arises primarily from settling cases "well enough" that people will abide by the final decision. Success does not require settling them "to perfection."

Law and the State

Social groups of all sorts—amateur play-reading groups, symphony orchestras, and political science departments—develop formal and informal conventions that provide a sense of structure so that work and play can proceed. The regularization of dispute settling in labor-management relations, by creating rules for collective-bargaining agreements and resolving industrial disputes in terms of the rules, has in this century substantially changed the workplace.

And yet we do not call these lawlike uses of rules "law." *Law* governs through rules made and enforced by the government, the State. What should it mean to a judge to define law this way? Why does it matter whether a unit of government on one hand or General Motors on the other creates and enforces a rule?

We can examine why it matters in two ways. The first method examines law as a practical aspect of politics; the second scrutinizes law in ethical and philosophical terms. Both try to see the world as it really is; both attempt to view law through the eyes of both the governors and the governed.

The political view of the importance of government in law is essentially one of degree. Law is the process that fosters and legitimates the interests of the powerful. Government matters simply because it provides the arena for the most important battles for power in society. One cannot gain position to make law in government without being powerful. Of course, elections try to equalize the unequal power that flows from differential distributions of wealth, but that is one small part of politics. Law results from the unending struggle for power in society because government and the power struggle are only different labels for a single phenomenon. When judges decide, they simply reinforce the interests of the powerful. From this standpoint, the content and quality of legal reasoning become no more than rationalizations for the exercise of judicial power.[10]

There is certainly some truth in the political appoach, at least if its proponents avoid the circular error of defining the powerful in terms of the interests that law promotes. I do, however, think this view seriously misleads us. The political aspect encourages us to think about law exclusively in power terms so that we do not recognize that ethics, beliefs about right and wrong, have a meaning and power of their own. It encourages us, for example, to think of the proceedings in the House of Representatives in 1974 concerning Richard Nixon's impeachment solely (as Nixon himself did!) in terms of relative party strength, the resources of the pro- and anti-Nixon forces, their strategies and tactics, and so on.

But is not the essence of Watergate very different? Did not Watergate uncover a feeling shared throughout the community that *if* the president violated a set of values, he should no longer hold office? The values were not absolute. No doubt many people who possessed the feeling could not articulate the values precisely, nor did everyone even agree on the standards by which to judge Mr. Nixon. Nevertheless, the community did share the belief that *some* structure limiting presidential power existed, that the president may have exceeded its limits, and that the situation absolutely had to be *judged*.[11]

This second ethical point of view makes the existence and quality of judgment absolutely central in the legal process.

[10]See Lawrence M. Friedman, *The Legal System* (New York: Russell Sage Foundation, 1975), and see also Arthur F. Bentley, *The Process of Government* (Chicago: University of Chicago Press, 1908).

[11]See Joseph R. Gusfield's review of Friedman's *The Legal System*, 29 *Stanford Law Review* 371 (1977), p. 381.

Viewed ethically, when government—rather than General Motors or the management of the Seattle Symphony—creates the rules, legal reasoning becomes more important because:

- The government's rules speak to the public, to the community, to everyone, in a way that General Motors' rules (or for that matter, the Pope's rules) do not.
- The community is the greatest source of disruption and uncertainty in our lives because it exposes us to the work of strangers that we individually cannot control: crimes, nuclear wars, and changes in moral standards. The community is the place where people's psychological need for confidence in structure is greatest, for it is the one place that binds everyone and beyond which we will find no social structure at all. The rules that the *government* makes and enforces must maintain confidence in structure, confidence that even strangers can share values.
- People need to maintain this confidence even when they cannot express precisely the "right" limit or value by which to judge a concrete situation. They take most seriously the idea that the community has value in it. Laws on the books do not alone satisfy the citizen's need for value. Rules help. Nevertheless, *law must maintain the confidence that the community can reconcile, can harmonize, four factors: its formal rules, the unique facts of concrete disputes, the "background" facts about society and its problems, and the ethical sense of right and wrong.*

The judicial process and legal reasoning therefore play a major part in preserving the confidence that the community can reconcile rules, facts of disputes, social conditions, and ethics. Our confidence does not rest entirely or immediately on the quality of legal reasoning. However, in the final analysis, legal reasoning, not just the existence of closure, performs the reconciliation. Unlike other social processes in and out of government, courts must make *some* decision, must reach some closure on the problems litigants bring to them. Regardless of the wisdom of the solution, we need to believe that our community contains points where decisions and action replace indecision and drift. This book has criticized so many conventional practices, habits, and assumptions in legal reasoning precisely because legal reasoning is so important. Reason must "break down the sense that legal argument is autonomous from moral, economic, and political discourse" or it will ultimately destroy our confidence in community.

In sum, the political view of law presumes that the State consists of people vying to have their specific wants, the policies they espouse, written into law. The ethical view, on the other hand, asserts that everyone, including the most apolitical of citizens, simply by virtue of living in a community, needs to believe that values hold the community together. In the political view, whatever decision occurs must be right. In the ethical view, the quality of judgment, the ability of judges to convince us they take the task of harmonizing seriously, is both problematic and very important.

Thus, the ethical view of the legal process holds that, despite its broad and complicated terrain, law must contain a method of applying the abstractions of law to human affairs. This does *not* require finding the perfect solution. It is much more important that the process *attempt* to reach acceptable reconciliations of facts, social conditions, laws, and ethical values. Viewing law as a process of resolving disputes in terms of rules made and enforced by the state helps us identify the special reconciling and harmonizing role of legal reasoning.

We must now shift our attention to the precise definitions of "reason" and "judgment." Before we do so, however, you should be certain that you understand the complexity of the problem which legal reasoning addresses.

The modern view of man teaches that neither judges nor anyone else ever will actually identify a structure that holds society together. Rules are ambiguous. People constantly disagree about the nature of social conditions and about ethical values. Virtually every problem, the more we think about it, reduces to an unsolvable riddle, a tension between opposing goods, an antinomy. Paul Freund eloquently identifies three such antinomies: triumph and fraternity, knowledge and privacy, and personal security and moral responsibility.[12] Duncan Kennedy reduces these to just one, the tension between individualism and altruism.[13] In this section, I have suggested that law need not resolve the unresolvable. I have urged that ongoing attempts to reach defensible but imperfect reconciliations of competing forces will suffice to maintain the necessary confidence in community structure.

WHAT IS REASON?

But, you ask, do people reason at all? Do not modern psychology and philosophy view man as essentially irrational? Wasn't Benjamin Franklin close to the mark when he wrote in his *Autobiography*, "So convenient a thing it is to be a *reasonable creature*, since it enables one to find or make a *reason* for everything one has a mind to do."?[14] Obviously, I think people reason or I could not.have written this book, so let me try to persuade you. Let me begin by describing human behavior that isn't reasoned.

One of the major roadblocks to understanding reasoning is that we tend to think reasoning somehow causes behavior. A person does X if he reasons but would do Y if he doesn't reason. Unfortunately, thinking about reason as a cause of behavior turns out to be extremely unmanageable. Any given event, of human or animal behavior or of matter in the physical universe, has countless causes. Take this simple-sounding question: What causes tides in the ocean? The combined gravitational pull of earth, moon, and sun, you say. But what is gravity and what causes it? What causes oceans, without which there would be no tides? What causes earth, sun, and moon in the first place? Similarly, if we assert that a student receives a better grade on a

---

[12]Paul Freund, "Social Justice and the Law," in Richard B. Brandt, ed., *Social Justice* (Englewood Cliffs, N.J.: Prentice-Hall, 1962), p. 94.

[13]Duncan Kennedy, "Form and Substance in Private Law Adjudication," 89 *Harvard Law Review* 1685 (1976), p. 1713.

[14]My thanks to Terrence Cook for this quotation.

test *because* he reasons (or that a judge produces a better result because he reasons), we have to think about other causes, such as education, family patterns, emotional state, and so forth that also "cause" this result.

Conceiving of reason, not as a cause but as a *description* of certain kinds of behavior will prove more manageable. This chapter's second paragraph provided alternative methods of describing decisions, procedures that are not reasoned. Paul Freund has articulated them best: *will* (power), *emotion, reck-lessness,* and *rapacity*.[15] Reason or any of these alternatives may describe a given behavior, a given choice, depending on how it is made and executed. Consider two examples:

First, suppose a king orders the execution of three prisoners. If he believes he has the prerogative to order executions at whim and does so, the decision would be willful, not reasoned. If he is crazed with anger at the time, he would act emotionally. If he flips a coin to decide, we might well call the decision reckless. If he enjoys seeing men die, we would call the decision rapacious, but not reasoned. If, however, he orders the execution in the belief that killing the prisoners will deter both them and others from unwanted behavior in the future, or if he believes the men lead political opposition that will crumble without their leadership, then we may say he reasons.

Second, consider Learned Hand's decision in the case of the sunken barges. Suppose he said to himself, "I hold the tugs unseaworthy for failure to carry radios because I'm the judge and I can decide any way I wish." Or, "I hold for the coal company because I am in love with the coal company president's daughter." Or, "I'll decide by flipping a coin." Or, "The coal company wins because it paid a bribe." These decisions also conform to Freund's four categories.

What distinguishes both the king's and Learned Hand's hypothetically unreasoned decisions from their reasoned decisions? You might say that the reasoned decision somehow pays attention to the facts, and that is certainly part of the answer. The main point, however, is that the reasoned decision rests

[15]Paul A. Freund, "Rationality in Judicial Decisions," in Carl Friedrich, ed., *Nomos VII: Rational Decision* (New York: Atherton, 1964), pp. 109–125.

primarily on an assessment of *consequences*. Reason is a form of calculation. The reasoned decision scans; it depends on an assessment of the consequences of alternative possibilities. The king who deliberately orders the executions to satisfy his perverse need to watch men die reasons only if he attempts to estimate the negative consequences of the killing and then concludes that they do not outweigh the fun of seeing the execution. Reasoning may be incomplete and partial. The king may not consider the possibility that a vengeful brother of the executed could slip past the guards and murder him in his sleep. Similarly, in Chapter V we reviewed five other solutions to the sunken barge problem besides Judge Hand's actual decision. We rejected these alternatives, but each was reasoned because each involved a calculation.

To conceive of reasoning as a form of calculation poses two related problems when we try to apply it to legal reasoning. First, people can reason to all kinds of ends, including cruel and selfish ones, as we have seen. But surely we do not say that judges reason in law properly when their scan indicates, for example, that they can rule for the party that offers the bigger bribe and escape discovery! Perhaps more realistically, we condemn a judge who ignores the facts of the dispute between the litigants in order to push his favored political philosophy, as the majority in *Lochner* appeared to do in Chapter VI. But do not forget that in this section we define only reason itself. *Not all reasoning is legal or judgmental reasoning.*

Second, how do we separate the good reasons from the real reasons? How do we see inside judges' heads? What if Learned Hand actually *had* taken a bribe in the tug case and then articulated his persuasive opinion to cover it up? If I have satisfied you that people do reason, I have hardly satisfied you that just any reasoning will do in law. To resolve both these problems, we must turn next to the nature of judgment.

WHAT IS JUDGMENT?

Imagine yourself in each of these three situations:

1. A midsummer afternoon in Wrigley Field. The Cubs versus the Cardinals. You are calling balls and strikes behind home plate.
2. A late Saturday night in Atlantic City in early September. You are judging the finals of the Miss America Pageant.
3. Eight-thirty in the evening, the home of your young family. The children are squabbling. They appeal to you for judgment:
   Laurie: "Mommie, Robbie bit me!"
   Robbie: "I did not!"
   Laurie: "You did too! Look! Tooth marks!"
   Robbie: "But Mom! Laurie took my dime!"
   Laurie: "I took your dime cuz you stepped on my doll and broke it."
   Robbie: "But it was an accident, dum-dum."
   Laurie: "I am not a dum-dum, you fathead!"

Each of these situations calls for judgment. Each judge makes decisions that affect the claims of others, and he decides before an audience that has some expectations about *how* the judge should decide. Without necessarily determining *what* the judge should conclude, the audience knows what the judge should look at and will test the judgment against these expectations. Even the children seeking justice from their mother do so.

To judge is to decide the claims of others with reference to the expectations of an audience that define the process of decision. We shall see shortly where this definition leads in law. For the moment, consider what these three nonlegal judging situations do and do not have in common.

First and most important, notice that the three are not equally reasoned. Reasoning, defined as a choice that depends on calulations about future consequences, influences the umpire calling balls and strikes only indirectly. Occasionally, he may reflect on the fact that if he calls a pitch wrong he may be beaned by flying beer bottles. Basically, however, he simply tries to fit physical—visual—evidence to a category, ball or strike, predetermined by the rule. He judges because the audience, baseball fans, has specific expectations of how umpires should behave. In most households the mother, at the other extreme, cannot escape from making some calculation about the effects of her decision on the children, or at least on her own sanity.

The second difference is that rules do not equally affect all three situations. The umpire works with an elaborate set of written rules about baseball, most of which he commits to memory. He decides most questions literally in a second or less by applying the rules to the facts. In baseball, time is of the essence, which is why its rules are so elaborate. Additionally, baseball allows for precise rules because, as in most sports, we can pinpoint what matters to us in time and space.

On the other hand, we cannot define male or female beauty so precisely in time and space. Beauty contest judges exercise more discretion because their rules do not so precisely tell them what to seek.[16] Finally, the squabbling children may invoke no family rule at all. The family may have no regulation forbidding or punishing Robbie's toothy assault on his sister and his lie, and no conventions governing Laurie's theft or their gratuitous exchange of insults. Expectations, not precepts, create the need for judgment.

Third, these three kinds of judges have different opportunities to make rules for the future. The parent can explicitly respond to the squabble by announcing what is right and wrong and declaring it official policy for the future. Such a setting of limits may be precisely what the children hope the judge will do. But beauty contest judges may do so only informally and the umpires hardly at all, given audience expectations of their roles.

The definition and discussion of the nature of reason made clear, I trust, that not all reasoning is legal reasoning. Legal

---

[16]There is another interesting difference: With rare exceptions, when he calls the game on account of rain or ejects an ornery manager or player, the umpire has minimal control over who wins. But the beauty contest judges *declare* the winner. This differential effect on the outcome explains why we have only one home plate umpire but several judges in contests of beauty and on our appellate courts. (Notice that when the umpire does make discretionary calls he is also more likely to reason than when he calls balls and strikes.) For a fascinating description of how a new sport, competitive female bodybuilding, failed to grow precisely because the relevant audience could not agree on how such contests should be judged, see Charles Gaines and George Butler, "Iron Sisters," *Psychology Today*, November, 1983, pp. 64–69.

reasoning involves judgment, deciding the claims of others in front of some audience, before a "public." We have also seen, from the example of the baseball umpire, that not all judgment involves reason. Law therefore employs reasoned judgment, and I shall develop that concept momentarily. First, however, we must pin down that quality inherent in all judging, whether reasoned or not: "impartiality."

Impartiality is not a mysterious concept. The *American Heritage Dictionary* defines "partial" as "pertaining to only part; not total; incomplete." To decide impartially is to leave the final decision open until all the information is received. It means that the information—the placement of the pitch, the beauty contestant's stage performance and the children's actual behavior—rather than a personal affection or preference for one "party"—determines the result.

While impartiality is not itself a difficult concept—we have all judged and been judged in our lives—it is often difficult for audiences to satisfy themselves that judges actually decide impartially. How can judges satisfy audiences that they decide impartially? Initially, a judge may succeed if his mistakes cancel out, if his errors favor both sides equally. But the loser, being the loser, will probably not take a balanced count of errors. The judge's only long-range security, therefore, is to care about and try as best he can to fulfill the expectations of judgment that the audience imposes.[17]

To judge is to be judged. The argument assumes, of course, that audiences can, in fact, distinguish their expectations of the process of decision from their hopes that one side—their side!—will win. I am convinced that people can do so, though I rely more on my experience as a sports fan, employee, teacher, and parent than I do on psychological experimentation. Teams can lose championships, employees can receive poor assignments,

---

[17]Robert G. Dixon, Jr., also identified judicial neutrality with judges' "style of operation," not the substance or impact of the outcome. See "The 'New Substantive Due Process' and the Democratic Ethic: A Prologomenon," 1 *Brigham Young University Law Review* 43 (1976), p. 76. Harold Berman and William Greiner describe this judicial style of decision as operating deliberately and publicly. Judicial decisions should reflect "an explicit community judgment and not merely an explicitly personal judgment." *The Nature and Functions of Law*, 3rd ed., (Mineola, N.Y.: Foundation Press, 1972).

students can receive disappointing grades, and children can be ordered to wash the dishes, all without doubting that the judges, by caring about standards of decision, have acted fairly.

Judgment need not free itself of all bias. Indeed, to judge impartially may mean to care about, to be passionately biased toward, the process of decision. Umpires may feel strongly about preventing pitchers from throwing at batters and retain their impartiality. Similarly, judgment need not be unselfish. The umpire who calls balls and strikes with superhuman care and effort may do so deliberately to advance his career, yet he remains impartial as long as his calls conform to the audience's criteria for balls and strikes.

People occasionally argue that the human animal cannot by nature judge impartially, but this argument misses the point. Social psychologists, indeed social scientists generally, know that role theory—conformity to group norms—powerfully predicts behavior. Others in the same role—other umpires, other judges, and other parents—compose the immediate group to which people in judging roles conform, but these groups are not isolated from the world around them, or at least they need not be isolated.

The roles vary tremendously, from being highly rule-oriented to being rule-free, as we have seen. In equally rule-oriented contexts, the rules themselves create very different expectations. Baseball fans would scream their disapproval equally to an umpire who called pitches by flipping coins as would the football fans protest a referee's choice of the receiving team to start the game *without* flipping a coin. The roles may vary on many dimensions, but judgment exists whenever they condition the way one human makes decisions affecting the fortunes of another before an audience.

REASON AND JUDGMENT IN LAW

Reason is a form of calculation. The reasoned decision is one we can describe as involving an attempt to estimate the consequences of alternate possible decisions and to choose among them by valuing some consequences above others. Reasoned

TABLE 1   Typology of Choices with Illustrations

	NONREASONED CHOICES	REASONED CHOICES
JUDGMENTAL CHOICES	Baseball home-plate umpire calling balls and strikes	Decisions in appellate legal cases
NONJUDGMENTAL CHOICES	Willful, emotional, reckless or rapacious decisions of king	Decision of college student to go to movie rather than study for exam

decisions may work exclusively to achieve selfish, biased, and partial results. Most reasoned decisions that people make do not pass judgment on people and their problems. Reasoning does not necessarily judge, and it need not meet the test of impartiality.

To judge is to decide the claims of others before an audience. The judgmental decision need not be reasoned, as the umpire's calling of pitches reveals. But judgmental decisions must be impartial, which means in the end they must, to appear impartial, conform to audience expectations of the process of decision. Sometimes the audience expects the decision to be reasoned; sometimes it does not. (See Table 1.)

Our three nonlegal judging situations described in the previous section reveal an interesting relationship between rules and reason. Reasoning plays an increasingly important role in judgment as rules become less and less precise. The precise rule defines all the facts the judge may seek, and it announces exactly what consequences flow from a finding of fact so that the judge makes no calculation at all. As rules become less precise, they leave the judge greater freedom to look at different possibilities and to choose, to assess the consequences, on his own.

In order to understand the place of reason in law, we must show that imprecise legal rules require reasoning in their application. But we have already done so in our study of appellate court decisions throughout this book. By contrast, at the trial level, where the parties and the judge together play historian and seek primarily to discover the facts in a dispute, most rules are much more precise. The trial judge's rulings on evidence resemble the umpire's calling balls and strikes in many instances. Furthermore, when an open legal question arises at trial, the judge and the parties may together agree to resolve it without examining the consequences in order to proceed with the fact-finding.

Since reasoning dominates appellate legal decisions, and since these decisions are judgmental, we must determine the audience's expectations of that decision process. But we have already done that, too! The audience of law, the community, expects the process to reassure it that society can reconcile and harmonize facts, rules, social conditions, and moral values. This is the test of judicial impartiality and hence of reason in law. When judges explain their results in judicial opinions, they must attempt to convince us that the result does *not* depend on a fact at issue between the parties that we know is false, does *not* depend on false assumptions about social conditions, does *not* depend upon a tortured reading of a rule, and does *not* depend on an ethical judgment that the community would reject. The result need not please everyone, but that is not the point. Judges cannot and need not discover one right solution that everyone somehow believes best. They convince us of their impartiality as long as they convince us that they have *attempted* to describe these four elements accurately and to reconcile them.

And now something like a complete picture of the legal process begins to take shape: Law is not a "natural science." We cannot experimentally test its propositions to demonstrate their truth or error. Nor is law a purely logical process that, like mathematics, is subject mainly to the test of internal consistency. Instead, the common law tradition gives us a process of asserting and persuading through language. Facts, rules, and values are processed through the judge's use of words to express his thoughts about them. Some thoughts may persuade more effectively than others, but we cannot prove them absolutely true or false in either the logical or empirical sense. Thus, when facts, rules, and values in a case are genuinely controversial, different judges can reach conflicting results in that case yet still reason impartially in law.

Thus judges reason badly when they pretend that law gives automatic "right answers" to legal questions in lawsuits. A judge who believes that law is a science or a quasi-mathematical logic misunderstands his role. This book has described many instances in which judges have reasoned inadequately. *The failures occur because our expectations of law have changed and judges are only now beginning to understand the changes. Occasionally they try to appear impartial in terms of roles the audience has abandoned. They pretend they have found the right rule, the one right solution to the conflict in the law itself. They continue to treat legal discourse separately from moral, economic, and political philosophy. They do not appreciate fully their common law heritage.*

Let me illustrate. Here are five criteria for guiding legal judgment. Each of them is inadequate, yet judges frequently approve them.

1. *Judges should not make new law.* When a judge finds that rules and precedents speak unambiguously to the case and when he has no evidence that conditions or values have changed so as to cast doubt on the meaning of the rules and precedents, then he may claim to avoid making law. But if conditions and values have changed, as they did in the mortgage moratorium case, then the judge who claims he avoids making law only increases the tension, the dissonance, between rules, events, and values. That increased tension changes law, makes new law. By increasing this tension in law, the judge who refuses to make new law only complicates and confuses the law with which lawyers and judges in the future must cope.

   As the previous chapters have shown, however, the judge will probably not find a clear legal answer in the first place. Each case contains some unique facts that might remove it from the scope of any established rule. Furthermore, the words of the established rules are often ambiguous. The precedents that could potentially give meaning to the rule or principle are in conflict. When law provides no clear solution, the only way the judge can assert the presence of harmony is to *create* law clear enough to resolve the case. The entire common law tradition accepts this lawmaking role.

2. *Judicial rulings should always be general, so that people in the same class receive the same treatment.* The problem here concerns the selection of an ethically acceptable class. A rule that blacks always lose and whites always win in litigation that pits one against the other is certainly general. It tells people in these two classes exactly what will happen to them. But the chosen class is wrong! It does not correspond to the audience's ethical restrictions on the definition of classes.

We expect judges to decide for the community. It is absolutely essential that judges articulate reasons for their results—justify their results—so that anybody in the community might, if they found themselves in the same circumstances, know how the courts would respond. The result must be generalizable in the sense that does not rest only on the unique characteristics of the individual parties. This is very different from expecting the court to articulate a rule or standard of overpowering generality that covers all people in all circumstances. Judges can, in other words, speak for the community at the same time they say that some extremely rare fact in the case before them produces a result that judges would not reach in otherwise similar cases. (Again, consider the key social condition, the Depression, in the mortgage cases in this light.) What makes the case speak for the community is the judge's justification for using that unusual fact as the basis for his conclusion. It is the deliberate, articulated, and public quality of reasoning that makes it legal, not its generality.

3. *Decisions should conform to the rules of logic; conclusions must always follow from the stated premises.* Strictly speaking, this command is true, but how helpful is it? What if the logic is correct but the premises are factually wrong or in doubt? A judgment in favor of capital punishment may flow with flawless logic from the premise that the death penalty deters murders, but there is considerable doubt that the death penalty really

does so. Furthermore, what if the original premise collides with an equally plausible alternative premise? Someone who reasons from the premise that "the early bird catches the worm," must reconcile the reasoning with the premise that "haste makes waste."[18] Again, it is the justification of the choice of premise that is so important.

4. *Decisions must not contradict history.* But we do not live in the past. Events, rules, and values constantly change. The judicial attempt throughout much of our legal history to derive results from natural law may have satisfied the expectations of the earlier community, but invocation of natural law does not necessarily satisfy us today. The need for the capacity to harmonize in the community exists always in the present.

5. *Decisions should reach the results that best serve the interests of society.* This criterion is much too broad. If a legislature passes an absurd law whose purposes seem quite at odds with social utility, the courts, absent constitutional restrictions, must apply the statute in terms of its questionable purpose. Furthermore, as we saw in the last chapter, courts do not possess the institutional capacity to make the kind of policy that every sort of social problem requires. The rules of evidence may prevent the courts from obtaining some key facts. Arbitration, negotiation, and straight political compromises in some instances best serve society. It is best to leave some issues entirely in private hands.

Law, as Gottfried Dietze thus puts it, "is a limitation upon rationality."[19] Just as the baseball audience (and baseball's rules) tells umpires to ignore certain facets of the game—the differences in the gracefulness of pitcher and batter, for example—we do not expect the legal process to care about certain social events and facts. The results of labor-management nego-

---

[18]Freund, "Rationality in Judicial Decisions," pp. 112–113.
[19]Gottfried Dietze, "The Limited Rationality of Law," in Friedrich, ed., *Nomos VII: Rational Decision,* pp. 67–88 at p. 67.

tiations may have tremendous social impact. Yet we do not expect judges to decide them or in some sense insure that negotiations reach equitable results. We leave this, instead, to the market and to politics. Decisions should serve the interests of society only in the broad sense that society benefits when courts respect legislative power and abstain from some issues altogether.

Let me summarize. Citizens living in communities need the reassurance that the community has the capacity to reconcile the concrete facts of a dispute with the conditions and events of life, the formal rules of the community, and the citizens' beliefs, often themselves in conflict, about right and wrong. I have asserted that this need is real in our political lives just as we need nourishment, sleep, and sex in varying degrees in the biological part of our existence. People do not care in this regard exclusively that public policy impose any specifically favored value of their own on society, though, of course, they often do care about policies. People, at a deeper level, are frightened by the prospect that their community may lose its structure its embodiment of place and of limits, altogether. People expect the kind of reasoning I have described from courts because other institutions only rarely face the task of dealing with the facts of specific human conflicts, rules, social conditions, and fundamental values all at the same time.

I do not mean that citizens daily review legal opinions to satisfy themselves as to the quality of legal reasoning, for, of course, they do not. But parties to lawsuits, and their friends, and the legal profession—the immediate audience—do care about the fairness of decisions. When legal parties, lawyers, and news commentators increasingly report dissatisfaction with judges; when, over thousands of people and thousands of cases the message emerges that judges somehow are "out of touch," then the community begins to lose confidence in its own capacity to reconcile the four factors. But if judges assume that no one decision matters, cumulative damage will occur.

Notice carefully what I am saying here. I am not saying that judges should carefully justify their decisions because judges are not democratically elected. Perhaps elected politicians can act willfully, emotionally, recklessly, or rapaciously because we assume electoral competition will correct such errors, but that is not the point. Many state judges are, after all, elected. We expect judges to reason because judging decides concrete cases. The legislature does not face the task of reconciling a general rule to the facts of a special case.

Legal reasoning as I have defined it matters primarily because communities need to retain confidence in limits, and reasoning can reinforce that confidence. Even for purely normative questions, questions of personal taste that cannot be resolved factually or scientifically, reasoning can improve judgment. For example, suppose that, offended by the rock music coming from my daughter's room, I tell her to turn off the music. She asks me why. I can, of course, say, "Because I say so." But I could, as an alternative, reason with her. If I say it's too loud, and mean it, I then give her the option to turn it down but not off, to satisfy us both. Or, I may say I don't like rock music. "Why not?" she then asks. "It's all beat. The tunes are monotonous." "But Dad, you play 'Bolero' on the hi-fi over and over." And suddenly, by reasoning with her honestly, I must confront what matters to me in music. Perhaps I will fail in that conversation to explain to myself or her a complete philosophy of aesthetics in music. However, I will begin to care about deeper structures and values in my life. By caring, my values may even change, but it is more important that I reassure my daughter of my capacity to care about structure and values. Do not characters in movies and literature become heroic when we believe they are in touch with values, although perhaps not ours, and live by them?

Now, take a case, any case, that this book has described and assess it in terms of the concepts discussed in this chapter.

Consider first some instances in which I have condemned judicial reasoning. Does not each one of these fail because the decision rests on assertions about facts, social conditions, rules, and/or ethical values that seem to us quite probably wrong?

- The second baseball antitrust case *(Toolson)* fails because we *know* baseball had by 1952 become a business, yet the court denied the truth of the fact in the case without providing a reason to deny it.
- *Lochner*, the bakers' hours case, fails because the judges ignored a social condition that seemed amply demonstrated: Baking long hours can endanger bakers' health.

- *Repouille,* Chapter II's second naturalization case, failed because the law created by the *Francioso* precedent made the character of the unique individual, not the general ethical category of his act, central to the case, but the court did not explain why it departed from that precedent.

- Finally, any decision fails if it invokes the stability and reliance argument when we can perceive no ethical justification for reliance. This is why *Fox v. Snow* (and *Toolson,* in part) failed, and why Chief Justice Vanderbilt's dissent in *Fox* is so powerful.

Now consider some cases this book has applauded:

- Does not the "slack action" case calling for uniformity in train limit laws *(Southern Pacific v. Arizona)* seem sound because we find plausible and relevant the fact that reorganizing trains at state borders will cost a great deal of time and money?

- Does not the case that rejected the root rule *(Lyman)* appeal to us because the physical and social character of land ownership, a social condition, makes it extremely cumbersome to determine who owns a tree or its fruit by digging in the neighbor's gladiolas to see how far the tree's roots extend?

- Does not the mortgage moratorium decision *(Home Building and Loan Association)* convince us that, given social conditions, the rule, the Constitution's contract clause, does not govern mortgage foreclosures in a depression?

- Do not *Hynes* (the case of the electrocuted diver) and *Barnette* (the second flag salute case) appeal to our ethical instincts? Do we not think that electrified railroads running along rivers *ought* to maintain their property to avoid electrocuting swimmers in the river, even if those swimmers physically touch a few feet of the railroad's property? Do we not think it ethically wrong for the state, through its public schools, to compel people to attend school and then compel them, because they obey the law, to abandon a fundamental religious belief?

Notice again that it is not the *logic*, or the *generality*, or the fidelity to *history*, or the drive for *social utility* that makes the reasoning in these cases appeal to us. They appeal primarily because in each instance they reassure us that courts can combine case facts, social events and conditions, rules, and ethical norms sensibly.

COMPLETING THE PICTURE

Several more puzzle pieces remain to be fitted in to make a complete picture of legal reasoning.

Getting Inside the Judge's Head

If the quality of legal reasoning is so important to society, how do we know that the reasons judges give for their decisions accurately report the process of deciding that actually occurred in their brains? Karl Llewellyn once wrote:

> Of course, only by happenstance will an opinion accurately report the process of deciding. Indeed, I urge flatly that such report is not really a function of the opinion at all.... Vital factors may go unmentioned; pseudo factors may be put forward; emphasis and weighing of factors may be hugely skewed; any statements of policy may be not for revelation but merely for consumption; the very alleged statement of "the facts" may be only a lawyer's argumentative arranged selection, omission, emphasis, distortion, all flavored to make the result tolerable or toothsome.[20]

In fact, we cannot expect the judge to report accurately the process by which he discovers his result because in all probability the judge himself will not fully understand the process of discovery. James Hopkins's description of the elusiveness of human discovery is telling:

> As Randall Jarrell has shown in describing the process through which he proceeded in creating his poem, "The Woman at the Washington Zoo," the artist cannot articulate

[20]Karl Llewellyn, *The Common Law Tradition* (Boston: Little, Brown, 1960), p. 56.

the series of backward and forward motions of thought which
constitute the events of the creative process. In the same
order...the judge finds it difficult to sort out the motions
which preceded the final choice of legal theory.[21]

However, if citizens need reassurance that judgment works in
their community, judges need not struggle to describe the
elusive process of discovery. It is the justification the judge gives
for the result that will succeed or fail to reconcile facts, conditions, rules, and values. We and the judge can distinguish the
process of justification. We can evaluate the judge's justification
on its own merits.[22]

Thus legal reasoning may be the process of putting into
words a justification for the result reached by some other,
undiscoverable, means, but we must not undervalue that process. The audience of the courts—the community's way of judging the judges, which in turn creates impartiality in law—does
not need or expect the judge to perform the impossible psychological feat of recreating the process of discovery. The judge's
rationalization, his justification of the result, is sufficient to
reassure the community that its courts possess the capacity to
harmonize the potentially conflicting forces within it in a given
case.

Modern Expectations of the Legal Process

By now I trust you understand that my prime motive in this book
has not been simply to catalog the various ways judges actually
decide cases. I have often criticized judicial results and justifications. Failures persist because law and courts have not yet
completely realized and incorporated into law the truth that
modern life forces us to face arbitrariness and meaninglessness
every day of our lives. In earlier legal history, the community
shared a consensus in the authority of God and hence of natural

---

[21]James D. Hopkins, "Fictions and the Judicial Process: A Preliminary
Theory of Decision," 33 *Brooklyn Law Review* 1 (1966), pp. 11–12.

[22]See Richard A. Wasserstrom, *The Judicial Decision* (Stanford: Stanford
University Press, 1961), pp. 25–29; and Robert S. Summers, *Instrumentalism in
American Legal Theory* (Ithaca, N.Y.: Cornell University Press, 1982).

law. The judge whose decision process probed for the truths of natural law followed the rules his audience expected. More recently, people believed that truth lay in agreement and that popular democracy would generate values the citizenry could share. But today those beliefs have dissolved. We live in a postliberal state whose bureaucratic machinery by its nature cannot provide ethical meaning.[23]

How, then, can communities achieve consensus and stability without order and belief?[24] I am not so naive as to think that judges and legal reasoning will somehow rescue us from meaninglessness. By virtue of its universality, its publicness, law cannot provide deeply personal individual solutions to the problem of meaninglessness. Ultimately, all human activities must adjust to modern conditions, or the quality of our lives will decline. Reasoning that denies truths that the community has come to accept will, however, make courts appear increasingly "out of touch."

What, then, are the directives we can give reasoning judges to help them catch up with the conditions of modern life? How can judges make their visions more "accurate and attractive?"

1. Abandon the pretense that a given decision has necessarily found the only acceptable legal solution and abandon the pretense that for each conflict there is an absolute principle that governs it. These pretenses only encourage judges to assume they have completed their work when they find a canon or factually similar precedent that can, without too much stretching, be imposed upon the problem. The pretenses nourish the idea that rules resolve problems when rules without justifications never do. If justification to the modern audience means reconciling facts, conditions, rules, and ethical values in the result, then even the case with the perfectly applicable rule, the "open-and-shut" case, must have an explanation why it is this way, why the rule fits the

[23]Roberto Mangabeira Unger, *Law in Modern Society* (New York: The Free Press, 1976), Chapter 3.
[24]Ibid., p. 170.

facts, and why neither social conditions nor ethical values exempt the facts from the rule.

2. Judges must accept with confidence the premise that they can remain impartial when law provides no single right answer to a legal question. The imprecision of words, the failure of the intent of lawmakers to yield precise guides, the very modest scope of horizontal stare decisis do not permit or obligate the judge to decide according to his whims. Professor Robert Cover has written:

> The judicial whim argument entails a common error or oversimplification. The critical dimension of the rule of law is not the degree of specificity with which an actor is constrained, but the very fact that the actor must look outside his own will for criteria of judgment. There is a difference—intelligible to most pre-adolescents—between the directions "Do what you want" and "Do what you think is right or just."[25]

To "look outside his own will for criteria of judgment": If we have any single key to legal judgment, it is here. It is this looking outside that enables judges to belie Benjamin Franklin's cynical statement about reason I quoted a few pages back. But how can people look outside their own will? The conventional answer, the one many thoughtful judges give, urges judges to practice certain "good" judicial habits. Judges must be patient. They must listen to both sides. They must develop the capacity to empathize, to get inside the skins of real people facing concrete difficulties. I do not mean to deprecate such habits, but I suspect they suffice more to make judging attractive than to make it accurate. To make his legal visions accurate, the judge must learn a different habit, that of relating directly to the social, economic, and political conditions that together compose the "outside."

---

[25] Robert Cover, Book Review of R. Berger, *Government by Judiciary*, *New Republic*, January 14, 1978, p. 27.

To go outside in this manner calls for a quiet revolution in legal reasoning, one that is already in progress but far from complete. Judges must abandon the assumption that the logical elegance of an argument contributes to its impartiality and legality. Instead, they must care, and care deeply, that the premises from which the argument flows are plausible and consistent with human knowledge insofar as knowledge on the point exists. In this vein Justice Thurgood Marshall once wrote in dissent, "It is perfectly proper for judges to disagree about what the Constitution requires. But it is disgraceful for an interpretation of the Constitution to be premised upon unfounded assumptions about how people live."[26] In complex cases the habit of caring about the external accuracy of premises will reqire judges to master difficult and unfamiliar materials. In many more instances, however, the judge who insists that his premises meet the standards of "common sense" and "good judgment" will reason effectively in law.

What I have called a quiet revolution in legal reasoning depends in turn on the success of a wider quiet revolution in the ethics of the practice of law and the accepted sense of what it means to be a lawyer at all. By our definition law is a certain kind of problem-solving process. We call people in the problem-solving business by names we do not often associate with lawyers: "ministers," "peacemakers," and so forth. Lawyers must define their mission in similar terms. The widely favorable professional and public reception to Fisher and Ury's *Getting to Yes,* cited above in footnote 9, is one small indication that lawyers and law professors believe in both the existence and the rightness of this shift in professional self-perception. In a compelling article in the *Journal of Legal Education,* Professor James R. Elkins has argued that law schools must make "moral discourse" a central part of legal

[26] *United States v. Kras,* 409 U.S. 434 (1973), p. 460.

education. He argues that law professors must abandon
the assumption that the proper question in the classroom is, "I don't care if it's right; is it legal?" These
advocates urge, in short, that the profession should
adopt peacemaking, not fighting, as its fundamental
organizing metaphor.[27]

3. "Know thyself." If, as we now know, the discovery of the
premise and the discovery of the result are one and the
same process in all reasoning, then judges should admit
the fact and justify their results in those terms. The
proper judicial opinion is the one that says, in effect:
"This is the result. The result is as acceptable as any
other placed before the court because it makes the
following assumptions about the elements at issue in
the case. Now here is why we find these assumptions
convincing." J. Braxton Craven, Jr., said it this way:

> I believe that there are only two kinds of judges at all levels
> of courts: those who are admittedly...result-oriented, and
> those who are also result-oriented but either do not know it
> or decline for various purposes to admit it. Those who are
> unaware of their result-orientation have an advantage; they
> get where they want to go without the inhibition of a
> conscious awareness of how they got there....A judge who
> is...introspective tends to be more flexible than his less
> perceptive brother who knows not what he does—if only
> because he is aware that he is constantly choosing, usually

---

[27]I strongly recommend Elkins's article, in part because he does not under-
estimate the difficulty of restructuring legal education. Indeed, he believes the
obstacles may be too high for formal organizations like law schools to leap at all.
See "Moral Discourse and Legalism in Legal Education," 32 *Journal of Legal
Education* 11 (1982). For a more optimistic vision of the possibility that lawyers
can and sometimes do successfully conceive of themselves as peacemakers, see
Thomas Shaffer, *On Being a Christian and a Lawyer* (Provo, Utah: Brigham
Young University Press, 1981). See also the widely publicized criticism of the
legal system by the former Harvard Law School professor and now president of
Harvard University, Derek Bok, "A Flawed System," *Harvard Magazine*, May–
June, 1983, p. 48. Cf. "The Trouble with Lawyers?," *Wall Street Journal*,
October 11, 1983, p. 1, and "Do Lawyers Court the Public's Contempt?," *Wall
Street Journal*, October 20, 1983, p. 31.

not between right and wrong but between two goods or two evils embraced within conflicting principles.[28]

Notice that by abandoning the pretense and admitting the psychological reality, the judge, as Craven implies, increases the extent to which he broods over the issues in the case. Making this admission forces the judge to re-examine the relevance and the accuracy of his assumptions. Doing so and admitting it only make the reconciling and harmonizing element of legal reasoning more prominent.

4. Accept the propriety of flexibility. Where judges determine that a "formality"—a priciple of general justice or stare decisis, for example—should resolve a case, they must explain what makes the formality appropriate in the case.[29] If, as I think we must, we believe in judicial fallibility, the absence of absolutes, and the fact that changed circumstances may make a previously reasoned opinion appear unreasoned now, then in some circumstances flexibility becomes essential.

Consider, for example, that the courts have in recent decades narrowed the grounds for justifiable homicide. Courts have moved away from the notion that people can kill to prevent trespassing on their property or can kill in their personal defense when less drastic remedies are available. The move coincides, I think, with the close of the frontier and the communal recognition of the need to raise the minimum standards of civilized conduct in complex societies.

As I complete this second edition, however, the media remind me to take another look. What of the problem of the infant born with severe physical and

---

[28]J. Braxton Craven, Jr., "Paean to Pragmatism," 50 *North Carolina Law Review* 977 (1972), p. 977. See also Joseph C. Hutcheson, Jr. "The Judgment Intuitive: The Function of the 'Hunch' in Judicial Decision," 14 *Cornell Law Quarterly* 274 (1929).

[29]For a convincing justification of formalities in contract law, see Lon Fuller, "Consideration and Form," 41 *Columbia Law Review* 799 (1941).

mental defects? What if the parents refuse to authorize emergency surgery to correct the physical defects of such an infant and a right-to-life organization brings suit to compel such surgery? Or what if the baby dies and a prosecutor files murder charges against the parents and/or the attending physicians? Judges have not escaped such cases. I do not want them to resolve these most perplexing issues by blindly reciting a precedent or a century-old penal statute. I want the judge, at least until the legislature steps in to create its own public policy, to wrestle with the facts about life-prolonging medical innovations and with the ethics about the value of preserving the lives of the severely retarded.[30] I don't want or expect the judge to convince me that his answers to these questions are completely and immutably correct. I may disagree, but I do want him to recognize that the issue requires him to try to answer these questions as conscientiously and completely as he can.

I am arguing that the modern view of reason, the modern expectation of judgment in communities, accepts openness and imperfections in reasoning, and recognizes that law should change with changes in the life with which law deals.

I do not for a moment doubt that courts should, barring clear constitutional violations, substitute the purpose of a statute as they see it for their own reasoning whenever a legislature in fact speaks to a problem. I am not proposing a new justification for judicial supremacy in politics and government. The antinomies in ethics, the absence of any undisputably moral principles to resolve many social problems make, as Alexander Bickel so clearly demonstrated, the legislature the primary source of modern law.[31] But courts cannot avoid judging, and so they cannot escape reasoning well or poorly.

Courts as well as other institutions must act to preserve the

---

[30]See "U.S. Panel Urges More Control by Patients over Life-Sustaining Medical Treatment," *Wall Street Journal*, March 22, 1983, p. 16.

[31]Bickel, *The Morality of Consent*, Chapter 1.

sense that the modern community has value in it, even though caring about the striving for values may itself be the only value the process preserves.

The position calls for judges to think openly about the institutional strengths and weaknesses of courts discussed in Chapter VI and to recognize that in many circumstances courts are not capable of meeting the demands of justice. The position also asks judges to take seriously the fact that decisions do guide other judges and practicing attorneys. The judge who justifies the correct result through a disguised manipulation of legal technicalities forecloses the opportunity to contribute to future understanding.

The approach I endorse here also questions the physical austerity, the formal distance, and archaic trappings of many courtrooms. My hunch is that the development of neighborhood legal centers and increased lay participation, particularly in criminal justice, can do much to improve fairness in the daily workings of courts.[32] My main point is that judges should treat legal reasoning itself as inevitably like human reasoning generally. Basically, this means that reasoning is no more than a dialogue about the questions "What matters?" and "Why?" It is perfectly possible to reason about values and thus to sharpen a mutual understanding of what matters in law just as my daughter and I can sharpen our mutual understanding by discussing values in music.

If modernity robs us of the security of religious, political, legal, or ethical absolutes, it does not rob us of the value of the attempt to articulate relative standards that make sense of what

---

[32]See Graham Hughes, *The Conscience of the Courts: Law and Morals in American Life* (New York: Doubleday, 1975); John T. Noonan, Jr., *Persons and Masks of the Law* (New York: Farrar, Straus & Giroux, 1976); James White, *The Legal Imagination* (Boston: Little, Brown, 1973); Phillippe Nonet and Philip Selznick, *Law and Society in Transition* (New York: Harper & Row, 1978). My approach parallels in many respects the "responsive law" model that Nonet and Selznick advocate. See also Richard Abel, ed., *The Politics of Informal Justice*, Vol. 1, (New York: Academic Press, 1982), especially Mark Lazerson, "In the Halls of Justice," pp. 119–163, showing how the traditional informality of the New York City Housing Court allowed landlords to evade tenant grievances and how recent formalization of the court's procedures forced landlords to respond to tenant grievances.

we know and believe. Judges should and can make the attempt. And modern judges often do. Let me conclude by letting a judge speak for himself:

> I have never had the misfortune to be closely associated with a truly conservative judge. I do not mean "conservative" in its ordinary sense. A more apt word is, perhaps, "sterile." I have in mind sterile intellectualism that is not in the least offended but, instead, is delighted that there may be no reason for decision other than that the rule "was laid down in the time of Henry IV." I have known very few such judges, and them only at a distance, but I have read others. This is the kind of judge who, if he is a trial judge, likes to say from the bench, "This is not a court of justice; it is a court of law." When I was a young judge (under age forty) I said it once or twice myself and am sorry for it. This is cold intellectualism that finds no room at the inn for people. This type of legal mind is concerned with "legal problems"—entirely unaware that the term is a misnomer, that there are only peoples' problems for which the law sometimes may afford answers. The life principle of such a judge is stare decisis. He fervently believes that it is far, far better that the rule be certain and unjust than that he tinker with it. It is a delight to him to construct painstakingly, with adequate display of erudition, an edifice of logic and precedent upon which justice may be sacrificed.... When one reads such an opinion, complete with pious disavowal of judicial power to usurp the legislative prerogative, the feeling comes through that the author is not sorry that he cannot and may even be glad that the legislature will not. Such a judge categorically rejects Holmes' aphorism that the life of the law is not logic but experience, and such a judge, of course, has never entertained the following thought of Yeats: "God guard me from those thoughts men think In the mind alone; He that sings a lasting song thinks in (the) marrowbone."[33]

SUMMARY

- How has this chapter defined law, reason, judging, and impartiality?
- How does the fact that law involves rules made and enforced by

---

[33]Craven, "Paean to Pragmatism," pp. 979–980.

the government help define the character and desired qualities of legal reasoning?

- In what circumstances do we not expect the decisions of a judge to be reasoned?
- What are five conventional criteria for sound legal reasoning? In what ways is each inadequate?
- What benefits flow from reasoning about problems, even when the problems involve values, like taste in music, about which no one can prove that one position is objectively right or wrong?
- Why does the problem of getting inside a judge's head turn out to be no problem at all?
- How can reason produce several inconsistent but equally justified resolutions of a legal conflict?
- What specific changes in judicial approach to legal reasoning will bring judges into greater awareness of modern conditions?

ILLUSTRATIVE CASES

Review each of the cases at the ends of the preceding six chapters. Analyze the effectiveness of the reasoning in each of these cases, using the terms and concepts presented in this chapter.

SOME EXPLORATORY PROBLEMS

1. Consider Lon Fuller's statement in *The Morality of Law,* "If I were asked...to discern one central indisputable principle of what may be called substantive natural law...I would find it in the injunction: Open up, maintain, and preserve the integrity of the channels of communication...."[34] Is this, in a nutshell, what reason in law is about?

2. Countries with seacoasts routinely claim some territorial limit out into the ocean. But from what point of land does one measure the limit? The approved practice in international law is called the *tracé parallèle,* a term that simply means that one traces a line parallel to the coast out at the stated legal distance

---

[34]*The Morality of Law* (New Haven: Yale University Press, 1964), p. 186. Fuller describes the minimal conditions that governing by rules must meet if it is to govern fairly. The book is required reading for further study in jurisprudence. See also "Jurisprudence Symposium," 11 *Georgia Law Review* 967–1424 (1977).

from shore. Foreign vessels that penetrate the line violate territorial waters. But now think about Norway, with its thousands of fjords and offshore islets. Instead of using the approved method, Norway drew a line connecting its outermost points and then extended the limit the prescribed distance out from that line. Given this method, a ship might penetrate Norwegian waters and still be many miles outside the *tracé parallèle* limit. Should Norway be required, in a suit brought by a foreign country whose fishermen were apprehended inside Norway's limit (but outside the limit prescribed by international law), to conform to the approved practice? What justification do you, as a judge of the International Court, give for your result? Should it matter that Norway in fact consistently publicized and enforced its peculiar way of defining its territorial waters for over 100 years before this suit was brought?[35]

3. Imagine a televised Saturday afternoon wrestling match pitting "Golden Boy" against "The Devil's Disciple." Is the referee of such a match a judge according to this chapter's definition? Does the answer depend on whether the "script" for the match actually allows either wrestler to win? Put another way, as long as the referee actually decides the match, is he not a judge because he decides on audience-based criteria, even though those criteria may not measure the wrestling skills of the contestants? Consider in this connection the remarks that a judge of horsemanship made to students attending a one-week horse school at the University of Georgia, July 10–15, 1983:

> When I judge horse showmanship my criteria are very personal. I can't say that any other judge has exactly my standards. But I do think it is fair for you to know what my standards are: First, the rider should be dressed comfortably so that the clothing does not interfere in any way with the ability to control the horse. Ruffles and other flashy [Western] gear never add points to a score I give. Second, don't rush into the ring to make a good impression. I judge the horse and rider as a unit. The first impression I get is usually the most important, and I want to see a unit that is calm and relaxed and under control....

Would a person who decided Western-style showmanship in such a manner be a judge? A good judge? Why or why not?

---

[35]See Stanley Paulson, "*Jus Non Scriptum* and the Reliance Principle," 75 *Michigan Law Review* 68 (1976).

Would such a person more resemble a baseball umpire calling balls and strikes or a Supreme Court Justice?

4. Readers familiar with the conventional wisdom about our legal system may have noted that this book pays relatively little attention to its asserted adversary character. My excuse is that the system has always been, at many of its stages, less adversarial than Judge Frank's "fight theory" (see page 286 above) suggests. And the last section of this chapter suggests that a shift from the fight metaphor is indeed happening.

In this regard Professor Geoffrey Hazard has asserted that modern judges already act more as pragmatic problem-solvers than the popular image of judging assumes. Hazard believes that judges, particularly appellate judges, want from attorneys not brilliantly crafted legal abstractions but helpful assessments of the practical realities of the situation. He feels that attorneys must learn to confront candidly the weaknesses in their own positions. He urges that attorneys can increase their chances of prevailing for their clients by cooperating with the judicial search for reasoned solutions to the problem represented in the case. They may do so by making the most concessions for the client consistent with winning.[36]

Professor Milner Ball's proposal for reforming our vision of the nature of law goes much further. He suggests that theater, not warfare or problem solving, is the proper metaphor for the legal process. Each case is an opportunity to stage in court a small morality play that reaffirms the values of our culture. In this context the object of argument is not to win a fight but to dramatize and concretize society's fundamental norms. In response to Professor Hazard, Ball and D. Robert Lohn have written:[37]

> In a performing, theatrical—as opposed to martial— setting, the advocate will find it as inapt to assault the other side as to assault the judge. If appellate advocates are actors representing (taking the parts of) their clients and the judge or panel of judges is the audience, then an attorney may view herself as engaged in a joint enterprise with the other advocate with whom she is pursuing a common cause, i.e., a

---

[36]"Arguing the Law: The Advocate's Duty and Opportunity," 16 *Georgia Law Review* 821, p. 830 (1982). See also Hazard's *Ethics in the Practice of Law* (New Haven: Yale University Press, 1978).

[37]"Legal Advocacy, Performance, and Affection," 16 *Georgia Law Review* 853, pp. 855–856 (1982).

performance (which is played also to the public at large as well as to the judges). The action then becomes dialogue rather than diapolemics, and the kinds of arguments offered will be drawn from a wholly different environment than that of battle and verbal warfare. We may identify this environment as one of cooperation and professional mutuality.

Theater lends itself to a sense of collegiality. One recent essay, for example, observes that theater elicits the reality of offering and receiving among the actors and between the actors and the audience.[a] This reality of connectedness may also be imagined as animating successful courtroom performances.[b] Within the context of such a reality, a brief that seeks to destroy the other side will fail—not for weakness, but for irrelevance. It is wholly out of place and not in keeping with the task at hand.

We hasten to point out that, if the brief is not a salvo, neither is it an abject surrender. There is need for strong individual performance in the joint effort of an appellate argument. A weak or stupid brief does not invite a good response and will have as depressing an effect as a poor, lifeless performance by an actor in an ensemble.

How persuasive do you find the theatrical metaphor? The essence of theater is deception, is it not? If you have difficulty accepting deceptiveness in the legal process, ask whether the

[a]The essay proposes that, although a city is "ambition and hubbub, buying and selling, greed and haste," it remains the case that "the real stuff of the city, that which makes it alive rather than dead, civilized rather than barbarous, a place of nourishment rather than of deprivation, is...the reality that comes of offering and receiving." *The Talk of the Town: Notes and Comments,* NEW YORKER, Mar. 15, 1982, at 33. This reality, the essay notes, is most vividly called forth through musical or theatrical performances "that take place in a room of some sort." Id.

[b]The success of the performance of a play or piece of music can be measured, it has been suggested, "by its ability to elicit connectedness." Id. A performance elicits the nexus of offering and receiving "by being, first, true and second, articulately true, so that people present not only recognize the truth of whatever is expressed...but also share it." Id. This standard for theater (being true and articulately true) is translated into the standard for judicial theater that it do justice and be seen to do justice.

Another word for connectedness is love. The love that it is the particular responsibility of judicial theater to evoke is civic affection....[Footnotes in original. Notice the similarity between the concept of "civic affection" and Tushnet's "attractiveness" in law.]

conventional processes of legal reasoning this book has criticized are not doubly deceptive for pretending to be accurate.
Theater, at least, freely admits the importance of deception in its
craft. And does not all human activity that pretends to impose
order on the chaotic buzz of atoms and molecules in the universe deceive simply by denying the reality of chaos?

5. Comment on the following story in *Newsweek:*

> California law permits doctors to end all treatment of
> patients whose brains are dead. But what is to be done with the
> seemingly hopeless comatose patient whose heart—and
> brain—won't die? Can doctors even stop feeding him?
> Seventeen months ago two Los Angeles physicians unplugged
> Clarence Herbert's respirator, cut off all his nourishment and
> let him die. Last August the Los Angeles district attorney's
> office filed murder charges against them, apparently the first
> time doctors have been criminally prosecuted for cutting off
> life-support devices. Now defense lawyers are trying to use a
> lengthy preliminary hearing to persuade a judge to dismiss the
> case, arguing that the doctors were merely following standard
> medical practice.
>
> Herbert had undergone successful abdominal surgery, then
> inexplicably slipped into a coma. Doctors immediately hitched
> him to a respirator, but after three days surgeon Robert Nejdl
> and internist Neil Barber concluded that their patient had
> suffered massive brain damage and would never recover.
> Herbert's wife approved the doctors' recommendation to
> unplug the machine—though she now says she was misled.
> Herbert's heart kept beating. The doctors then removed his
> intravenous tubes, and he lived for six more days without
> sustenance. The prosecution contends that the doctors did not
> have the right to stop feeding a person who had not died, and
> they produced expert witnesses who said Herbert had a small
> chance to recover. They also say that the doctors' aim was to
> bury a potentially nasty malpractice claim. "They did
> everything they could to make him die," says a spokesman for
> the D.A.'s office.
>
> The defense has countered by denying all charges of
> malpractice and bringing on its own expert witnesses. Last
> week Father John Paris, a medical-ethics professor at the
> College of the Holy Cross, testified that Barber and Nejdl had

followed American Medical Association guidelines. He added that since the prosecution, "physicians are so frightened that they aren't taking any patients off machines." The hearings are expected to last another three weeks.[38]

6. Is there any objective evidence that judges actually conform as role theory predicts? When we observe differences in the formal definitions of judicial roles within the legal system do we find that judges actually behave differently?

We certainly do. Here are two examples, both of which deal with differences in the degree to which judges think their role gives them discretion to articulate new law. First, British judges much more commonly speak in terms of adherence to precedent. Archibald Cox, lecturing in Great Britain, said that judges in the United States:

> are less attentive to the letter of the law or to precedent. They move freely in wider orbit. Both bench and bar make greater use of statistical and other social studies, and the line between law and policy is often blurred.[39]

Second, although the law on any given point cannot be any more or less ambiguous at the appellate than at the trial level in the United States, trial judges are much less adventuresome in the creation of new law than are appellate judges. Trial judges work, after all, at the bottom of a judicial hierarchy. To trial judges, precedents tend to speak not simply as examples from the past but as commands from their superiors. Hence the trial court in *Tarasoff,* finding no law that allowed recovery against psychiatrists for their failure to warn the potential victims of their patients, in effect threw out the case at the outset. The California Supreme Court, on the other hand, used the same facts to expand the law. The laws of role theory govern judges no less than the rest of us.

---

[38]"Did the Patient Die—Or Was He Murdered?" *Newsweek,* February 14, 1983, p. 76. See also *Superintendent of Belchertown State School v. Saikewicz* 370 N.E. 2d 417 (Massachusetts, 1977), in which a court denied physicians' request to administer painful chemotherapy to a 67-year-old terminally ill cancer patient. The patient was born severely retarded and had never learned to talk.

[39]Archibald Cox, *The Role of the Supreme Court in American Government* (New York: Oxford University Press, 1976), p. 1. See aso Gareth Jones, "Should Judges Be Politicians?: The English Experience," 57 *Indiana Law Journal* 211 (1982).

7. I have urged greater judicial appreciation for the place of common sense in legal analysis. But what, more precisely, is common sense? Michael Boudin has speculated that, in addition to the obvious components of age and experience, common sense consists of such qualities of mind and character as:

1. a sense of proportion and moderation;
2. the ability to think about multiple factors at the same time;
3. a willingness to order and attach different weights to competing elements in a problem;
4. the ability to devise alternative solutions;
5. a sense of mental self-discipline and an instinct for order, pattern, and reason.[40]

Boudin's descriptions do not quite add up to a definition. The search for a precise definition of common sense today goes on at the highest levels of computer science. The competition among companies to produce computers containing true artificial intelligence capacity has run into several difficulties. How, for example, can a computer be programmed to differentiate between these two statements: "Time flies like an arrow" and "Fruit flies like apricots"? With enough time and money, such simple linguistic problems can be programmed out, but there remains the problem of teaching the machine to use the right information at the right time, to teach a hypothetical walking encyclopedia filled with information about gravity and cliffs not to walk off the edge of a cliff. The *Wall Street Journal* calls the search for an understanding of common sense "a preoccupation of artificial-intelligence researchers." In their attempt to apply to computers what is known about common sense in humans, researchers have found that they do not understand common sense operations in the human brain. It seems that the brain does not resemble current computer designs in the first place.[41] So, if I have frustrated you by failing to provide an authoritative definition of "reason," I urge you to pursue a career not in law but in computer science.

8. The ethical component in legal reasoning presents challenges to judges every bit as complex as the challenge to see accurately

[40]"Common Sense in Law Practice," *Harvard Law School Bulletin*, Spring, 1983, pp. 22–24.
[41]"Scientists Are Laboring at Making Computers Think for Themselves," *The Wall Street Journal*, March 29, 1983, p. 1 and p. 22.

the factual elements in a case. Ethical principles compete with one another, as the antinomies in law cited above show, yet judges must make informed choices among them. Let us therefore return to the problem raised in *Repouille.* If a judge must go outside himself, how can he choose an ethical principle from society? Should he use public opinion polls? Should he care equally about mass and elite opinion? And what if society contains multiple ethical views on a subject—like abortion—so that no single opinion commands a majority? Should courts mirror the "ethos" of the polity, or do courts properly lead and contribute to the creation of the "ethos" of society?

9. What characterizes a good lawyer? Stewart Macaulay has reviewed some empirical studies showing how lawyers define and differentiate their status and prestige within the profession. See "Law Schools and the World Outside Their Doors."[42] But my question concerns skill, not status. What is the essence of this skill? In addition to the several answers this chapter has already provided, consider the following passage. It is from an essay titled "Thomas More's Skill."

> *Skill, character and knowledge.* This lawyer skill is not a matter of principles. Lawyers use legal principles, but they use them more to garnish their work than to carry it out. Lawyers, when being candid, admit scant regard for legal principles. Nonlawyers may think that lawyers disdain principles, or that we disdain the idea of government under law. But the lawyer thinks of legal principles as something to be taken apart and made to fit the client's needs. The lawyer thinks this work *is* government under law. Principles and facts are the lawyer's raw materials. What is sacred in the law is not legal principles. The sacred thing in the law, to a lawyer, is the fact that those who have power are bound to respect skill and knowledge in the wielding of power—skill and knowledge even among those who merely wield power, who do not have it. This is, at last, we think, the political side of a respect for *character.* With regard to what is *legal,* principles come last, Thomas More understood that. He lived it. It was important to him. Bolt understands that; it is part of the reason he thinks that More's life might stand up as an illustration of the courage to preserve one's soul—one's unbudgeable self—in the modern world.[43]

[42]32 *Journal of Legal Education* 506 (1982).
[43]Thomas Shaffer, *On Being a Christian and a Lawyer, supra,* Chapter 18 (written in collaboration with Stanley Hauerwas), p. 195.

I can think of no more suitable way to close this book than to urge readers to explore further the nature of legal skill by reading two of this century's finest plays, Robert Bolt's *A Man for All Seasons* and Herman Wouk's *The Caine Mutiny Court-Martial.* In each drama a heroic lawyer's skill is very much an extension of his character. In both dramas circumstances force the heros, Thomas More and Barney Greenwald, into adversarial positions. Each hero sees clearly the destruction that adversarial argument brings. Each hero agonizes profoundly because each sees clearly the great costs that rejection of the value of cooperation brings.

Bibliography

Abel, Richard, ed. *The Politics of Informal Justice.* New York: Academic Press, 1982.

Adamany, David. "Legitimacy, Realigning Elections, and the Supreme Court." 1973 *Wisconsin Law Review* 790 (1973).

Ball, Milner. *The Promise of American Law.* Athens, Ga.: University of Georgia Press, 1981.

Ball, Milner, and Lohn, D. Robert. "Legal Advocacy, Performance, and Affection." 16 *Georgia Law Review* 853 (1982).

Becker, Theodore L., and Feeley, Malcolm, eds. *The Impact of Supreme Court Decisions.* 2nd ed. New York: Oxford University Press, 1973.

Bennett, W. Lance, and Feldman, Martha S. *Reconstructing Reality in the Courtroom.* New Brunswick, N.J.: Rutgers University Press, 1981.

Bentley, Arthur F. *The Process of Government.* Chicago: University of Chicago Press, 1908.

Berger, Raoul. *Government by Judiciary: The Transformation of the Fourteenth Amendment.* Cambridge: Harvard University Press, 1977.

Berman, Harold, and Greiner, William. *The Nature and Functions of Law.* 3rd ed. Mineola, N.Y.: Foundation Press, 1972.

Beveridge, Albert J. *The Life of John Marshall,* Vol. 1. New York: Houghton Mifflin, 1916.

Bice, Scott. "Rationality Analysis in Constitutional Law." 65 *Minnesota Law Review* 1 (1980).

Bickel, Alexander. *The Least Dangerous Branch.* Indianapolis: Bobbs-Merrill, 1964.

Bickel, Alexander. *The Morality of Consent.* New Haven: Yale University Press, 1975.

Bishin, William. "The Law Finders: An Essay in Statutory Interpretation." 38 *Southern California Law Review* 1 (1965).

Bok, Derek. "A Flawed System." *Harvard Magazine,* May-June, 1983, p. 48.

Bok, Sissela. *Secrets: On the Ethics of Concealment and Revelation.* New York: Pantheon Books, 1982.

Boudin, Michael. "Common Sense in Law Practice." *Harvard Law School Bulletin* 22 (1983).

Boyum, Keith, and Mather, Lynn. *Empirical Theories About Courts.* New York: Longman, 1983.

Calabresi, Guido. *A Common Law for the Age of Statutes.* Cambridge: Harvard University Press, 1982.

Canon, Bradley. "A Framework for the Analysis of Judicial Activism." In *Supreme Court Activism and Restraint,* edited by Halpern and Lamb. Lexington, Mass.: Lexington Books, 1982.

Cardozo, Benjamin N. *The Nature of the Judicial Process.* New Haven: Yale University Press, 1921.

Cardozo, Benjamin N. *The Paradoxes of Legal Science.* New York: Columbia University Press, 1928.

Carp, Robert, and Rowland, C.K. *Policymaking and Politics in the Federal District Courts.* Knoxville: University of Tennessee Press, 1983.

Carter, Lief H. *The Limits of Order.* Lexington, Mass.: Lexington Books, 1974.

Carter, Lief H. "When Courts Should Make Policy: An Institutional Approach." In *Public Law and Public Policy,* edited by John A. Gardiner. New York: Praeger, 1977.

Carter, Lief H. *Administrative Law and Politics.* Boston: Little,

Brown, 1983.

Chafee, Zechariah. "The Disorderly Conduct of Words." 41 *Columbia Law Review* 381 (1941).

Choper, Jesse H. *Judicial Review and the National Political Process: A Functional Reconsideration of the Role of the Supreme Court.* Chicago: University of Chicago Press, 1980.

Cohen, Felix. "Transcendental Nonsense and the Functional Approach." 35 *Columbia Law Review* 809 (1935).

Cover, Robert. Book Review of R. Berger, *Government by Judiciary. The New Republic,* 14 January 1978, p. 27.

Cox, Archibald. "Some Aspects of the Labor Management Relations Act, 1947." 61 *Harvard Law Review* 1 (1947).

Cox, Archibald. *The Role of the Supreme Court in American Government.* New York: Oxford University Press, 1976.

Crane, Frederick E. "The Magic of the Private Seal." 15 *Columbia Law Review* 24 (1915).

Craven, J. Braxton. "Paean to Pragmatism." 50 *North Carolina Law Review* 977 (1972).

Cross, Sir Rupert. *Statutory Interpretation.* London: Butterworths, 1976.

Currier, Thomas S. "Time and Change in Judge-Made Law: Prospective Overruling." 51 *Virginia Law Review* 201 (1965).

Curtis, Charles. "A Better Theory of Legal Interpretation." 3 *Vanderbilt Law Review* 407 (1950).

Davis, Kenneth C. "Facts in Lawmaking." 80 *Columbia Law Review* 931 (1980).

Dickerson, Reed. *The Interpretation and Application of Statutes.* Boston: Little, Brown, 1975.

Dietze, Gottfried. "The Limited Rationality of Law." In *Nomos VII: Rational Decision,* edited by Carl Friedrich. New York: Atherton Press, 1964.

Dixon, Robert G. "The 'New Substantive Due Process' and the Democratic Ethic: A Prologomenon." 1 *Brigham Young University Law Review* 43 (1976).

Donnelly, Jack. "Human Rights and Human Dignity: An Analytical Critique of Non-Western Conceptions of Human Rights." 76 *American Political Science Review* 303 (1982).

Douglas, William O. "Stare Decisis." 4 *Record of the Association of the Bar of the City of New York* 152 (1949).

Eisenstein, James, and Jacob, Herbert. *Felony Justice.* Boston: Little, Brown, 1977.

Elkins, James. "Moral Discourse and Legalism in Legal Education." 32 *Journal of Legal Education* 11 (1982).

Ely, John Hart. *Democracy and Distrust.* Cambridge: Harvard University Press, 1980.

Feeley, Malcolm M. "The Concept of Laws in Social Science." 10 *Law and Society Review* 497 (1976).

Fisher, Roger, and Ury, William. *Getting to Yes: Negotiating Agreement without Giving In.* New York: Penguin Books, 1981.

Fiss, Owen. "Foreword: The Forms of Justice." 93 *Harvard Law Review* 1 (1979).

Fleming, John G., and Maximov, Bruce. "The Patient or His Victim: The Therapist's Dilemma." 62 *California Law Review* 1025 (1974).

Frank, Jerome. "Words and Music: Some Remarks on Statutory Interpretation." 47 *Columbia Law Review* 1259 (1947).

Frank, Jerome. *Courts on Trial.* Princeton: Princeton University Press, 1949.

Frankfurter, Felix. "Some Reflections on the Reading of Statutes." 2 *Record of the Association of the Bar of the City of New York* 213 (1947).

Freund, Paul. "Social Justice and the Law." In *Social Justice,* edited by Richard B. Brandt. Englewood Cliffs, N.J.: Prentice-Hall, 1962.

Freund, Paul. "Rationality in Judicial Decisions." In *Nomos VII: Rational Decision,* edited by Carl Friedrich. New York: Atherton Press, 1964.

Fried, Charles. "Two Concepts of Interests: Some Reflections on the Supreme Court's Balancing Test." 76 *Harvard Law Review* 755 (1963).

Friedman, Lawrence M. *The Legal System.* New York: Russell Sage Foundation, 1975.

Friedman, Lawrence, and Macaulay, Stewart. *Law and the Behavioral Sciences.* Indianapolis: Bobbs-Merrill, 1977.

Fritschler, A. Lee. *Smoking and Politics.* Englewood Cliffs, N.J.: Prentice-Hall, 1975.

Fuller, Lon. "Consideration and Form." 41 *Columbia Law Review* 799 (1941).

Fuller, Lon. *The Morality of Law.* New Haven: Yale University Press, 1964.

Gadamer, Hans-Georg. *Truth and Method.* New York: Seaburg Press, 1975.

Galanter, Marc. "Why the 'Haves' Come out Ahead: Speculations on the Limits of Legal Change." 9 *Law and Society Review* 95 (1974).

Gilmore, Grant. "Products Liability." 38 *University of Chicago Law Review* 103 (1970).

Goodhart, Arthur L. "Determining the *Ratio Decidendi* of a Case." 40 *Yale Law Journal* 161 (1930).

Gray, John. *The Nature and Sources of the Law.* New York: Macmillan, 1927.

Grey, Thomas C. "Do We Have an Unwritten Constitution?" 27 *Stanford Law Review* 703 (1975).

Grey, Thomas C. "Origins of the Unwritten Constitution: Fundamental Law in American Revolutionary Thought." 30 *Stanford Law Review* 843 (1978).

Grossman, Joel B. "Social Backgrounds and Judicial Decision-Making." 79 *Harvard Law Review* 1551 (1966).

Gusfield, Joseph R. Review of Friedman's *The Legal System.* 29 *Stanford Law Review* 371 (1977).

Hall, Jerome. *Foundations of Jurisprudence.* Indianapolis: Bobbs-Merrill, 1973.

Hand, Learned. *The Bill of Rights.* Cambridge: Harvard University Press, 1958.

Hart, Henry M., Jr., and Sacks, Albert M. *The Legal Process: Basic Problems in the Making and Application of Law.* Cambridge: Harvard Law School, 1958.

Hart, H.L.A. *The Concept of Law*. Oxford: Clarendon Press, 1961.

Hazard, Geoffrey. *Ethics in the Practice of Law*. New Haven: Yale University Press, 1978.

Hazard, Geoffrey. "Arguing the Law: The Advocate's Duty and Opportunity." 16 *Georgia Law Review* 821 (1982).

Hochschild, Jennifer. *What's Fair: American Beliefs About Distributive Justice*. Cambridge: Harvard University Press, 1981.

Hopkins, James D. "Fictions and the Judicial Process: A Preliminary Theory of Decision." 33 *Brooklyn Law Review* 1 (1966).

Horack, Frank E., Jr. "The Disintegration of Statutory Construction." 24 *Indiana Law Journal* 335 (1949).

Horowitz, Donald. *The Courts and Social Policy*. Washington, D.C.: The Brookings Institute, 1977.

Howard, J. Woodford. "Adjudication Considered as a Process of Conflict Resolution." 18 *Journal of Public Law* 39 (1969).

Hughes, Graham. *The Conscience of the Courts: Law and Morals in American Life*. New York: Doubleday, 1975.

Hutcheson, Joseph. "The Judgment Intuitive: The Function of the 'Hunch' in Judicial Decision." 14 *Cornell Law Quarterly* 274 (1929).

Hyde, Lewis. *The Gift: Imagination and the Erotic Life of Property*. New York: Vintage Books, 1983.

Jones, Gareth. "Should Judges Be Politicians?: The English Experience." 57 *Indiana Law Journal* 211 (1982).

"Jurisprudence Symposium." 11 *Georgia Law Review* 967–1424 (1977).

Kempin, Frederick G. *Historical Introduction to Anglo-American Law in a Nutshell*. 2nd ed. St. Paul: West, 1973.

Kennedy, Duncan. "Form and Substance in Private Law Adjudication." 89 *Harvard Law Review* 1685 (1976).

Knapp, Charles L. *Problems in Contract Law*. Boston: Little, Brown, 1976.

Lasswell, Harold. *Power and Personality*. 1st ed. New York: Norton, 1948.

Lazerson, Mark. "In the Halls of Justice." In *The Politics of Informal Justice,* edited by Richard Abel. New York: Academic Press, 1982.

Lempert, Richard. "A Right to Every Woman's Evidence." 66 *Iowa Law Review* 725 (1981).

Levi, Edward. *An Introduction to Legal Reasoning.* Chicago: University of Chicago Press, 1949.

Levin, Martin. *Urban Politics and the Criminal Courts.* Chicago: University of Chicago Press, 1977.

Lewis, Anthony. *Gideon's Trumpet.* New York: Random House, 1964.

Llewellyn, Karl. *The Common Law Tradition.* Boston: Little, Brown, 1960.

Llewellyn, Karl. "Remarks on the Theory of Appellate Decision and the Rules or Canons about How Statutes Are to Be Construed." 3 *Vanderbilt Law Review* 395 (1950).

Macaulay, Stewart. "Noncontractual Relations in Business: A Preliminary Study." 28 *American Sociological Review* 55 (1963).

Mason, Alpheus, and Beany, William. *American Constitutional Law.* Englewood Cliffs, N.J.: Prentice-Hall, 1978.

McDonnell, Julian B. "Purposive Interpretation of the Uniform Commercial Code: Some Implications for Jurisprudence." 126 *Pennsylvania Law Review* 795 (1978).

Merryman, John Henry. *The Civil Law Tradition.* Stanford: Stanford University Press, 1969.

Murphy, Arthur. "Old Maxims Never Die: The 'Plain Meaning Rule' and Statutory Interpretation in the 'Modern' Federal Courts." 75 *Columbia Law Review* 1299 (1975).

Murphy, Walter. *Elements of Judicial Strategy.* Chicago: University of Chicago Press, 1964.

Murphy, Walter. "The Art of Constitutional Interpretation." In *Essays on the Constitution,* edited by M. Judd Harmon. Port Washington, New York: Kennikat Press, 1978.

Murphy, Walter, and Pritchett, C. Herman. *Courts, Judges and Politics.* 3rd ed. New York: Random House, 1979.

Nonet, Phillippe, and Selznick, Philip. *Law and Society in*

Transition. New York: Harper & Row, 1978.

Noonan, John T., Jr. *Persons and Masks of the Law*. New York: Farrar, Straus & Giroux, 1976.

"Note—Congressional Reversal of Supreme Court Decisions: 1945–1957." 71 *Harvard Law Review* 1324 (1958).

Paulson, Stanley. "*Jus Non Scriptum* and the Reliance Principle." 75 *Michigan Law Review* 68 (1976).

Perry, Michael J. *The Constitution, the Courts, and Human Rights*. New Haven: Yale University Press, 1982.

Phelps, Arthur. "Factors Influencing Judges in Interpreting Statutes." 3 *Vanderbilt Law Review* 456 (1950).

Plucknett, Theodore F.T. *A Concise History of the Common Law*. 5th ed. Boston: Little, Brown, 1956.

Rosett, Arthur I., and Cressey, Donald R. *Justice by Consent*. Philadelphia: Lippincott, 1976.

Sarat, Austin. "The Role of Courts and the Logic of Court Reform." 64 *Judicature* 300 (1981).

Schaefer, Walter V. "Precedent and Policy." 34 *University of Chicago Law Review* 3 (1966).

Schaefer, Walter V. "Prospective Rulings: Two Perspectives." In *The Supreme Court Review*, edited by Philip B. Kurland, Gerhard Casper, and Dennis J. Hutchinson. Chicago: University of Chicago Press, 1983.

Scheingold, Stuart A. *The Politics of Rights*. New Haven: Yale University Press, 1974.

Scheingold, Stuart A. *The Politics of Law and Order*. New York: Longman, 1984.

Shaffer, Thomas. *On Being a Christian and a Lawyer*. Provo, Utah: Brigham Young University Press, 1981.

Shapiro, Martin. "Stability and Change in Judicial Decision-Making: Incrementalism or Stare Decisis?" 2 *Law in Transition Quarterly* 134 (1964).

Shapiro, Martin. "Courts." In *Handbook of Political Science*, edited by Fred Greenstein and Nelson Polsby, volume 5, pp. 321–371. Reading, Mass.: Addison-Wesley, 1975.

Shapiro, Martin. *Courts: A Comparative and Political Analysis*. Chicago: University of Chicago Press, 1981.

Spaeth, Harold. *Supreme Court Policy Making.* San Francisco: Freeman, 1979.

Stone, Julius. *Legal System and Lawyers' Reasonings.* Stanford: Stanford University Press, 1964.

Summers, Robert S. *Instrumentalism in American Legal Theory.* Ithaca, N.Y.: Cornell University Press, 1982.

"Symposium." 42 *Ohio State Law Journal* 3 (1981).

"Symposium." 90 *Yale Law Journal,* Part 2 (1981).

Tribe, Lawrence. "Seven Pluralist Fallacies: In Defense of the Adversary Process." 33 *University of Miami Law Review* 43 (1978).

Tribe, Lawrence. "The Puzzling Persistence of Process-Based Constitutional Theories." 89 *Yale Law Journal* 1063 (1980).

Tushnet, Mark. "Following the Rules Laid Down: A Critique of Interpretivism and Neutral Principles." 96 *Harvard Law Review* 781 (1983).

Unger, Roberto Mangabeira. *Law in Modern Society.* New York: The Free Press, 1976.

Wasby, Stephen L. *The Impact of the United States Supreme Court.* Homewood, Ill.: Dorsey, 1970.

Wasby, Stephen L. "Horowitz: The Courts and Social Policy." 31 *Vanderbilt Law Review* 727 (1978).

Wasserstrom, Richard A. *The Judicial Decision.* Stanford: Stanford University Press, 1961.

White, James. *The Legal Imagination.* Boston: Little, Brown, 1973.

Woodward, Bob, and Armstrong, Scott. *The Brethren: Inside the Supreme Court.* New York: Simon & Schuster, 1979.

Index

Index of Cases

Boldfaced page numbers indicate pages on which a significant excerpt from an opinion in the case begins. All other page numbers denote in-text case references. This index excludes cases of minor significance, for example, cases cited within other quoted cases and materials. Case citations are provided in the text.

CREDITS